LAS VEGAS GUIDE

BE A TRAVELER - NOT A TOURIST!

PRAISE FOR OPEN ROAD'S
LAS VEGAS GUIDE

"Very helpful in providing information such as what foods the various buffets around town offer, the types of entertainment and gaming found at each of the hotel/casinos, and points of interest that exist off the Strip.

Thorough explanations and tips on casino gambling ... especially useful to those who are in Vegas for a short time and need to pick their spots." – **Books of the Southwest**

"I want to commend you ... by purchasing your guide, I was able to save over $300 on food and beverages, and came home $900 richer." – **W. Pratt, South Carolina**

ABOUT THE AUTHORS

Larry Ludmer is a professional travel writer who makes his home in Las Vegas. He is the author of Open Road guides to Arizona, New Mexico, Colorado and Utah.

Ed Kranmar is a travel writer who has trekked the length and breadth of the Southwest. He often accompanies Cardoza on his trips to the desert gambling mecca, studying the constantly changing Las Vegas scene to bring you an up-to-date, insiders' perspective.

Avery Cardoza is the best-selling author of many how-to-win gaming books and advanced strategies, and is recognized as one of the top gambling authorities in the world. He is also head of Cardoza Publishing, the world's foremost publisher of gambling books, and Cardoza Entertainment, designer of pioneering gambling software. A Las Vegas resident, he has spent many years conducting extensive research into the mathematical, emotional, and psychological aspects of winning.

BE A TRAVELER, NOT A TOURIST - WITH OPEN ROAD TRAVEL GUIDES!

Open Road Publishing has guide books to exciting, fun destinations on four continents. As veteran travelers, our goal is to bring you the best travel guides available anywhere!

No small task, but here's what we offer:

• All Open Road travel guides are written by authors with a distinct, opinionated point of view – not some sterile committee or team of writers. Our authors are experts in the areas covered and are polished writers.

• Our guides are geared to people who want to make their own travel choices. We'll show you how to discover the real destination – not just see some place from a tour bus window.

• We're strong on the basics, but we also provide terrific choices for those looking to get off the beaten path and experience the country or city – not just see it or pass through it.

• We give you the best, but we also tell you about the worst and what to avoid. Nobody should waste their time and money on their hard-earned vacation because of bad or inadequate travel advice.

• Our guides assume nothing. We tell you everything you need to know to have the trip of a lifetime – presented in a fun, literate, no-nonsense style.

• And, above all, we welcome your input, ideas, and suggestions to help us put out the best travel guides possible.

LAS VEGAS GUIDE

BE A TRAVELER - NOT A TOURIST!

Larry Ludmer,
Ed Kranmar & Avery Cardoza

OPEN ROAD PUBLISHING

This book is once again dedicated to the Shuffler, the Doubler, and Grandma Kranmar.

5th Revised Edition
Copyright©1999 by Larry Ludmer, Ed Kranmar & Avery Cardoza
- All Rights Reserved -

ISBN 1-892975-10-6
Library of Congress Catalog Card No. 99-74385

Front cover photo by FPG International. Bottom back cover photo courtesy of Las Vegas News Bureau. Top back cover photo by Nathaniel Stein. Map on page 14 courtesy of Las Vegas Convention Center; other maps by James Ramage.

We have made every effort to be as accurate as possible, but we cannot assume responsibility for the services provided by any business listed in this guide; for any errors or omissions; or any loss, damage, or disruptions in your travel.

TABLE OF CONTENTS

1. INTRODUCTION   13

2. OVERVIEW   14
Gambling   14
Hotels   14
Food   16
The Strip & Other Sights   17
Excursions & Day Trips   17
Nightlife & Entertainment   17
Sports & Recreation   18
Shopping   19

3. SUGGESTED ITINERARIES   21

4. A SHORT HISTORY   24
Beginnings   24
The Railroad   24
Gambling Comes to Town   25
Howard Hughes   26
The Dawn of the Mega-Resorts   26
Las Vegas Today   27

5. PLANNING YOUR TRIP   29
When to Visit   29
What to Pack   30
Las Vegas Tourism Information   30

A Little Advance Planning   32
Booking Your Vacation   33
Getting the Best Airfare   33
Flying to Las Vegas   35

6. BASIC INFORMATION   37

Alcoholic Beverage & Gaming Laws   37
Banking, Money & Credit Cards   37
Emergencies   38
Foreign Visitors   39
Fun Books & Discounts   40
Health   40
Newspapers & Magazines   41
Places of Worship   41
Safety   42
Taxes   43
Telephones   43
Time of Day   43
Tipping   43
Other Special Considerations   44
    Disabled Travelers   44
    Traveling with Children   44
    Senior Citizens   44

7. ARRIVALS & DEPARTURES   46

Geographic Orientation   46
Arriving & Departing By Air   46
From the Airport to the City   47
Car Rentals   48
Arriving & Departing By Bus   48
Arriving & Departing By Car   49
Directions   49

8. GETTING AROUND TOWN   51

On Foot   51
By Car   52
Bus & Trolley   53

Taxis & Limousines   55
Hotel Monorails & Trams   55
Guided Tours   56

9. WHERE TO STAY   57

The Strip   60
   Very Expensive   60
   Expensive   65
   Moderate   70
   Inexpensive   76
Off-Strip   78
   Very Expensive   78
   Expensive   78
   Moderate   80
   Inexpensive   83
Downtown   85
   Expensive   85
   Moderate   86
   Inexpensive   87
Around Las Vegas   88
   Very Expensive   88
   Moderate   89
   Inexpensive   92
Henderson   93
   Moderate   93
   Inexpensive   94

10. WHERE TO EAT   96

Restaurant Price Categories   96
The Strip   97
   Very Expensive   97
   Expensive   100
   Moderate   107
   Inexpensive   112
Off-Strip   113
   Expensive   113
   Moderate   114
   Inexpensive   118
Downtown   118

Expensive   118
Moderate   118
Around Las Vegas   119
Expensive   119
Moderate   120
Inexpensive   121
Buffets   123
The Strip   125
Off-Strip   128
Downtown   129
Around Las Vegas   130
Henderson   130

11. GAMBLING IN VEGAS   132

Casino Basics   132
Money Management   134
A Quick Guide to Casino Action   135
Winning Strategies for the Main Games   137
Blackjack   137
Craps   142
Slots   148
Keno   151
Poker   153
Baccarat   157
Roulette   160
Video Poker   163

12. SEEING THE SIGHTS   167

The Strip   167
Hotel/Casino Attractions   168
Other Strip Diversions   194
Off-Strip   195
Downtown   198
Around Las Vegas   200
Henderson   202

13. NIGHTLIFE & ENTERTAINMENT   207

Production Shows   208

Lounge Acts & Other Shows   214
Celebrity Entertainment   217
Nightclubs & Dance Halls   218
Comedy Acts   220
Gentlemen's Clubs   221
Cultural Offerings   222
Odds & Ends   222

14. SHOPPING   223

The Strip   223
Off-Strip   226
Downtown   226
Around Las Vegas   226
Henderson   227
I'm Looking For...   227
How About Those Souvenirs?   229

15. SPORTS & RECREATION   230

Bicycling   230
Boating   231
Bowling   231
Bungee Jumping   231
Golf   231
Hiking   233
Horseback Riding   233
Hot Air Balloons 233
Rafting   234
Skiing & Ice Skating   234
Sky Diving   235
Spectator Sports   235
College Sports   236
Swimming   236
Tennis   237
Miscellaneous   238

16. EXCURSIONS & DAY TRIPS   239

Day Trips   240
    Hoover Dam   240

Lake Mead   242
Red Rock Canyon   244
Spring Mountain Attractions   245
Mt. Charleston   246
Valley of Fire State Park   247
Laughlin   248
Primm   250
Ghost Towns & Indian Reservations   251
Further Afield   252
Grand Canyon   252
Death Valley   253
Southwestern Utah   254

17. LAS VEGAS FOR KIDS   255

Child Care Facilities   255
Arcades   256
Amusement & Theme Parks   256
Attractions for Kids   257
Some Hotel Suggestions   258

18. WEDDING CHAPELS   259

Going to the Chapel   259
Independent Chapels   260
Best Hotel Wedding Chapels   262

19. ANNUAL EVENTS   264

Calendar of Annual Events   259
Theater & Music   262
Conventions   263

MAPS

Nevada & the Southwest   15
The Strip   62-63
Las Vegas & Vicinity   241

SIDEBARS

Ladies of the Night   18

The Best of Las Vegas   20

Lt. John Fremont   24

Thinking of Moving to Vegas?   28

Las Vegas Climate at a Glance   30

Quick Tips for Planning Your Trip   31

Comps, Las Vegas Style   45

When is the Next Train to Vegas Due?   50

Garage Secrets   53

Your Magic Locator Guide   56

Hotel Room Rate Ranges   59

What Does the Asterisk Mean?   60

Time Shares & Extended Stay Accommodations   95

News Flash: Power Chefs Open New Power Restaurants   107

Where's that Restaurant We Always Liked?   113

Hotel Coffee Shops – A Tasty & Inexpensive Alternative   115

Restaurant Row...Oriental Style   122

The Best Buffets in Town   131

Eye in the Sky   135

Gaming Availability by Hotel/Casino   136

Blackjack: Master Strategy Chart   141

House Edge in Craps Chart   148

Slots Clubs   149

Slots City   150

Ranks of Poker Hands   153

Baccarat Banker Rules   159

Baccarat Player Rules   159

Roulette Payoff Chart   163

Payoffs: Jacks or Better: 8-5 Machine   164

Winning Hands in Video Poker   165

Jacks or Better: 9-6 Flattop Strategy   166

Coming Soon...   193

America's Fastest Growing City   203

Developments at Lake Las Vegas   204

Casino-Only Establishments   206

Afternoon Delights   218

Gambling Paraphernalia   229

More About UNLV   236

Travel Distances to Area Excursions   240

The Desert Tortoise   248

Laughlin Casinos at a Glance   250

Divorce, Vegas-Style   263

Convention City   265

Hotel Implosions: The New Vegas Extravaganza!   268

1. INTRODUCTION

Las Vegas is America's most exciting city, with more than 30 million visitors each year having the time of their lives! We'll show you all that this great town has to offer. If you follow our advice, and we have plenty of it, you'll be sure that you, too, will tell your friends that you had the time of *your* life.

Of course Las Vegas is built around gambling, but the city that never sleeps is much more. With the proliferation of gaming in so many other places, Vegas has gone way beyond just being the Mecca of gambling. It is a complete year-round destination resort that has something for everyone. For families with children there's good clean fun to be found in its theme parks and video arcades. Grown-ups, if they wish, can also discover Sin City from the mild topless production shows at the big casinos to much more risque forms of entertainment. A trip to Vegas can also be a raft trip on Lake Mead, a breathtaking hike in the Valley of Fire or a visit to the "Eighth Wonder of the World" – monumental Hoover Dam.

We'll show you unexplored Vegas; where to go Country and Western dancing; how to rediscover Elvis and Liberace; and where to find delicious 99 cent shrimp cocktails. You'll find out where to go to enjoy some of the country's finest golfing, tennis, boating and swimming, and if it's solitude and nature you want, where to go to explore your soul in the vast magnitude of the desert.

For people who never sleep or love to gamble, Vegas is paradise. While other travel guides may tell you how to play, we'll show you how to maximize your chances of winning. Armed with Avery Cardoza's inside tips, you'll learn everything you need to know to walk into the casino with confidence.

It all adds up to excitement and thrills. We'll show you all the possibilities to help make your trip to Vegas one of the best you've ever taken!

2. OVERVIEW

Few cities in the world have the kind of heart-charging excitement and limitless possibilities that Las Vegas has, and the Entertainment Capital does it without breaking a sweat. We'll give you a quick preview here of all that Vegas has in store so you can see how to plan your vacation and get the maximum enjoyment from it. A respected Wall Street gaming analyst put it best a few years ago when he said that you go to Atlantic City or any number of other gaming venues to gamble, but that you "go to Las Vegas to have fun."

GAMBLING

You can gamble day or night, 24 hours – the casinos never close. With almost 40 casinos on The Strip alone and more than 150 in total, the novice gambler or pro alike will find non-stop action and excitement in any one of them.

Sit down at any table, and you've got action. In our gaming chapter we'll show you how to play and increase your chances of winning at blackjack, craps, poker, roulette, slots, video poker and keno. Nevada is also the only place in the United States where you can legally bet on sporting events other than racing.

HOTELS

Las Vegas boasts nine of the ten largest resort hotels in the world and completely dominates the top 25. Best of all, you'll generally find excellent value wherever you stay. Casinos lure players to their premises by offering inexpensive rooms, food and entertainment. The casino operators figure, and generally correctly, that their guests are a captive audience for their casino games. If you're a gambler be sure to follow our money-management tips. While prices have risen quite dramatically in the past few years, Las Vegas is still a relative bargain when compared with most other resort destinations or large cities.

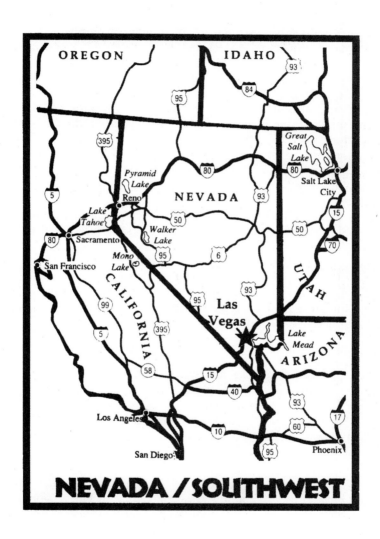

NEVADA / SOUTHWEST

On The Strip the hotels are more than just places to stay and eat. Majestically lined up one after the other, they are more often than not major attractions in themselves. From the new world class **Bellagio** and its fine art collection to the ultra-chic **Mirage** with its exploding volcano, lush tropical forest and Siberian tigers; to the working class **Excalibur** with its medieval castle theme featuring knights in shining armor; from the glory of ancient Rome at **Caesars Palace** and its adjacent magnificent Forum Shops to the splendors of ancient Egypt at the **Luxor**; and from the dazzling skyline of **New York, New York** and its thrilling roller coaster to the plazas, canals and gondolas of **The Venetian**; or the famous sights of **Paris**, the hotels of The Strip are a remarkable sight.

But not all of the great hotels are even located on the famous Strip. Take part in a colorful carnival at **The Rio** with its fabulous Masquerade Village. Or journey through space at *Star Trek: The Experience* at the **Las Vegas Hilton**. Downtown's **Golden Nugget** is the class of the area and has great dining as well as the largest gold nugget on public display in the world. See a million dollars in cold cash at **Binion's Horseshoe**. You can even stay further afield at such interesting locales as **Sunset Station** with its beautiful Mediterranean architecture or sample an African safari theme at **The Reserve**.

It's been said that Las Vegas is the most egalitarian city in the world. Perhaps the greatest eveidence of this is the fact that you can find a guy in a tee shirt and jeans rubbing elbows with a tuxedo clad high roller. There's something for everybody and whatever your taste or budget, you'll find it in Las Vegas!

FOOD

Not only is the gambling non-stop, so is the food. At any time, day or evening, you can satiate your appetite with a T-bone steak at 3:00 am for just a few bucks or you can sample the offerings at some of the most lavish buffets anywhere, often for under ten dollars.

But the most recent trend in Las Vegas dining has been the debut of dozens of fine restaurants featuring a variety of cuisines prepared by some of the most renowned chefs in the world. Even a noted food critic from the *New York Times* recently had to admit (grudgingly, we surmise) that Las Vegas has taken its place alongside New York and Paris as one of the world's great dining cities. The choices are almost endless and the prices range from ridiculously low to more than a hundred dollars per person, but are generally less than you would find for equivalent dining in most large cities. *Bon appetit!*

THE STRIP & OTHER SIGHTS

We've already touched on the magnificent hotels on The Strip and elsewhere in our hotel overview. That didn't even scratch the surface. There's big-top and midway fun at **Circus Circus** along with an indoor theme park. The "City of Entertainment," the **MGM Grand** also has a theme park and many other attractions, as would be expected from the world's largest hotel. The beautiful gardens of the **Flamingo Hilton** and the outstanding vintage car collection at the **Imperial Palace** are a couple of other sure to please places.

But the hotels and the accompanying atmosphere that make up The Strip aren't the only worthwhile things to be seen in and around town. Such diverse attractions as the **Showcase** (exhibits about Coca-Cola, M&M's candy and indoor "mountain" climbing) can be found on the fabulous Strip while downtown's famous **Glitter Gulch** has been greatly enhanced by the presence of the multi-million lights and sounds of the **Fremont Street Experience**. Around town are the **Liberace Museum** as well as numerous other more "mainstream" museums, zoos and much, much more.

EXCURSIONS & DAY TRIPS

There's a whole lot of Vegas sights beyond the lights of the city that are worth exploring. Among the best are a visit to **Hoover Dam** and the **Lake Mead National Recreation Area**, the colorful rock formations of **Red Rock Canyon National Conservation Area** and the **Valley of Fire State Park**. A short trip to nearby **Mt. Charleston** brings summer visitors into a much cooler world – and skiing during the winter.

If you haven't had enough of the casinos you can take a two-hour trip to the Colorado River boomtown of **Laughlin**. Or stay closer and partake of the action in **Primm** on the California State line, just over a half hour's drive from The Strip.

Longer excursions can take you to **Death Valley**, **Zion National Park** and even the **Grand Canyon** although these, and others, are best done via overnight excursions. Regardless, the choices are almost endless.

NIGHTLIFE & ENTERTAINMENT

What's a visit to Las Vegas without taking in a show or two? Extravagant shows have been an important factor in making the desert oasis what it is today. Choose between big name celebrities or production shows that range from magic to high-tech and include several of the traditional Las Vegas style revues with beautiful feathery costumes and gorgeous, often topless, show girls. Or take in some less expensive lounge shows that feature up and coming entertainers. Comedy clubs, celebrity impersonators, and even performers in drag round out this part of the entertainment scene.

For more participant oriented evening fun, Las Vegas has no shortage of classy nightclubs with dancing. These range from small local places to extravagant glitter domes in some of the biggest casinos. The music ranges from country western to heavy metal and everything in between.

And, for those whose tastes are more on the wild side, there is still plenty of sexy entertainment that earned Las Vegas its "sin city" name. In short, there's something for everyone.

LADIES OF THE NIGHT

This may come as news to many, but prostitution is illegal in Clark County, of which Las Vegas is very much a part. But just over the county line, well, that's another story. Some of the famous "ranches" of Nevada call adjacent Nye and Lincoln Counties their home. The town of Pahrump, located about 60 miles from Las Vegas, is one of the closer communities featuring this type of legal diversion. Within Las Vegas itself you can certainly find your pick of strip clubs and other adult entertainment. The Yellow Pages, street vendors handing out racy brochures and newspaper boxes all along The Strip will let you know that there is no shortage of businesses providing "entertainers" for a price.

While street prostitution has been heavily cracked down on in recent years (after all, Vegas does try to promote a family atmosphere to at least some extent), the many out-call entertainment services are a thinly veiled front for a much more intimate kind of companionship.

SPORTS & RECREATION

On and off The Strip there's everything any prime vacation spot of comparable size can offer – -miniature golf, city parks offering a full range of activities, fun and sun in the hotel swimming pool, even spectator sports.

Some of the finest golf courses anywhere are in the Las Vegas area, which is why the LPGA and many other leading tournaments come to town every year to hold some of their world-class contests. There are almost thirty excellent courses in the Las Vegas Valley.

And since the weather is so good year round, you can also enjoy great tennis, swimming, hiking, boating, and just about anything else that comes to mind – including bungee jumping or indoor skydiving. When the weather turns a bit cold and snowy up in the mountains west of town, you've got first-rate skiing and other snow-bound activities in **Mt.**

Charleston's Lee Canyon. On a nice winter day you can swoosh down the slopes in the morning and water ski on Lake Mead in the afternoon.

SHOPPING

As in the case of dining, recent developments have put Las Vegas high up on the list of the most important shopping destinations in America, if not the world. It used to be there were a few regional malls, plenty of souvenir shops and hotel gift shops. That has certainly changed. The **Forum Shops** at Caesars Palace may well be the most remarkable shopping center in the world – fun even if you don't intend to buy anything.

But that's only for starters. It seems that every hotel that opens up now has to have a major shopping center within it. The **Grand Canal Shoppes** at the Venetian is the latest world-class shopping venue to join the list. Some of the greatest names in upscale shopping can easily be found. For the bargain hunter there are several outlet malls in addition to the more traditional shopping centers. Whatever it is you're looking for (and whatever price you're willing to pay), you're going to find it in Las Vegas.

THE BEST OF LAS VEGAS

With apologies to some other great places...

Best Buffet	*See the special best buffet sidebar in Chapter 10*
Best Steak House	*Prime (Bellagio), Alan Alberts, The Range (Harrahs)*
Best Gourmet Restaurant	*Le Cirque (Bellagio), Michaels (Barbary Coast), Isis (Luxor)*
Best Italian Restaurant	*Canaletto, Battista's, Pasta Palace*
Best Seafood Restaurant	*Rosewood Grille, Emeril's (MGM)*
Best Shrimp Cocktail	*Golden Gate Hotel (still only 99 cents!)*
Best Dancing/Nightclub	*Ra (Luxor), Western Dance Hall (Sam's Town), The Beach*
Best Traditional Revue	*Jubilee!, Enter the Night*
Best Production Show	*Mystere, "O", EFX*
Best Magic Show	*Siegfried & Roy, Lance Burton*
Best Excursion	*Red Rock Canyon*
Best Shopping	*Forum Shops at Caesars, Grand Canal Shoppes (Venetian)*
Best Thrill Ride	*Manhattan Express, Big Shot*
Best Motion Simulator	*Race for Atlantis, Search for the Obelisk*
Best Free Show	*Battle of Buccaneer Bay (Treasure Island), Masquarade Village Sky Parade (Rio), Fremont Street Experience*
Best Exterior Hotel Architecture	*New York New York; Venetian; Paris*
Best Interior Hotel Architecture	*Luxor; Venetian; Caesars Palace*
Best Casino Decor	*Bellagio; Mandalay Bay*
Best Place to Stay (hotel)	*Caesars Palace; Rio; Bellagio*
Best View of Las Vegas	*Voo Doo Cafe & Lounge (Rio)*
Best Way to Pass the Time	*Walking The Strip at night*
Best Guidebook	*Las Vegas Guide, Open Road Publishing – what else?*

3. SUGGESTED ITINERARIES

In the old days many people came to Las Vegas for a couple of days. Some stayed as many as four but it was rare to see anything much longer than that, except for a few high rollers on an extended gambling junket. Because of the explosion of things to see and do in Las Vegas over the past several years the typical visitor is now spending more nights here than used to be the case. How long you should plan to stay in town depends on, in addition to your available time and budget, exactly what you want out of your visit. You can see the highlights in a few days but that won't allow for any extended amount of shopping, visiting some of the beautiful nearby attractions, taking part in the many recreational opportunities or just plain relaxing.

The lists below will help you plan a trip which covers things to see, both major and minor. It doesn't specifically allow time for gaming, shopping or recreational pursuits. However, some of that can be done in the morning or evening hours after you've done your sightseeing. Going to shows is almost always an evening affair and if that is part of what you'd like to schedule, should fit right in.

Keep in mind that different people operate at varying speeds. What takes one person an hour could occupy another individual for three times that long. These itineraries should allow sufficient time for the average visitor to see a full day of sights, with a short lunch break in the middle. To save the most amount of time and to get the most out of your day, try to arrange your activities (where possible) by organizing sites you want to see that are located nearby to one another. If you're going to be combining some of the area's scenic sights with hotel attractions then it makes sense to alternate days. That is, The Strip on one day, Hoover Dam and Lake Mead on the next, and then back to The Strip on the following day.

If you have....

TWO DAYS

- Bellagio
- Caesars Palace/Forum Shops
- Luxor
- Mirage (see the Volcano *only*; detailed exploration of the hotel will be for three day trip)
- New York, New York (exterior *only*; interior visit will be for three day trip)
- Paris
- Rio
- Treasure Island (Battle of Buccaneer Bay *only*; remainder for three day visit)
- Venetian/Grand Canal Shopper

THREE DAYS

Do all of the things above and add the following (be sure not to forget the parts of the Mirage, New York, New York and Treasure Island that were omitted from the two-day itinerary).

- Circus Circus
- Excalibur
- Fremont Street Experience
- Mandalay Bay
- MGM Grand

FOUR DAYS

Everything in the three day visit, plus:

- Hoover Dam and Lake Mead National Recreation Area
- Showcase
- Stratosphere

FIVE DAYS

Everything in the four day visit, plus:

- Flamingo Hilton
- Imperial Palace Auto Collection (remainder of hotel optional)
- Las Vegas Hilton *Star Trek: The Experience*; (remainder of hotel optional)
- Red Rock Canyon National Conservation Area

SIX DAYS

Everything in the five day visit, plus:
- Hard Rock Hotel
- Harrah's
- Liberace Museum
- Sam's Town
- Tropicana

SEVEN DAYS

Everything in the six day visit, plus:
- Henderson Factory Four (Henderson casino/hotels optional)
- Primm

Even a week long visit to Las Vegas is longer than most people will actually do so we won't bother to make any suggestions for trips beyond that length. If you are going to be staying that long in the area then just pick out additional attractions from later in this book. We would strongly suggest that trips of more than a week include an overnight or two-night excursion to some of the further afield natural attractions in neighboring states.

If you're here for a shorter period of time but plan to come back, something that the majority of Las Vegas visitors do, then you can pick up where you left off from the above itineraries. When working The Strip sights, and you plan to see all of the important hotels, you can avoid a lot of running around by grouping them by geographic location rather than the above day-by-day itinerary. For instance, one day can be devoted to the Tropicana Avenue intersection, another to the Flamingo Road intersection, and so on.

4. A SHORT HISTORY

BEGINNINGS

The first whispers of modern day Las Vegas (Spanish for *The Meadows*) can be traced back to the late 1820's, when traders found a shortcut en route from New Mexico to Los Angeles along the old Spanish Trail. These folks became the first non-Indians to set foot in the area later to be known as Las Vegas. This new shortcut went right through Paiute Indian territory, and eventually doomed the Paiute, as more traders came to settle in the area. They were followed by Mormon missionaries who started to come in ever-increasing numbers. To this day visitors are surprised to learn that Mormons make up a significant part of the population.

An ill-fated attempt to colonize Las Vegas Valley failed in the early 1850's, as the Mormon settlers' first mission fell into disarray. The main cause was crop failures which worsened tensions among and between the missionaries and miners and finally caused the entire settlement to disband.

LT. JOHN FREMONT

*Southern Nevada was first mapped by the U.S. military. Army cartographer **John Fremont** was assigned the task, and after two trips he had produced maps of the entire region. On his first visit he camped around what is today Las Vegas Springs outside of town. His perseverance and outdoor skills were rewarded many years after his death by having streets and hotels named after him. Pretty cool being an explorer, huh?*

THE RAILROAD

As in so many other places in the Wild West, it was the advent of the mighty Iron Horse that established Las Vegas and put it on the map, even if it was a pretty small dot! Chosen as a crossroads in the late 1800's due to a relatively plentiful water supply and, of course, strategic location, a railroad town soon sprung up and Las Vegas was off and running. A few years later, in 1905, the town became a city when the San Pedro, Los Angeles and Salt Lake Railroad (later to become the Union Pacific Railroad) made it a hub of sorts – a railroad division point.

Mining had been important in the development of Nevada but most activity took place well to the north of Las Vegas. Nonetheless, there was some silver mining in the area until relatively recently. It never did, however, follow the often stormy boom and bust pattern of many western towns that were based entirely on mining.

GAMBLING COMES TO TOWN

The seminal year in the history of Las Vegas was 1931. That year construction begun on Hoover Dam and Governor Fred Balzar legalized gambling. A separate bill in 1931 also influenced events to come: it allowed a divorce to become legal and binding after just six weeks, the nation's first quickie divorce law.

This came into play immediately when Hollywood movie moguls and screen stars began making the divorce pilgrimage, first to Reno, and then, with the completion of the Hoover Dam in 1935 (bringing in its wake new hotels and casinos), to Las Vegas.

Gambling did not really take off in Vegas for quite a few years, largely because conservative Mormons controlled the politics and much of the business of the city. The first hotel/casino on The Strip opened in 1941, the **El Rancho Vegas**. The innovative El Rancho was a big hit and showed other developers the tremendous potential of combining a casino with a hotel and a showroom. Don't overlook the increasing availability of air conditioning as a factor in Las Vegas' growth after World War II.

With the opening of mobster Benjamin "Bugsy" Siegel's **Flamingo Hotel** in 1946, Las Vegas replaced Reno as the king of Nevada's gambling cities, a title it never relinquished. Bugsy's big, glitzy casino, the first of its kind in Vegas, was the first to attract high rollers. They now had a luxurious place where they could spend their money in style. There was now bait to attract the *whales*, the term used in today's casino parlance for the highest of the high rollers. Las Vegas had come of age.

The city prospered, but its reputation as a gangster hangout and center of prostitution grew too. The association in the public's eye of mobsters with Las Vegas held back the city's growth. In fact, Las Vegas was often referred to in this period as **Sin City**.

HOWARD HUGHES

The 1950's and '60's were a time of especially colorful characters, people like **Nick the Greek**, one of the most famous gamblers in Vegas; the **Binion family**, owners of the famous Binion Horseshoe Casino; and **Howard Hughes**, the iconoclastic and secretive billionaire who arrived on the scene in 1967 and lent Las Vegas the legitimacy it had long been seeking. Vegas was seen in a new light and began a remarkable period of growth that continues to this day.

Rumor has it that Hughes moved to the Desert Inn, one of the ritziest hotels on The Strip, rented out all the rooms on the top floor and decided to stay for a while. Hughes did not gamble. The owner, Cleveland crime boss Moe Dalitz, wanted Hughes out so he could move some whales into his best suites, but Hughes enjoyed the creature comforts and was not interested in moving. So, the story goes, he bought the hotel for $13 million.

Hughes then went on a buying spree that ended with the controversial billionaire buying a good portion of Las Vegas, including six hotel/ casinos, lots of land, the local airport, and practically everything else not nailed down to the desert floor. In effect, he bought out the mob. That, and the implementation of tougher standards for casino owners and management, scrupulously enforced by the **Nevada Gaming Commission** and the **Nevada Control Board**, effectively legitimized the business.

THE DAWN OF THE MEGA-RESORTS

There were other great men to follow in Hughes footsteps and shape the city of Las Vegas. But Howard Hughes, Old Spruce Goose himself, the man who changed the face of Vegas, occupies the highest rung on the grandiose ladder of Las Vegas myth-making.

The end of the Hughes era ushered in another epoch – the public corporation controlled casino/hotel industry that prevails today. When Caesars Palace opened in 1966 it was the first of the truly great Las Vegas hotels. They didn't use the term mega-resort back then and perhaps the original Caesars Palace wasn't quite in that class but it did set the standard by which everything else that followed had to compete by (including its own expansions). While Howard Hughes was clearly the most important individual in the previous era, the mega-resort era was first pushed along by **Kirk Kekorian** who built the original MGM Grand Hotel. (That property is now Bally's, while the current MGM Grand sits about a mile further south.) **Steve Wynn**, chairman of Mirage Resorts, is the real father of today's Las Vegas scene. After using the money garnered by his sale of the Golden Nugget in Atlantic City to build the amazing **Mirage** in 1989, Wynn went on to build **Treasure Island** (1993) next door and he had two of the city's biggest successes.

CORPORATE VEGAS

Just as in banking and many other industries, consolidation among several big players has been the name of the game in casino/hotel ownership in recent years. It is a trend that is likely to continue. For now, the lineup card looks something like this (only Las Vegas area properties are listed):

Boyd Gaming: *California Hotel, Fremont Hotel, Main Street Station Hotel, Sam's Town, and The Stardust as well as several smaller non-hotel casino properties scattered throughout Las Vegas and Henderson.*

Mandalay Resort Group: *Circus Circus, Excalibur, Luxor and Mandalay Bay and a half-interest in the Monte Carlo. Formerly known as Circus Circus Enterprises.*

Harrah's Entertainment: *Harrah's, The Rio, and the Showboat.*

Mirage Resorts: *Bellagio, Golden Nugget, The Mirage, Treasure Island, Holiday Inn Boardwalk, as well as half of Monte Carlo.*

MGM Grand: *Besides the humongous Grand, this company owns New York, New York.*

Park Place Entertainment: *A recent spin-off from Hilton Hotels Corporation, they own Bally's, the Flamingo Hilton, Las Vegas Hilton, and Paris. Just acquired Caesars Palace.*

Station Casinos: *Boulder Station, Palace Station, Sunset Station and Texas Station.*

LAS VEGAS TODAY

The demolishing of older resorts and their replacement with ever larger and more fantastic hotel/casinos continues almost without let-up. Once filled with numerous large open spaces, The Strip now has few parcels left to build on. With approximately 119,000 hotel rooms, Las Vegas has more rooms to stay in than any other place in the world. It is a city that constantly keeps reinventing itself and which manages to always stay a step ahead of the competition.

The growth of gaming has spawned other development and industries as well. The current population of **Clark County** is now more than 1,300,000, with slightly more than one-third living in Las Vegas proper (but the suburbs that have sprawled out from Vegas are for all intents and purposes part of the city). You may be interested to know that The Strip itself is not within the city limits of Las Vegas but in an unincorporated area of Clark County, most of which is called Paradise. Try that on your friends at trivia time. At the current rate of influx, some observers believe that the city's population could surpass two million in the next ten years.

Tourism is alive and well. About 30 million visitors a year fill the casinos' and the state's coffers. However, with the numbers being so high, the rate of growth has slowed a bit. The typical visitor is younger than in the past and stays longer.

The federal government employs quite a few locals. More than 12,000 people work at **Nellis Air Force Base** and the **Nevada Test Site**, with tens of thousands more indirectly employed. The **University of Nevada at Las Vegas** (UNLV), founded in 1963, is also a significant employer as is the county government. Favorable tax laws have created a large warehousing industry.

Regardless of all this, gambling is the driving economic force in Vegas – about $6 billion in gambling revenues are generated each year. This amazing and exciting city has come a long way from its sleepy origins as a railroad town. *The Meadows* no longer, Las Vegas has truly come into its own as a world class resort destination and a place to live and work.

THINKING OF MOVING TO VEGAS?

Interested in moving to Las Vegas? Well, you won't be alone. Over the past few years an average of about 5,000 people moved into the Valley each month. The rate has only dropped a little in the most recent year and Las Vegas is likely to remain one of the fastest growing areas in the country for some time to come. Henderson, Las Vegas' neighbor to the immediate south claims the title of fastest growing city in America, but more about that in a later sidebar.

The attractions for new residents are many. The availability of jobs and the excitement of living in Action City are among the most obvious, but not exclusive. Although the overall cost of living is lower in many other places, many major items are cheap for Las Vegas residents. These include the absence of a state income tax, low real estate taxes and low utility costs. Even water is cheap, a big surprise to most people since Las Vegas is one of the driest areas in the country.

Savvy consumers can find inexpensive places to eat without trouble and plenty of entertainment at costs far less than in most cities. Las Vegas attracts young singles and families as well as a large number of senior citizens. It seems that the desert life is pleasing to a whole bunch of people including one of your authors, who settled into Henderson in 1995.

5. PLANNING YOUR TRIP

WHEN TO VISIT

Assuming that you can arrange a visit to Las Vegas whenever you want, there are two major considerations in determining when to make your trip. These are the weather and crowds. To a large extent the two are related. There are, with some notable exceptions, more visitors in the cooler months than during the hot summers. However, the presence of some of the big conventions, for example, can be a less than ideal time to visit. November's Comdex is the best example. If you like crowds, then you don't have to be concerned with avoiding any particular time. If there is an advantage to coming at a busy time, it is that the electricity in the air and the general carnival atmosphere of Vegas is even better when the place is jumping with its largest visitor counts.

Although Vegas is never lacking for lots of visitors, one of the slowest periods is the time from after Thanksgiving weekend to just before Christmas. Those who want to shun the hordes might find that a good time to come to town but it has a drawback if you plan to see a lot of shows – many, especially the bigger production shows, take a hiatus during the middle part of December.

Now to the weather. Las Vegas Valley sits in the middle of the desert, actually the meeting point of three deserts: the **Mojave**, the **Sonoran** and the **Great Basin**. As you might guess, then, the temperature here can get pretty hot. The city is surrounded by mountains, the highest peak of which is **Mt. Charleston**, northwest of the city, at just under 12,000 feet. There is very little rainfall – about 4-1/4 inches per year and an average of 294 days of sunshine, including partially sunny days. It is dry, windy and hot much of the time.

July and August are the hottest months when the daily maximum temperatures almost always easily tops 100 degrees. Be prepared: dress lightly and wear a hat. You can have rain showers at this time of the year but rainy days are almost unknown. The heat is mitigated to some extent by the low humidity. Even during the August "monsoon" season, when moisture from Arizona flows into the Valley, it is unusual for the humidity to rise beyond the 20's for any length of time. (You'll hear the locals complaining about the oppressive humidity when it gets to around 25 percent – they don't know what humidity is!)

January and December are the coolest months; the average maximum is 60 degrees, but it can go below freezing so bring at least one warm jacket or sweater if you're planning to visit anytime during the winter. The spring and autumn months are the most temperate, with average temperatures in the 70's and 80's.

The worst thing about the Las Vegas weather isn't the heat and certainly not the lack of rain – it's the wind. The heating conditions and the surrounding mountains make for many windy days. Sustained winds of 25mph are not uncommon. On the other hand, the wind seems to take to extremes. It can be windy for a day or a week and then revert to calm or near calm conditions for days at a time. The change is, more often than not, quite abrupt.

LAS VEGAS CLIMATE AT A GLANCE

	Average Daily Maximum	Average Daily Minimum	Precipitation
January	54	34	0.48"
February	59	35	0.22"
March	66	42	0.69"
April	81	54	0.21"
May	90	63	0.28"
June	102	72	0.12"
July	105	78	0.35"
August	104	75	0.49"
September	87	62	0.28"
October	80	54	0.20"
November	62	40	0.44"
December	60	36	0.36"

WHAT TO PACK

The days when people came to Las Vegas dressed to kill are long since gone although you'll see just about every kind of dress, especially on a Saturday night. Don't be surprised to see a couple in jeans and tees sitting next to a well dressed couple. It happens all the time. You can wear just about anything you want to in Las Vegas although some of the fancier restaurants have dress codes (we'll let you know in the Where to Eat chapter). Showrooms don't require fancy outfits either although they do frown on tank or halter tops, cut-off jeans and other similar non-attire.

We usually suggest packing light when going on vacation, however, if you're going to stay put in Las Vegas for several days and don't have to worry about constantly packing and unpacking, you might be more inclined to bring along a few more changes of outfits than is usual for touring.

In the summer make sure you have light colored clothes that breathe. Shorts and tees are quite the order of dress for the day but they aren't always the best choice. They seem the logical choice given the relentless heat and sunshine. But in reality, it makes more sense to cover up a little more skin and keep those rays off of you as much as possible. Sunscreen is advisable and sunglasses and a hat are a must. It's unlikely you'll need a jacket during the evening unless you chill quite easily. The wintertime is another matter. A light wind breaker is always a good idea and a little bit warmer outer wear can come in handy during the evening.

QUICK TIPS FOR PLANNING YOUR TRIP

• *Don't bet more than you can afford to lose.*

• *Big conventions bring in a ton of people, especially the annual* **Comdex Convention** *(November) and the* **Consumer Electronics Show** *(January). Super Bowl weekend is another jam-packed time. You should make reservations well in advance during these periods because it's extremely difficult to get rooms if you just show up at these times.*

• *The spring and fall are the busiest seasons. With around 119,000 rooms, it's usually possible to locate accommodations – but to get a room in your desired hotel, you should book in advance. Friday and Saturday evenings can be difficult times to get a room at just about any time of the year.*

• *Remember, Las Vegas is in the desert. It gets really hot in the summer so it's a must to drink plenty of fluids – and alcoholic beverages don't count towards your daily requirement of fluids.*

• *Heavy traffic and long lights, especially on The Strip will definitely slow you down, particularly in the evenings. Take alternative routes where possible (see the Getting Around chapter for more information).*

• *Book the most popular shows in advance. The bigger ones often sell out early.*

LAS VEGAS TOURISM INFORMATION

Before you go, you might want to contact the **Las Vegas Convention and Visitors Authority**, the largest "official" source of information on Glitter City. Their mailing address is *3150 Paradise Road, Las Vegas, NV 89109; Tel. 702/892-0711.* They also have a Room Reservation Service, *Tel. 800/332-5333.* The Convention folks can give you an up-to-the minute update on special events and show schedules for the time you'll be in Las Vegas. You might want to request a general information packet, or more specifically "Events & Attractions" and "Showguide." They contain schedules for two-month periods (for example, October-November).

Other useful folks to call, depending on your needs:

Las Vegas Chamber of Commerce, *711 E. Desert Inn Road; Tel. 702/735-1616*, who can fill you in on facts and figures about the area if you're more interested in relocation than visiting.

Nevada Commission on Tourism, *Capitol Complex, Carson City, NV 89104; Tel. 800/638-2328*, if you want more detailed information about things to do outside the city limits or somewhere else in Nevada.

Las Vegas Events, an events hotline of sorts, *Tel. 702/731-2115*; find out by phone what's going on during your intended stay.

Finally, although there are many different web sites with information on Las Vegas, most of them are rather specific and not suited to general planning. The exception is the comprehensive *http://www.lasvegas.com* which has a multitude of information that will interest the cyber traveler and cyber planner. If you like to make your reservations on-line but aren't sure which hotel you wish to stay at then log on to Travelscape at *http://www.lvrs.com.* We've also included some individual hotel web sites in the hotel listings.

Once you're in town you can still contact any of the above information sources. However, it's easier then to consult the local newspapers or magazines for the latest scoop. See the appropriate section in the next chapter.

A LITTLE ADVANCE PLANNING

We usually recommend a fairly good amount of advance planning when it comes to having an itinerary. For Las Vegas, however, it isn't as important to do so as for a road vacation. You'll probably find that certain activities are more to your liking than others once you've been in town for a while. However, you should use this book to at least jot down the things that you feel will most appeal to you and at least have a daily framework for what you plan to do. Or, take the easy way and try one of our sample itineraries.

BOOKING YOUR VACATION

The first question to ask yourself is whether or not you need a travel agent. We usually prefer self-booking because it isn't at all difficult to read airline schedules, select and contact a hotel and make whatever other reservations are necessary, such as a car. However, many people feel uncomfortable about doing these things and prefer to let a travel professional do their work.

While most travel agents are familiar with Las Vegas (it is, after all, a frequent destination of many customers) you can't always assume that the agent knows more than you do. In fact, after reading this book you'll likely know more then he or she does. So, use an agent that has been recommended by others. Another good indication of reliability is to ascertain if the agent is a member of the American Society of Travel Agents (ASTA). Membership in that group or other industry organizations should be considered as a minimum requirement when selecting a travel agent.

Regardless of which travel agent you choose, their services should be free of charge to you. Some agents have begun instituting fees in recent years because airlines and other travel industry payers have been reducing commissions to agents. We don't doubt that it's becoming harder for agents to make a living but it shouldn't be at your expense when the majority still do it without charging the customer. This especially applies to booking a Las Vegas trip which is an easy task for the agent.

Travel agents will generally recommend a package plan when going to Vegas. This includes airfare, hotel and sometimes a rental car. They also throw in various coupon books (see the Funbooks section in the next chapter for more on this topic) which are of dubious value. You can often get a great deal using such packages but it isn't always the case. You should check out (either through the agent or on your own) what it would cost if you purchase each component separately. Not only may it be the same price or even lower, but it allows you to tailor it more specifically to your own needs. That can even be worth paying a little extra for.

Las Vegas is the kind of place where being on your own is best. There are few comprehensive guided tours and they aren't worth discussing. If you do not rent a car and wish to see some things outside of the city then you can purchase day bus tours from numerous operators. These will be discussed later and can be arranged at just about any Strip hotel.

GETTING THE BEST AIRFARE

Even travel agents have trouble pinning down what the best airfare is on a given flight on a given day. It's like trying to hit a moving object. If you call one airline ten times and ask what it will cost to fly from New York to Las Vegas on the morning of July 10th and return on the afternoon of July 16th, you'll probably get several different answers. It wouldn't surprise us to hear that you got ten different responses! Unfortunately, such is the state of the airline fare game. The car rental companies and even hotels aren't much better. There are, however, some things to keep in mind when searching for the best fare.

When you fly is important. Travel to Las Vegas will be cheaper during the mid-week than on weekends or shoulder days (Monday and Friday). The time of the year can also have a big effect. If you travel during the busiest times of the year the airfare will likely be higher. Night flights are considerably less expensive than daytime travel if you don't mind arriving on the "red-eye" special. Even then it might not be as cheap as it seems. For example, if you arrive in Las Vegas at eleven in the evening you'll be paying for an extra night's hotel that you may not have had to if you flew in the next morning. So be sure to check all the angles.

Advance confirmed reservations that are paid for prior to your flight are almost always the cheapest way to go. The restrictions on these low fares vary considerably. In general you must book and pay for your tickets at least seven to 30 days in advance. In most cases they require that you stay over a Saturday night. They usually are non-refundable or require payment of a large penalty to either cancel or even make a change in the flight itinerary.

You can sometimes find big bargains by doing the opposite strategy – waiting for the last minute. If the airline has empty seats on the flight you select they're often willing to fill it up for a ridiculous low price. The problem with this is that you don't know if there will be an available seat at the time you want to go. In recent years there has been a "shortage" of flights to Las Vegas, especially long distance direct flights from the east coast. If you have hotel and other reservations this can be a dangerous game to play. Also, even if you do get a ticket at the last minute it can wind up being at a sky high price.

In this era of deregulation, airfares from one airline to another can sometimes be radically different, although carriers flying the same routes will often adjust their fares to the competition more often than not. Whenever possible, try to go with a low-fare airline, several of which have extensive service into Las Vegas.

One thing you should always be on the lookout for regardless of who you plan to fly with are promotional fares. Scan the newspapers or just call the airlines. It's always best to phrase your inquiry something like "what's the lowest available fare between Las Vegas and x on date y?'

Finally, we know that those accustomed to first class air are going to squirm in their seats at this but the cost of first class is simply not worth it – you're only going to be on the plane for a few hours. This isn't a week long cruise where you want to be pampered every minute. Go coach, bring along a good book (such as this) and enjoy the flight.

FLYING TO LAS VEGAS

Las Vegas is served by more than 20 airlines. Here's a rundown on the major carriers including which cities they serve non-stop to Las Vegas.

- **America West**, *Tel. 800/247-5692; web site: www.americawest.com.* Las Vegas is a major hub for this airline and flies non-stop to Atlanta, Baltimore, Boston, Chicago, Columbus, Dallas/Ft. Worth, Denver, Detroit, El Paso, Ft. Lauderdale, Houston, Indianapolis, Kansas City, Los Angeles, Mexico City, Miami, Minneapolis, New York/Newark, Oakland, Omaha, Orlando, Philadelphia, Phoenix, Portland, Reno, Sacramento, St. Louis, Salt Lake City, San Diego, San Francisco, Seattle/Tacoma, Tampa, Tucson and Washington. Many of their long distance non-stops are overnight flights.

- **American Airlines**, *Tel. 800/433-7300; web site: www.aa.com.* Non-stop service to Chicago, Colorado Springs, Dallas/Ft. Worth, Los Angeles, Oklahoma City, Portland, Reno, San Diego, San Francisco, San Jose, Seattle and Tucson. Except for Chicago, Dallas and Los Angeles, all of the other cities were recently added to American's route system by their acquisition of Reno Air. Unfortunately, they won't be providing the same low cost fares. The merger was scheduled to be completed by the time this book reaches the shelves; if not, Reno Air's number was *Tel. 800/RENO-AIR.*

- **Continental Airlines**, *Tel. 800/525-0280; web site: www.continentalair.com.* Non-stop service to Cleveland, Houston (their hub and transfer point to dozens of other localities), and New York.

- **Delta Airlines**, *Tel. 800/221-1212; web site: www.delta-air.com.* Non-stop service to Atlanta, Boston, Cincinnati, Dallas/Ft. Worth, Los Angeles, New Orleans, New York, Orlando, Portland, Salt Lake City and Tampa. Good connections to their entire route system.

- **National Airlines**, *Tel. 888/757-5387, web site: www.nationalairlines.com.* A new airline with Vegas as its hub. Serves Chicago, New York, San Francisco, with more cities planned.

- **Northwest Airlines**, *Tel. 800/225-2525; web site: www.nwa.com.* Non-stop service to Detroit, Los Angeles, Memphis, Minneapolis/St. Paul, Seattle and San Francisco. They also have initiated non-stop service to Tokyo, Japan.

- **Southwest Airlines**, *Tel. 800/359-5786; web site: www.southwest.com.* The largest airline in Las Vegas and a popular low cost one as well. Non-stop service to Albuquerque, Amarillo, Austin, Baltimore/Washington, Boise, Chicago (Midway), Cleveland, El Paso, Houston, Kansas City, Los Angeles, Lubbock, Midland/Odessa, Nashville, New Orleans, Oakland, Omaha, Orlando, Phoenix, Portland, Reno, Sacramento, Salt Lake City, St. Louis, San Antonio, San Diego, San Jose, Seattle/Tacoma, Spokane, Tampa, Tucson and Tulsa.

- **TWA**, *Tel. 800/221-2000; web site: www.twa*.com. Non-stop service to New York and to their system hub in St. Louis.
- **United Airlines**, *Tel. 800/241-6522; web site: www.ual.com*. Non-stop service to Chicago, Denver, Fresno, Los Angeles, Palm Springs, San Francisco and Washington with connections to their entire route system.
- **USAirways**, *Tel. 800/428-4322; web site: www.usairways.com*. Non-stop service to Charlotte, Philadelphia and Pittsburgh.

Some other airlines serving Las Vegas include **Air Canada**, *Tel. 800/776-3000;* **Alaska Airlines**, *Tel. 800/426-0333;* **American Trans Air**, *Tel. 800/225-2995;* **Frontier Airlines**, *Tel. 800/432-1359;* **Hawaiian Air**, *Tel. 800/227-7110;* **SkyWest**, *Tel. 800/453-9417* and **Sun Country Airlines**, *Tel. 800/359-5786*. The latter was one of the major charter airlines but recently converted to a scheduled carrier. They currently serve Las Vegas from Minneapolis, Milwaukee, Dallas and Detroit.

There are a few airlines offering air tours from Las Vegas to the Grand Canyon and other nearby scenic areas. These will be discussed in the Chapter 16, *Excursions & Day Trips*.

6. BASIC INFORMATION

You'll encounter a variety of useful and interesting information in this chapter that will make you a more informed traveler. Major topics that are covered in their own chapter (such as hotels, dining, shopping and entertainment, to name a few) won't be included here.

ALCOHOLIC BEVERAGE & GAMING LAWS

The minimum drinking age is 21 years and if you look underage bartenders will not be bashful to request proper identification. The same restrictions apply to gambling. Parents should take note that Nevada gaming regulations prohibit children from loitering in the casino. You are not allowed to play if your children are present. Although virtually every casino is designed so that you have to pass through it in order to get anywhere, children can walk in the casino so long as they do not stop in an active gaming area. Casinos operate 24 hours a day, 365 days a year. Likewise, alcoholic beverages are always available.

BANKING, MONEY & CREDIT CARDS

After spending all of your money on shopping and shows (not to mention gambling), you may well need to replenish your cash stockpile. Most banks are open from 9:00 am to 5:00 pm weekdays (with some later hours on Friday) and from 10:00 am to 1:00 pm on Saturday. Some are even open on Sunday.

You should have no trouble using traveler's checks in casinos to buy chips. If you have good credit you may be able to take out a line of credit at most casinos, but call first and make sure that you can provide them with the necessary documentation (usually something like credit cards or a driver's license; some may require a bank statement).

Almost all casinos now have automatic teller machines (ATM's) where you'll be able to use either your local ATM card if it's part of one of the large national networks or your VISA, MasterCard or other major credit card. Watch out, though: a number of hotel ATM machines charge fees beyond the nominal charge you may find elsewhere. The fees on cash advances for charge cards are, likewise, similary exorbitant.

Credit cards are almost universally accepted in Las Vegas. All hotel and restaurant listings in this book will indicate if credit cards are accepted. In cases where four or less are valid the names of the card will be shown. *Most major credit cards accepted* indicates five are valid (including American Express, Discover, MasterCard and VISA) while the acceptance of six or more cards will be indicated by *Major credit cards accepted*. The same cards valid for use in paying your hotel bill will always be accepted for show tickets at that hotel. The acceptance of at least some credit cards at other attractions will be indicated only if the price is $20 or higher.

EMERGENCIES

No one likes to think about emergencies when the skies are blue and you're having a swell time but it's always good to know what to do in case trouble arises. Coordinated emergency services (police, ambulance and fire) throughout the Las Vegas area and all of Nevada can be reached by dialing **911**. The Las Vegas Metro Police Department non-emergency number is *Tel. 702/795-3111*.

General care hospitals in the Las Vegas Valley are:
- **Desert Springs Hospital**, *2075 E. Flamingo Road. Tel. 702/733-8800*
- **Lake Mead Hospital**, *1409 E. Lake Mead Blvd., North Las Vegas. Tel. 702/ 649-7711*
- **Mountainview Hospital**, *3100 N. Tenaya Way. Tel. 702/255-5000*
- **St. Rose Dominican Hospital**, *102 E. Lake Mead Drive, Henderson. Tel. 702/564-2622*
- **Summerlin Hospital Medical Center**, *657 Town Center Drive. Tel. 702/ 233-7000*
- **Sunrise Hospital & Medical Center**, *3186 Maryland Parkway. Tel. 702/ 731-8000*
- **University Medical Center**, *1800 W. Charleston Blvd. Tel. 702/383-2090*
- **Valley Hospital**, *620 Shadow Lane. Tel. 702/876-4357*

If you need a doctor or dentist for non-emergencies, call the **Clark County Medical Society**, *Tel. 702/739-9989* or the **Clark County Dental Society**, *Tel. 702/255-7873*. In addition, there are literally dozens of walk-in medical centers throughout the city. They can be found in the yellow pages. A few are located on The Strip in some of the major hotels. Both the Imperial Palace and Caesars Palace have such facilities.

There are many 24-hour pharmacies around but the most convenient one for the majority of visitors will be the **Walgreens** located on The Strip at *3765 Las Vegas Blvd. South*. In addition to prescriptions, you can get other items such as sunscreen and aspirin for a lot less money here than at the hotel sundry shops.

FOREIGN VISITORS

Our friends from abroad, especially those from just over the northern frontier, love Las Vegas like few other American cities. For many, the allure of Vegas is not just the prospect of a quick buck; for better or worse, many foreigners perceive Las Vegas as the quintessential American city.

More visitors from Canada go to Vegas than any other country, with more than one million tourists arriving each year. Next in line are Great Britain, Germany, Japan, Mexico, France, Spain and Brazil.

If you need to change money, you'll get a better rate at most banks or foreign exchange shops than you will in the hotels and casinos. One exception is the **American Foreign Exchange** *in the Las Vegas Hilton; Tel. 702/892-0100.*

It's a good idea to bring traveler's checks for the bulk of your cash, or even better, you can use most major credit cards at cash machines. You can exchange money at most hotels and banks, and of course at the airport.

The United States uses a 110-volt alternating current system which can blow the socks off electrical equipment not designed for it. Chances are you'll need a transformer for any electrical appliances you bring in, including electric razors. Also, we use a two prong outlet with one prong slightly larger than the other. You can purchase cheap adapters in many places.

Passports & Visas

If you are visiting the US from abroad (other than Canada and Mexico), you will need a **valid passport** and, depending upon the country, a **visa**. The American embassy in your home country or your own immigration authorities will know if there are any visa requirements. There are limits on what you may bring in: $400 in duty-free gifts; one liter of alcohol (the booze will count against your $400 total); and 200 cigarettes or 100 cigars. You'll have to report on a customs form if you are carrying in more than $10,000 in US currency.

The authorities are also touchy about bringing in agricultural produce and meat products, so if your plans call for importing some kind of foodstuff (or your pet plants), do yourself a favor and contact the **US Customs Service**, *1301 Constitution Ave., NW, Washington, DC 20229; Tel. 202/566-8195.*

FUN BOOKS & DISCOUNTS

Fun books are free coupons given out in many hotels and casinos as well as other locations.. You can probably pick one up in your hotel lobby or just ask one of the receptionists or employees. You can also usually find them in the complementary tourist magazines like *What's On* or *Today in Las Vegas*. Some hotels go so far as to have an employee in the street handing them out to passers-by.

The coupons offer things like free drinks, gambling incentives such as three-for-two dollar plays at the tables, free pulls at slots, discounts on meals, and the like. *The Discover Nevada Bonus Book*, available from the Nevada Commission on Tourism, also has lots of coupons. Many package tour plans and/or airlines flying to Las Vegas will also distribute a fun book to their passengers. Keep in mind that although you do get something for nothing, it isn't such a big deal. They can save you a couple of bucks here and there and maybe a little more if you're not to choosy as to where you eat. For example, the better hotel buffets and restaurants are rarely, if ever, included in the coupon books.

Also be wary of "free trips" that are offered to you as part of many group travel arrangements. Often it's just a way of taking you to an off-Strip casino to gamble all day. If you like to gamble, fine, but otherwise you'll just be trapped at a place you don't really want to be until they take you back to your hotel.

HEALTH

A week long stay in Las Vegas isn't much different from the stand-point of health precautions than staying in any other city in the United States. However, there are some potential pitfalls that, while not necessarily unique to Las Vegas, can be something that visitors will often fall into. **Sunburn** or **heat exhaustion** during the summer are definite threats. Drink plenty of fluids. Water is best but fruit juices also count towards your daily requirement. Take your sunbathing in the morning and in small doses. Use a good quality sunscreen. If you are going to be taking part in demanding forms of outdoor recreation during the hotter months, again, try to do it in the cooler morning hours. Wear protective clothing including a hat. Avoid contact with wild animals in the surrounding area. Some of them can carry disease.

The widespread availability of **alcohol** (including free drinks when you play) can be a temptation that some people will have trouble resisting. Pace yourself. Don't overdo it. It's likely that you'll wind up drinking a bit more in Las Vegas than at home but know your limitations or have a family member cut you off at the appropriate time. And remember that drinking alcoholic beverages does not count toward your water intake requirements. Alcohol can actually cause dehydration.

NEWSPAPERS & MAGAZINES

The *Las Vegas Review Journal* (or RJ to the locals) is the city's largest newspaper and publishes every morning. If you happen to be in town on a Friday then it's a good idea to pick up a copy because the pull-out tabloid section titled "Neon" has a comprehensive listing of current entertainment and other useful information. The *Las Vegas Sun* is an afternoon newspaper that publishes weekdays and has a section in the weekend editions of the RJ. Its visitor information value is, however, sparse compared to the former. A number of other newspapers are published for residents but also have information that can be useful for visitors, especially those seeking alternative life-styles. *Las Vegas Weekly* is the best of the publications in that category.

Every hotel distributes one or more free magazines that feature information on current entertainment and happenings as well as general tourism information. The biggest is *What's On*. It is published every two weeks. This can be a valuable source of information but a word of caution is advised: having read this publication for several years we are of the opinion that articles and reviews contained in it definitely seem to favor the hotel/casinos that advertise in it the most. *Las Vegas Style* (monthly) and *Las Vegas Today* (bi-weekly) both also offers some good information. *Showbiz Magazine* comes out every week and is almost as huge as *What's On*. It concentrates mostly on entertainment rather than on things to see and do.

PLACES OF WORSHIP

This may be Sin City in the eyes of many, but people *do* live here and there are scores of houses of worship representing all major denominations. According to local lore Las Vegas has more churches and synagogues per capita than any other city in America! There are even a few churches located on or very near to The Strip. Here are some of the bigger and better-known houses of worship should the urge hit you (or you need some help in getting on a winning streak):

- **Guardian Angel Cathedral**, *336 Cathedral Way, between Desert Inn Road and Convention Center Drive; Tel. 702/735-5241.* This Catholic church sits not quite on The Strip. The church draws big crowds, particularly for Saturday afternoon Mass.
- **St. Joan of Arc**, *315 S. Casino Center Blvd; Tel. 702/382-9909,* a Catholic church.
- **First Baptist Church**, *300 S. 9th Street; Tel. 702/382-6177*
- **First Southern Baptist Church**, *700 E. St. Louis Ave.; Tel. 702/732-3100*
- **Reformation Lutheran Church**, *580 E. St. Louis Ave.; Tel. 702/732-2052*
- **First United Methodist**, *231 S. Third Street; Tel. 702/382-9939*

• **Temple Beth Shalom**, *1600 E. Oakey Blvd.; Tel. 702/384-5070*
• **Shrine of the Most Holy Redeemer**, *55 E. Reno Ave., Tel. 702/891-8600.*
  This Catholic church is located just east of The Strip, a block south of
  Tropicana Avenue.

SAFETY

Any big city has crime and Las Vegas is no exception. Yet, considering
the number of tourists that come through each year, the safety record for
visitors is exceptional. The police (and hotel security forces which assist
them) do a good job in protecting tourists. After all, it is the city's
lifeblood. While some simple precautions are in order, Las Vegas is
probably the only city in America where you can walk down the main
street at one in the morning with a thousand dollars in your wallet and not
get mugged! On the other hand, feeling too secure is never a good idea
– anywhere, so familiarize yourself with this brief list of safety tips:

• Avoid contact with panhandlers. Although most of them are harmless
  there have been some incidents in the past. If they come up to you just
  ignore them and keep walking. Panhandlers will be found on The
  Strip but even more so in the downtown area.
• Even though mostly everyone on The Strip and other popular areas is
  carrying a good deal of cash, don't attract attention to yourself by
  flaunting it. Keep money hidden until you have to spend it and don't
  wear expensive jewelry when wandering around outside.
• Stick to The Strip or the main part of Fremont Street late at night. There
  are some areas in Las Vegas you don't want to be in, especially at
  night.
• Lock your hotel room and use the deadbolt lock where provided. Do not
  let anyone in your room unless they have properly identified themselves as a hotel employee. Even then, if you did not request service
  of some kind, verify their presence by calling the front desk.
• Use hotel safe deposit boxes for large amounts of cash and valuable
  jewelry when you aren't going to be needing them.
• Acquaint yourself with the layout of the hotel. Identify the nearest fire
  exit and be sure everyone in your party, including children, knows
  what to do in case of a fire. (Fire precautions and escape routes are
  posted in each room.) Do not use elevators during a fire; always take
  the stairs.
• The busy and exciting surroundings can make it easy to get distracted
  as a pedestrian. Always exercise caution when crossing streets,
  especially The Strip and other major thoroughfares. Wait for the
  signal that it is safe to cross. (Las Vegas has many wide, multi-lane
  streets.) Use pedestrian bridges whenever available.

• Although this is the desert and there is little rainfall, sudden downpours (especially summer thunderstorms) can result in flash flooding. While this isn't a major problem in tourist areas such as The Strip, be careful in outlying areas. Never cross a road that is flooded and stay away from all natural or man-made depressions and washes. You could quickly get swept away in a torrent from only a few minutes of heavy rain.

TAXES

The sales tax in Las Vegas is 7.25 per cent and is added to the cost of all purchases (with a few exceptions). There is no sales tax on services. An additional 2% tax is levied on the cost of hotel rooms. But the worst tax that the state of Nevada soaks visitors for is the 17.25% (including the sales tax) on entertainment. This includes all shows and even restaurants which offer a formal entertainment program. Well, someone has to help pay for the residents' services!

TELEPHONES

Surprise – telephones in Vegas are just like everywhere else in the country. Beginning in 1999, Nevada will be split into two area codes. The one you have to be most concerned with is 702, which covers Clark County and encompasses the entire Las Vegas area. All other parts of Nevada will be in the 775 area code and will require dialing "1" before the area code and number. The "1" prefix is also required for all toll free calls (800, 877 and 888 exchanges).

TIME OF DAY

Las Vegas is in the Pacific Time Zone (three hours earlier than the east coast) and observes Daylight Savings Time. It's a good idea to wear a watch because it isn't easy to find a clock in any casino!

TIPPING

Las Vegas didn't invent the "folding favor" but tipping is a way of life in this city. So, more than ever the question that we must ask ourselves is: how much should I tip this guy or gal? Tipping varies from country to country so here are a few rules for tipping Vegas-style. Of course, if you hit the million-dollar jackpot you'll probably want to be more generous than the advice given here!

Gratuities are not built into the check at restaurants unless you have a party of more than a certain number, usually ten or more, although this varies from place to place. For good restaurant service, 15% is the norm. You can be a big tipper by leaving 20% or more, which many people do if they feel the service is outstanding. Don't forget to tip your server at a buffet (the person who brings your drink and clears away the plates for the next round of eating). Many people think they don't have to, but it is customary to leave about a dollar a person for dinner. At the bar, leave a dollar for each round of drinks ordered.

For taxis, the standard tip is 10%; 10-15% for limousines. Give your bellhop a dollar or two for bringing your bags to your room, $3 if you have a number of heavy bags; and leave anywhere from $7 to $10 a week for efficient maid service in your hotel room. The Gaming chapter has some additional suggestions for tipping at the table.

In the old days you had to give an exorbitant tip to the maitre'd hotel in showrooms in order to get a good seat. Fortunately, most rooms have gone to an assigned seating system so you don't have to tip the individual taking you to your seat. Those shows with cocktail service will often include the gratuity in the price of the ticket. If not, a dollar per drink is sufficient.

OTHER SPECIAL CONSIDERATIONS

DISABLED TRAVELERS

If you or someone you're traveling with is disabled, you might want to call ahead and find out what special services are available and where. Las Vegas is better than many other cities in adapting its buildings and services for the disabled.

Write or call one of the following agencies:
- **Nevada Association for the Handicapped**, *6200 W. Oakey Blvd., Las Vegas, NV 89102. Tel. 702/870-7050*
- **Southern Nevada Sightless Inc.**, *1001 N. Bruce Street, Las Vegas, NV 89101. Tel. 702/642-0100*

TRAVELING WITH CHILDREN

Besides making sure that you have something to occupy your little ones for the trip to Las Vegas, Chapter 17 will provide you with plenty of things to see and do that children will enjoy.

SENIOR CITIZENS

Discounts for senior citizens are often available for the asking. This includes airfare, hotels, restaurants, car rental, area attractions and even some shopping. So it pays to get some details from the right sources. Vegas is a great town for discounts so seniors can usually do pretty well for themselves here. Identification cards from such organizations like the **American Association of Retired Persons** (AARP) are often useful. These organizations sometimes even have special travel services for seniors.

Whether you're seeking general information or specific activities and events for seniors, a good source is the **Senior Citizens Center of Las Vegas and Clark County**, *450 E. Bonanza, four blocks from Casino Center Blvd. Tel. 702/229-6454.*

COMPS, LAS VEGAS STYLE

The bigger brother of fun books are comps, gambling jargon for freebies, which are available to those who will be doing some serious gambling. Casinos will gladly supply you with comps for meals (to include the better eating establishments), shows, rooms and even airfare. But it doesn't come easy or free: you've got to earn it by showing the casinos a sufficient level of action, or play.

What about your acquaintance who constantly gets comped for the whole deal – airfare, room, shows and food? Jealous? Don't be. These comps are earned the hard way, and in all likelihood these gamblers drop so much money at the tables that the casinos are glad to comp them the whole shebang – again and again. Wouldn't you? A running joke in Las Vegas is the guy who laments that his free breakfast cost him $389!

If you're looking to earn comps by gambling it will mean more than just gambling at your own pace. But if you're already a big player then comps are the way to go. The casinos will be more than happy to make you feel comfortable if you give them the chance at your gambling dollar.

How do you go about getting comps? It's simple – ask for them. The casino will let you know the deal. Or if you're already in the casino playing, don't be afraid to ask for some comps. A subtle suggestion to the pit boss such as, "How's the food in the grill?" or "How's the show?" should get the message across. If your play is seen as adequate, hey, have a good meal – on the house.

Another type of comp is the slot club. See the sidebar on this in Chapter 11.

7. ARRIVALS & DEPARTURES

GEOGRAPHIC ORIENTATION

Las Vegas sits in the southeastern tip of the state of Nevada, near the confluence of three states: California to the west, Utah to the northeast and Arizona to the east and southeast. Situated in a beautiful valley about 2,100 feet above sea level, Las Vegas has low humidity – about 29 percent on average but usually lower in the summer – and ranges from hot to mild.

The highest mountains which rim the valley are to the west of The Strip. These are the **Spring Mountains**, with 11,918-foot high **Charleston Peak** being the tallest of the group. Several smaller ranges lie to the east with the dominant landmark being **Sunrise Mountain**. The southern border of the valley is the **Railroad Pass**. Just to the south of the pass is Boulder City, the **Lake Mead National Recreation Area** and **Hoover Dam**. The northern end of the valley doesn't have such a sharp beginning – it more or less fades away into other mountain rimmed desert valleys.

There aren't any significant rivers in the Valley – only a few **washes** which are usually dry except after torrential rains – and no natural lakes. There are a number of nice man-made lakes throughout the Valley.

ARRIVING & DEPARTING BY AIR

The point of entry and exit for many of the 30 million visitors to Las Vegas is the large and modern **McCarran International Airport** (*general information: Tel. 702/261-5743; terminal paging: Tel. 702/261-5733*). McCarran is one of the busiest airports in the United States, remarkable for a city of Las Vegas' size.

More than 20 airlines serve Las Vegas and there are many additional charter lines. With the addition of the spanking new "D" gates in 1998, McCarran retains its leading position as one of the most modern, attractive and efficient airport facilities in the world. Moving walkways help you with the long distances between gates and two automated rail systems connect the main terminal with the "C" and "D" sections.

The airport is spotlessly clean and you can indulge your gambling appetite right off the plane. Slot machines are ringing, clanging, banging and bojangling everywhere. But our advice on airport slots is to skip them – they're generally "tight," meaning that the payoff is low.

When departing Las Vegas by air don't cut your time too short. Getting to your destination gate can be a long trip and with the crowds that often abound at peak periods you may find yourself having to run to catch your plane.

FROM THE AIRPORT TO THE CITY
Limos & Taxis

The city's bus service has two lines that go out to the airport but they aren't a convenient way to get to The Strip or most other hotels. McCarran is close in, however, just one mile from the southern part of The Strip and about five miles from Downtown. You might want to consider taking one of the main **limousine services** in front of the terminal ($3.50 per person to The Strip and about $5.00 to Downtown). The main services are **Ambassador Limo**, *Tel. 702/362-6200*, **Bell Transportation**, *Tel. 702/385-5466* and **LV Limo**, *Tel. 702/739-8414*. More expensive limo service is available from **Presidential**, *Tel. 702/731-5577*.

The **Gray Line** airport shuttle, *Tel. 702/739-5700*, runs about the same price as a limo but isn't as much fun. You need to reserve the shuttle at least one day in advance. Other similar shuttle services are provided by **Ray & Ross Transport**, *Tel. 702/646-4661* and **Bell Trans Shuttle**, *Tel. 702/739-7990*. Gray Line and other shuttle buses pick you up on the street across from the baggage claim area.

Taxis are also readily available at the terminal, but it'll cost you about twice as much as one of the limo or shuttle services. Among the larger taxi companies you'll see at the airport and around town are:
- **Ace Cab**, *Tel. 702/736-7708*
- **Desert Cab**, *Tel. 702/376-2687*
- **Western Cab**, *Tel. 702/382-7100*
- **Whittlesea Blue Cab**, *Tel. 702/384-6111*

You should definitely inquire with your hotel before you arrive to see if they offer free limo or van pickup from the airport. Such services used to be rare but they are becoming more common in recent years.

CAR RENTALS

If you want to rent a car, a number of car rental agencies have cars waiting for you just outside the airport and at selected hotels in the city.

It's always a good idea to call ahead and book a car, especially during peak periods such as weekends and major holidays. Following are among the many car rental agencies you'll find in town, separated by national chains and local operators. The local phone number is either a central reservation point for all locations or is the office nearest the airport.

Note: [A]=airport location; [S]=Strip location; [O]=Other location. An airport location doesn't always mean that the car will always actually be within the airport confines – sometimes it is a short shuttle bus ride away.

National Chains
• **Alamo**, *Tel. 800/327-9633 or 702/263-8411.* A
• **Avis**, *Tel. 800/831-2847 or 702/261-5595.* A-S-O
• **Budget**, *Tel. 800/527-0700 or 702/736-1212.* A-S-O
• **Dollar**, *Tel. 800/800-4000 or 702/739-8408.* A-S
• **Enterprise**, *Tel. 800/736-8222 or 702/795-8842.* A-S-O
• **Hertz**, *Tel. 800/654-3131 or 702/736-4900.* A-S
• **National**, *Tel. 800/227-7368 or 702/261-5391.* A
• **Thrifty**, *Tel. 800/367-2277 or 702/896-7600.* A

Major Local or Regional Companies
• **Advantage**, *Tel. 702/386-5775.* A
• **Allstate**, *Tel. 800/634-6186 or 702/736-6147.* A-O
• **Ladki**, *Tel. 800/245-2354 or 702/587-1100.* A-S-O
• **US Rent A Car**, *Tel. 800/777-9377 or 702/798-6100.* A
• **Value**, *Tel. 800/468-2583 or 702/733-8886.* A

ARRIVING & DEPARTING BY BUS

Greyhound buses serve Las Vegas from all directions. The main bus terminal is located Downtown at 200 S. Main Street near Jackie Gaughan's Plaza Hotel. It is the cheapest way to travel by far. *Tel. 702/384-8009 for the bus station; Tel. 800/231-2222 for reservations.* Greyhound has also added some service into neighboring Henderson. The bus stops at the Sunset Station Casino, *1301 W. Sunset Road.*

The bus company has also expanded its working arrangement with Station casinos and has begun service to the other properties in this chain (Palace Station near the Strip; Texas Station in North Las Vegas; and Boulder Station on Boulder Highway.)

ARRIVING & DEPARTING BY CAR

If you're coming by car make sure that you have a full tank of gas, a spare tire and plenty of water because gas stations are few and far between on some stretches of the road and you wouldn't want to get caught short in the middle. Even if your car is in great shape, bring plenty of water as emergency protection against overheating. It's a hot desert out there.

Driving long distances in the glaring sun can be hard on your eyes, so don't forget a good pair of sunglasses. And we certainly hope your air conditioning is working. Summer temperatures will climb into the 100's just about every day and you might soon get to know what dough goes through to become bread.

Driving conditions are generally good but you should be aware that there can be occasional dust storms and winter snowstorms in the high passes. In the event of a dust storm, make sure your lights are on and drive cautiously. If visibility decreases to the point where you cannot see then slowly pull off the road and wait for it to subside. You will also probably encounter at some point the almost inevitable road construction delay as well as heavy traffic. The latter, however, seems to be a bigger problem getting out of town after a busy weekend than when coming in.

Here are some numbers you might want to call for road conditions depending upon which way you're coming into town:
- **Nevada**: *Tel. 702/486-3116*
- **California**: *Tel. 213/628-7623 or 916/445-1534*
- **Arizona**: *Tel. 520/779-2711*
- **Utah**: *Tel. 800/492-2400*

DIRECTIONS

From **Los Angeles** take any major highway to I-10 heading east (the San Bernadino Freeway) past Ontario and then take I-15 north all the way into town. The trip is about 290 miles and should take about 4-1/2 hours without heavy traffic. The speed limit is 65 mph up to the Nevada line where it goes up to 75 mph for a short time until you get nearer to Las Vegas.

There's sometimes heavy fog near the Angeles Forest and, in the winter, passes in the high desert above 4000 feet may get snowed in and require chains. Sometimes they may be closed altogether for short periods.

From other points in **Southern California** you'll still want to hook up with I-15 at the earliest opportunity and take it all the way into town as discussed above.

From **northeastern Nevada** take US Highway 93 south until you hit I-15 and then go south on I-15.

From **Utah** take I-15 south until you see the neon of Las Vegas.

From **Phoenix or Tucson** go north on US 93 past the Lake Mead National Recreation Area. This runs into I-515 and you can take either the Flamingo Road or Tropicana Avenue exits and proceed west to The Strip. I-515 continues directly into Downtown if you're staying in that part of town.

From the **east** (and if your route takes you past Flagstaff, Arizona, just south of the Grand Canyon), take I-40 to Kingman and then go north on US Highway 93 as indicated above.

WHEN IS THE NEXT TRAIN TO LAS VEGAS DUE?

*A good question! Amtrak service to Las Vegas via the Desert Wind from Chicago to Los Angeles was discontinued a few years ago. There are plans in the works to restore service between Los Angeles and Las Vegas. The public and private partnership wants to upgrade the tracks and use high speed Spanish-built **Talgo** cars on the route. In addition to the former terminal station in Downtown there might be one or more stops near some Strip hotels.*

But right now it's still in the talk stage – just like the super monorail or mag-lev trains that crop up for discussion purposes every now and then. In the meantime, we'll keep listening. For now, Amtrak does provide connecting bus service from Los Angeles.

8. GETTING AROUND TOWN

Las Vegas is an easy town to get around in. Many of the big hotels on **The Strip** are within walking distance from each other, as are the casinos in the smaller **Downtown** area, though you'll need transportation between The Strip and Downtown and to get to surrounding areas and excursion destinations.

ON FOOT

It's easy to walk The Strip or Downtown. You won't need transportation within these areas unless you're at a hotel away from The Strip's center, are feeling a bit lazy, or you've been withered by a hot desert sun that gets as high as 115 degrees in the summer. In such instances, taxis or a city bus will do the trick. You will be doing lots of walking, however, if you're going to be touring The Strip hotels. Even when they're "next door," the properties are often so huge that it takes quite a bit of walking to get around. Wear comfortable shoes!

Keep in mind that it is over four miles from one end of The Strip to the other so you either have to do it in small sections or rely on another means of transportation. Downtown is a couple of miles north of the northern end of The Strip.

We won't hesitate to repeat ourselves from earlier and remind you to always be alert for traffic when crossing The Strip. Drivers are just as preoccupied as pedestrians and this can lead to tragic consequences. Fortunately, this problem doesn't exist at the intersection of Tropicana Avenue and partially at Flamingo Road, the busiest Strip intersections, where pedestrian bridges allow walkers to avoid the traffic and cars to avoid the pedestrians. The bridges, which are handicapped accessible, also offer great views of The Strip scene, day and night. The second half of the bridge project at Flamingo Road is now scheduled to be completed some time in 2000.

BY CAR

Despite the good results you can get sightseeing on foot, there is still nothing like the flexibility of a car. This convenience becomes a necessity if you're going to be venturing further afield and don't want to go the guided tour route. Las Vegas is an easy place to get around by car since the major streets are generally in a grid pattern and there are only a few important routes that you need to be familiar with. So let's start with a brief lay-of-the-land description.

Las Vegas Boulevard South is the main street of interest to visitors. That's the official designation of what is simply called "The Strip" – by both visitors and residents. It runs from north to south and is paralleled to the west by I-15. The other major arterial highway is I-515 (also US 93 and US 95) which runs from east to west just north of downtown (where it crosses I-15) and then turns southeasterly and runs roughly parallel to the old Boulder Highway through Las Vegas and on into Henderson. I-215 will eventually be a beltway system. Right now it runs from just west of the southern end of The Strip in the vicinity of the airport and through Henderson to I-515.

The major east-west thoroughfares that cross The Strip are (from south to north), Tropicana Avenue, Flamingo Road, Sands Avenue (Spring Mountain Road west of The Strip), Sahara Avenue, and Charleston Boulevard. Another important route is Desert Inn Road; however, in the area by The Strip it is a controlled access highway that goes underneath Las Vegas Boulevard without direct access to it.

To avoid some of the traffic on The Strip you can use **Industrial Road** for accessing some hotels on the west side of The Strip. Avoiding The Strip and traffic in general may soon start to be an easier task. In addition to the Industrial Road alternative, **Frank Sinatra Drive** is under construction and will run from Russell Road all the way to Flamingo between I-15 and the hotels. This should be finished in the year 2000 along with a new overpass on Hacienda Avenue across the Interstate. The latter should relieve some traffic on Tropicana Avenue. I-15 itself is also going through several widening projects. We might also mention at this juncture that you're likely to encounter road construction just about everywhere in the Valley as the public works folks mightily struggle to keep up with the incredible growth. The east side of The Strip doesn't have as good an alternative system of routes, but Koval Lane can be used in a similar manner between Tropicana and Sands Avenues.

Traffic is commensurate with what you would expect in a big city. But a good system of highways and broad streets keep it manageable. Although the locals complain an awful lot, it isn't really all that bad for a big city, except on The Strip at peak times (which occurs between 6:00 and 10:00 pm) and in the aforementioned construction areas. Perhaps the most exasperating part of coping with Las Vegas traffic are the long traffic signals at major intersections. With every-way lights it seems that you never get the green. Just be patient and your turn will come. The flip side of this is that a lot of cars can get through turns and you don't have to fight your way to make a left. Right hand turns are permitted on red unless indicated otherwise.

At least parking is never a problem. All of the hotels have plenty of free parking (but in Downtown you'll have to validate your parking in the casino). The Strip hotel garages are always behind the hotel itself but, due to the size of many resorts, it can be a little more than a short walk. All hotels have free valet parking which avoids the walking but, of course, it is customary to buy your car back from the valet parker for a buck or two.

GARAGE SECRETS

We already alluded to how big the hotels are. The same goes for the garages, and some places are easier to park in than others. It isn't always best to park where you'll be for a couple of hours – sometimes a nearby hotel will give you less headaches when it comes to getting in and out.

The newer hotels usually have a central or side ramp that accesses all levels of the garage so you don't have to get dizzy going round and round from one level to another. A few examples of these are Bellagio, Caesars, The Mirage, and Treasure Island. Some, such as the Luxor and Excalibur have only two level garages so, they're easy too. Avoid the MGM Grand garage if you can. It's big, confusing and has a naturally crowded design, although a new wing to open in 1999 should help the problem to at least some extent. (If you're going to the Grand try parking at The Tropicana instead.)

Almost all garages have direct access to the casino/hotel, often without going out into the street. To avoid waiting for elevators you should try to park on the garage level that has the bridge to the casino. Of course, these levels tend to fill up faster. If you're not going to park on the bridge level than the best alternative strategy is to head for a higher level which fills up slower and is, therefore, easier to find a space on. If you're parking at Mandalay Bay, avoid the front elevators nearest to the casino unless you're parked right near them. They're always jammed, so it's better to use the elevators in the center of the garage.

BUS & TROLLEY

Buses are an easy and cheap way to get around town. The Regional Transportation Commission of Clark Country runs the **Citizens Area Transit** bus system that is called **CAT** (*Tel. 702/228-7433 for route* *information and schedules*). Trips often take longer on The Strip than the scheduled time but the system is fairly reliable.

The Strip has two routes. The main one is #301 and runs from the Vacation Village Hotel and Casino (at Sunset Road about two miles south of where most of the hotels begin) all the way to the Downtown Transportation Center (DTC). Service is frequent and runs 24 hours a day. The Strip Express bus (#302) covers the same route but has limited stops, so be sure to ask the driver before boarding if it will let you off where you are going. The fare is $1.50 and exact change is required. Discount cards for frequent travelers are available at the DTC (Stewart and Casino Center Boulevard).

One other line that you may be able to make use of is the 402 Crosstown Express. This line has limited stops but connects many of the city's major shopping centers. CAT has almost 40 other routes that go to just about every part of the Las Vegas Valley. Other routes generally do not have service between the wee hours of 1:30 am and 5:30 am. Trip frequency varies by line from about 15 minutes to an hour. In recent years CAT has generally been increasing the frequency of service on many lines. The fare for all lines other than routes in the 300 series is $1.00 and free transfers between routes are available. Virtually all buses are handicapped accessible and they also have bike racks.

There are two "trolley" services to choose from, depending upon where you are. The privately owned and operated **Las Vegas Strip Trolley** (*Tel. 702/382-1404*) covers The Strip from the Sahara Hotel to the Mandalay Bay, with the added feature of dropping you off at the doorstep of most major hotels. This can save a fair amount of walking over CAT buses but it takes even longer as it can be a time consuming affair driving into and out of each hotel drop-off point. The charge is $1.50 (exact change required). The Strip Trolley begins at 9:30 am and runs until 2:00 am. The **Downtown Trolley** (*Tel. 702/229-6024*) is a bargain at 50 cents (over age 65 it's 25 cents). The trolley covers most of Downtown. It's run by the city and closes down at 10:00 pm. Both trolleys are actually buses made to look like old-time trolley cars.

If you're not staying on The Strip and do not have a car, then be sure to make an inquiry as to shuttle services provided by the hotel you are staying at. Many off-Strip properties, especially those not too far from The Strip, provide free transportation to and from the hotel. Some of the Strip hotels also have regular bus service to their non-Strip affiliated hotels or otherwise. Two examples are the service between the Stardust (Strip) and Sam's Town (Boulder Highway); and between the MGM Grand (Strip) and Sunset Station (Henderson). The Rio provides service from the hotel to The Strip at the corner of Harmon Avenue. There are quite a few others, too, such as the one run by Coast Hotels.

TAXIS & LIMOUSINES

Taxis are plentiful and easy to get either on The Strip or Downtown. They're a bit tougher to get outside the main tourist paths – in fact, at other locations it's best to call for one. On The Strip they're lined up at virtually every hotel waiting for fares. The current cost is $2.20 for the initial drop of the meter and then $1.50 for each mile thereafter, with nominal extra charges for more than three passengers. Then they also tack on 35 cents for each minute of waiting time. As in most cities, hold on to your hat – Las Vegas cabbies are justly famous for their aggressive approach to negotiating Strip traffic! The names and telephone numbers of the main taxi companies were listed in the section on getting into town from the airport.

If taking a cab is not your bag, go for a limo. They're a fun way to travel in style, if you can afford it or simply want to splurge. The rates are reasonable compared to some cities – a range of $35-45 an hour to much more for some huge stretch limos, depending on the amenities offered.

The standard limo offers a comfortable ride and a few amenities like stereo sound and a car phone. The stretch limos (which run about $60-$80 per hour) include bar service, cellular phone, color TV, stereo and other amenities. Sound too high for you? Well, what the heck – you're in Vegas. Treat yourself to one limo ride, have your picture taken, and make copies for all your friends back home. Telephone numbers of limo operators are also in the section on getting into town from the airport.

HOTEL MONORAILS & TRAMS

You can't live in Las Vegas without reading about one of a seemingly endless number of proposals to build an elaborate monorail system serving The Strip as well as other areas. It doesn't exist yet and may not ever come to fruition. However, slowly but surely the hotel owners are taking matters into their own hands as isolated transit systems crop up here and there.

The first of these systems to come on line was the monorail connecting Bally's with the MGM Grand. It now also serves Paris. The sleek Disneyland-style monorail runs daily from 9:00 am until midnight. Another system connects Monte Carlo with the Bellagio. The futuristic looking high-tech cars contrast sharply with the traditional interiors of these two hotels. It runs 24 hours a day at approximate five minute intervals. Mandalay Resort Group just completed a tram along its "Miracle Mile" with stops at the Excalibur, Luxor and Mandalay Bay. Another tram, this one a real short ride, can take you between The Mirage and neighboring Treasure Island (24 hours). All of the hotel transit systems are free of charge.

YOUR MAGIC LOCATOR GUIDE

To help arrange things more easily for you, all information on where to stay and eat, seeing the sights, nightlife and entertainment, as well as shopping, will be divided into five geographic sections in each of the chapters on the aforementioned topics. These are as follows:

The Strip: *Las Vegas Boulevard South extending from Russell Road at the southern end to the intersection of Main Street (a little north of Sahara Avenue) in the north.*

Off Strip: *Areas adjacent to or very near The Strip. Establishments will either be on streets that cross Las Vegas Boulevard South or along the Paradise Road corridor between Tropicana Avenue and the Convention Center. Also covers Las Vegas Boulevard south of Russell.*

Downtown: *The old "casino center" area centered around Fremont Street.*

Around Las Vegas: *Everything not included in the three above areas or in the following one. This area also covers the so-called "Boulder Strip" – Boulder Highway from its beginnings at Fremont Street all the way to the Henderson line.*

Henderson: *Anything within the city limits of Henderson, the Las Vegas Valley's biggest community after Las Vegas itself.*

GUIDED TOURS

There are several bus companies offering guided tours that you might want to consider in lieu of renting a car. All offer city tours, trips to Hoover Dam and other locations within hailing distance of Las Vegas. Many offer longer excursion trips as well. For more information, see the section on excursions.

The more reliable tour operators for day trips are listed below. All arrange for pick-up at major hotels. If you're not staying at one of those then they'll tell you to meet them at their nearest pick-up point.

• **Cactus Jack's Wild West Tour Co.**, *Tel. 702/731-2425*
• **Gray Line**, *Tel. 702/384-1234*
• **Guaranteed Tours**, *Tel. 702/369-1000*
• **Sightseeing Tours Unlimited**, *Tel. 702/471-7155*

If you're interested in a more unusual type of tour that almost borders on "adventure," then consider **ATV Action Tours**, *Tel. 702/566-7400.* This firm specializes in highly personalized trips in sport utility vehicles for two to ten people. Besides the usual sights around Las Vegas, ATV Action will take you to the Extra-Terrestrial Highway, "Area 51," ghost towns, or just about any other place you might be interested in.

9. WHERE TO STAY

You're not going to read about pirate ship battles and volcanoes in this chapter. This is about hotels as places to stay (as in sleep). Many of the hotels are, of course, important visitor attractions and, if they fall into this category, you will be referred to Chapter 12 for details. For those hotels that are not included under sightseeing, there will be a more complete general description of the property included in this chapter.

Most of the major hotels have a "theme" whether or not it's in the lower price category, such as the Excalibur, or the upscale Bellagio. The themes are almost as numerous as the hotels. Ancient civilizations or historical eras, famous cities, carnivals, and tropical motifs are among the most popular. The theme vogue has even spread off-Strip in recent years although not to the same extent. Downtown, on the other hand, remains essentially a place of hotels without a particular genre.

Because gaming brings in such a load of money to the hotels, Las Vegas room prices are generally low by comparison with other major cities or resort destinations. Even with the new age of hotels that cater to the *Conde Naste* crowd and the accounting principle that each cost center of the hotel/casino has to carry its own weight, prices have remained generally attractive to the cost conscious traveler. This is especially so when compared to other resorts or major cities. It doesn't mean, however, that you're going to get away cheap. Just less than you might expect if you've traveled extensively but haven't yet been to Vegas.

We've arranged the hotels by cost as shown in the table below. The rates shown and, hence, which category the hotel is listed in, are based on the so-called **rack rate**. Since there is such a huge variation in the rack rate we've categorized each hotel by its average annual rack rate. The standard room charges are based on double occupancy. But in Las Vegas nothing is what it seems.

In effect, there is almost no rack rate. The price for the same room in the same hotel can vary by an extraordinary amount depending upon when you stay there. Weekends and holidays are, of course, higher priced as are the busier months of the year. Special events like Super Bowl Sunday, the National Rodeos Final or major conventions also raise the price. On the other hand with all of the competition these days the rates are frequently discounted from the rack rate. Travel agent arranged packages often get good rates but you can get it on your own if you pick out the proper time. The harsh reality of the situation is that if reservations for a particular night are slow, the rates will drop. But, if potential customers for that same night should suddenly pick up, the rates will rise accordingly. With computers tracking occupancy and trends, the hotels can and do change on a moment's notice. In short, the listed hotel prices are just a guide and may well bear little resemblance to the rate you actually get.

When you have about 119,000 hotel rooms in one place, it obviously allows the buyer some space for maneuvering. Even so, things pretty well fill up at busy times and aren't ever really that slow. The overall occupancy rate is around 90 percent (down a couple of percentage points from the pre-100K room era). That figure, however, is still the envy of the hotel industry which, on a nationwide basis, has an occupancy rate in the low 70's. In addition, The Strip rate is higher than 90 – it's more like 95% filled – because the total figure is brought down by the large number of smaller hotels and motels that only average occupancy in the 60's or 70's. They are a good choice of last resort should The Strip be booked when you want to be in town.

Having said that, it should be apparent that advance room reservations are the way to go. If you are not booking through a travel agent you can make reservations with all of the major hotels through their toll free reservation number. In addition, there are several general booking services for Las Vegas.

These are:

• **Accommodations Express**, *Tel. 800/211-3836 or 702/795-7666*
• **A to Z Reservation Service of Las Vegas**, *Tel. 800/634-6727 or 702/736-2226*
• **Hotel Reservations Network**, *Tel. 800/511-5323*
• **Las Vegas Convention & Visitors Bureau**, *Tel. 702/386-0770*
• **Las Vegas Reservations Systems**, *Tel. 800/233-5594 or 702/369-1919*

While you can probably do as well or better rate-wise by contacting hotels directly in advance, these reservation systems can be especially useful in finding a place to stay should you ignore our previous advice and come into town without a confirmed booking. And as a reminder once again, on-line reservations are available at *http://www.lvrs.com*. Many hotels also offer their own web sites where you can get rate information and book your stay.

For those of you who like to stay in a national chain because you feel comfortable with their known facilities, they are well represented in the Las Vegas area. Among those present are Best Western, Choice Hotels (Comfort, Econolodge, Quality Inn and Rodeway), Days Inn, Marriott Hotels (Courtyard, Fairfield Inn, Marriott Suites and Residence Inn), Hampton Inn, Hilton Hotels, Holiday Inn (including a Crowne Plaza), Howard Johnsons, LaQuinta, Motel 6, Ramada Inn, Sheraton, Super 8 and Travelodge. Many have multiple properties (Best Western, for example has seven different locations) and a number are included in the recommended places to stay.

The variety of accommodations in Las Vegas runs the gamut from the most basic motel units to super-luxurious suites that are bigger than most mansions. Just about the only type of accommodation you won't find in this town is the bed and breakfast inn. It seems that type of lodging doesn't go with the atmosphere and has just never caught on. The only area B&B is located in Mt. Charleston, not exactly a convenient place to stay if you're going to be spending most of your time on The Strip and adjoining areas.

HOTEL ROOM RATE RANGES

Very Expensive	*More than $150*
Expensive	*$101-150*
Moderate	*$65-100*
Inexpensive	*Less than $65*

All costs are for one night based on double occupancy and are exclusive of taxes. See the general write-up above for more information on Las Vegas hotel room rates.

A little explanation about each of the hotel listings that follows is in order. We'll concentrate first on the guest rooms. Under *Dining* will be a list of all the hotel's restaurants and other eating facilities. The most prominent type of cuisine will also be shown.

Finally, the *Facilities* section will give you an indication of the hotel's recreational opportunities and entertainment venues (including casino). A "cocktail lounge" is really just a bar (no entertainment), as opposed to a "lounge with entertainment." The latter, however, is differentiated from a "nightclub" (which has dancing) and a "showroom." A showroom may features either a major production or big-name celebrity entertainment.

> ## WHAT DOES THE ASTERISK MEAN?
> *An **asterisk** (*) next to a restaurant listing in this chapter indicates that there is either a separate listing of the restaurant or it is featured in a sidebar in the Where to Eat chapter.*

All of the other listings under facilities are self-explanatory. While most of the major hotels have meeting/business facilities, this aspect of the property will generally not be discussed. If you're planning a meeting you should contact the hotel's sales department.

THE STRIP

Very Expensive

BELLAGIO, *3600 Las Vegas Blvd. South. Tel. 702/693-7111, Fax 702/ 792-7646. Toll free reservations 888/987-6667. Web site: www.bellagioresort.com. 3,005 Rooms. Rates: $159-499. Major credit cards accepted. Located at the southwest corner of Flamingo Road. For Attractions, see Chapter 12.*

Given the elaborate and luxurious nature of Bellagio, you would expect nothing less in the way of accommodations. Bellagio won't disappoint in this regard as the guest rooms are among the loveliest in Las Vegas. The standard room measures a fairly generous 510 square feet and has attractive furnishings along with fine fabrics and wall coverings. The bathrooms have a separate tub and stall shower along with marble tile floors and elegant fixtures. The sleeping area contains a huge armoire that hides a complete entertainment system as well as an in-room safe. All rooms are grouped into one of four basic color patterns (as are all other classes of accommodations) which range from colorful to the more gentle to look at earth tones that are so popular in the southwest. Comfortable chairs and plenty of desk space are two nice features.

The Tower upgrade room (about $25 more) is a little bit fancier and has a whirlpool tub. Aside from that, for prices ranging from $375 and beyond, are various classes of suites. The smallest suites aren't out of the affordable price range for many people and are sumptuous homes away from home that feature his and her bathrooms and a TV that pops out of a piece of furniture so as not to block your view when it isn't in use. Many rooms have excellent views of The Strip, Bellagio's beautiful pool area, and the mountains. Getting back to the small suite, we especially like the double columns near the entrance that set off the foyer from the combined sitting/sleeping area.

More elaborate suites consist of multi-room units ranging from the one and two bedroom penthouse suites (minimum 1,500 square feet) all the way up to the luxurious private villas that are reserved for special guests of the hotel. Amenities depend upon the level of accommodations (things like slippers and terry cloth robes start at the small suite level), but fine quality toiletries and little conveniences like electronically controlled draperies are pretty well standard throughout all classes of accommodation.

Dining: Aqua (seafood), Cafe Bellagio* (24 hour), Osteria del Circo* (Italian), Jasmine* (Chinese), Le Cirque* (French), Noodles (Asian), Olives* (Mediterranean), Picasso* (French/Spanish), Prime* (steakhouse), Sam's American, and Shintaro (Japanese). Also, the Buffet*, and several locales for fast-food, snacks, espresso bar, ice cream and pastries.

Facilities: Casino, cocktail lounges, lounges with entertainment, showroom, health spa and fitness center, swimming pools, beauty salon, gift/logo shop, shopping, wedding chapel, and game arcade.

THE DESERT INN, *3145 Las Vegas Blvd. South. Tel. 702/733-4444, Fax 702/733-4435. Toll free reservations 800/634-6906. 821 Rooms. Rates: $220-300. Major credit cards accepted. Located between Sands Avenue and Convention Center Drive. For Attractions, see Chapter 12.*

First rate accommodations done in an attractive and warm country English style. The chaise lounges found in many units are unusual, even for Las Vegas. Many of the guest units are multi-room suites that range from real nice to exclusive. Some of the latter even have their own swimming pools. The Desert Inn has long been known for its excellent guest service. For that reason (and perhaps its smallish casino), the DI appeals to a small, exclusive group of travelers and rarely attracts the throngs found in most Strip establishments. To a lot of people, that's also a plus.

Dining: Howan (Oriental), Monte Carlo* (French), and Portofino (Italian). Also has coffee shop/buffet combination.

Facilities: Casino, cocktail lounge, lounge with entertainment, showroom, fitness center and health spa, swimming pools, golf, tennis, beauty salon, gift/logo shop and shopping.

FOUR SEASONS HOTEL, *3960 Las Vegas Blvd. South. Tel. 702/632-5000, Fax 702/632-5222. Toll free reservations 877/632-5200. 424 Rooms. Rates: $200-600. Major credit cards accepted. Located on the 35th through 39th floors of the Mandalay Bay, just north of the intersection of Russell Road. There is a separate entrance and check-in.*

The hotel within a hotel concept does have precedents elsewhere but it is the first such arrangement of its type in Las Vegas. The Four Seasons, however, is much more than just a few floors of another hotel. It has its own separate entrance and check-in, elevators serving only its floors, and numerous facilities that are located in their own public area away from those of Mandalay Bay. On the other hand, there is a direct connection

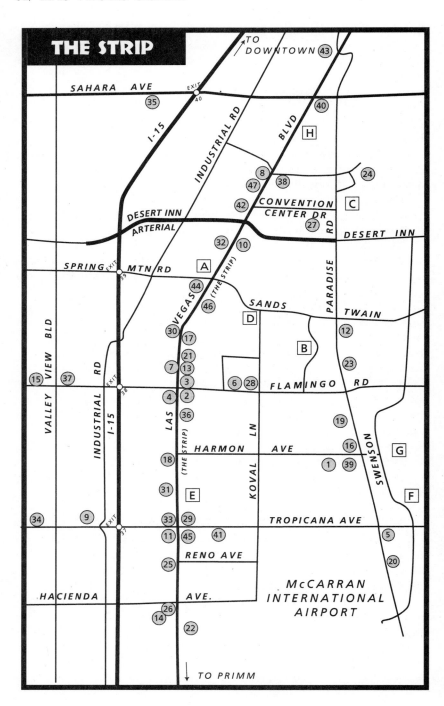

1. Alexis Park
2. Bally's
3. Barbary Coast
4. Bellagio
5. Best Western McCarran
6. Bourbon Street
7. Caesars Palace
8. Circus Circus
9. Wild Wild West
10. Desert Inn
11. Excalibur
12. Fairfield Inn
13. Flamingo Inn
14. Four Seasons
15. Gold Coast
16. Hard Rock
17. Harrah's
18. Holliday Inn Boardwalk
19. Holliday Inn Crown Plaza
20. Howard Johnson's Airport
21. Imperial Palace
22. Klondike Hotel
23. LaQuinta Inn Convention Ctr.
24. Las Vegas Hilton
25. Luxor
26. Mandaly Bay
27. Marriott Suites
28. Maxim
29. MGM Grand
30. Mirage
31. Monte Carlo
32. New Frontier
33. New York, New York
34. Orleans
35. Palace Station
36. Paris
37. Rio
38. Riviera
39. St. Tropez
40. Sahara
41. San Remo
42. Stardust
43. Stratosphere
44. Treasure Island
45. Tropican
46. Venetian
47. Westward Ho

A   Fashion Show Mall
B   Howard Hughes Center
C   Las Vegas Convention Center
D   Sands Expo & Convention Ctr.
E   Showcase
F   Thomas & Mack Center .
G   UNLV
H   Wet 'N Wild

between the two, so that Four Seasons guests have easy access to, for example, the casino at Mandalay Bay. Thus, Four Seasons claim that it is a non-gaming hotel is really a technicality. But, the entry of Four Seasons onto The Strip is another important example of the increasing sophistication of the Las Vegas market.

Set on its own grounds that rival Mandalay Bay for exotic beauty, the Four Seasons brings with it a high level of service that is recognized world wide as a leader in the hotel industry. Nice little touches such as nightly turn-down service, bottled water and a cold towel after you return from a morning jog, free use of poolside cabanas and much more, make this a luxurious place to stay. Afternoon tea service is offered daily in the Lobby Lounge.

The luxurious rooms and 86 suites (starting at $500) offer striking views of the mountains and desert as well as of The Strip. The large and beautifully appointed rooms feature such amenities as in-room safe, iron/ironing board, non-allergenic foam or down pillows, hair dryer, terry cloth bathrobes, oversized towels and more. The huge bathrooms have deep tub, separate glass enclosed shower and attractive marble vanities. The furnishings are highlighted by canopy draperies over the bed, a rich wood armoire, night tables and chairs.

Dining: First Floor Grill (American) and Verandah Cafe (24 hour). In addition, light snacks will be available at The Club Bar, Lobby Lounge and at a poolside grill.

Facilities: Cocktail lounge, swimming pool (in addition to access to Mandalay Bay's beach and wave pool), and health and fitness center.

THE VENETIAN, *3355 Las Vegas Blvd. South. Tel. 702/733-5000, Fax 702/733-5404. Toll free reservations 800/494-3556. Web site: www.venetian.com. 3,036 Rooms. Rates: $159-289. Major credit cards accepted. Located just south of the intersection of Sands Avenue. For Attractions, see Chapter 12.*

Advertised as an all-suite hotel, the Venetian will meet opposition to that claim from some people because the "standard" unit doesn't actually have separate rooms. However, we see no reason to quibble over labels given the high level of luxury at this newly opened resort.

Consisting of a spacious 700 square feet (which is almost double the average hotel room size), the suite begins with a gracious marble foyer entrance area. The rooms have crown moldings and baseboards, and a wrought iron railing separating the bedroom area from a sunken living room. The bedroom features draped bed canopies, huge closet, armoire with Venetian floral designs and a safe. The living room has an entertainment center (each suite has two 27" TVs), mini-bar, fax machine/copier, three telephones and much more – all extremely tasteful and providing the comforts of home. A plush sofa converts into a queen-sized bed so that the entire family can stay in the same suite. The marble floored bathrooms are equally impressive with their gold fixtures and generous use of marble accents.

The 4.5 acre outdoor pool area (with five separate swimming pools) is located on the third floor roof of the casino building. It is designed in the style of a Rensaissance Venetian garden and contains lovely grounds.

Dining: 14 restaurants, including Canaletto* (Italian), Delmonico Steak House*, Grand Lux Cafe* (24 hour), Lutece (modern and classic French), Pinot Brasserie* (International), Postrio* (California with Asian and Mediterranean influences), Royal Star (Chinese), Star Canyon* (southwestern), Taqueria Canonita (Mexican), Valentino (Italian), Warner Brothers Soundstage* (American), and Zeffirino* (Italian). Food court.

Facilities: Casino, cocktail lounges, lounge with entertainment, multi-function entertainment complex with lounge, showroom and nightclub, swimming pools, gift/logo shop and shopping. The **Canyon Ranch SpaClub**, one of the world's premier operators of upscale health resorts, comes to town for the first time in this 63,000 square foot health spa and fitness center, the most elaborate to date in Las Vegas. It features massage, skin care, body treatment rooms, movement therapy and every other imaginable way of improving yourself. It also has a beauty salon and medical center as well as an indoor swimming pool for water aerobics and lap swimming.

Expensive

BALLY'S LAS VEGAS, *3645 Las Vegas Blvd. South. Tel. 702/739-4111, Fax 702/794-2413. Toll free reservations 800/634-3434. Web site: www.ballyslv.com. 2,818 Rooms. Rates: $99-299. Major credit cards accepted. Located at the southeast corner of Flamingo Road. For Attractions, see Chapter 12.*

Large, commodious and brightly decorated rooms are the hallmarks of Bally's. Since this hotel doesn't have a theme around which to design its rooms, they opt for a simple "touch of class" – Bally's advertising slogan (that's even publicized on the side of one of the monorails that runs to the MGM). The standard rooms are among the better ones of any major hotel. They are also amongst the biggest in size. But if you like a little bit more room and luxury, you can always opt for one of the Royal Penthouse Suites. They'll only set you back around $2,500 a night!

Dining: al Dente* (Italian), Bally's Steak House, Chang's (Chinese), Seasons* (Continental), and Sidewalk Cafe (24 hour). Big Kitchen Buffet* and several fast-food outlets in casino and along shopping arcade.

Facilities: Casino, cocktail lounge, lounge with entertainment, showroom, health club and spa, swimming pool, tennis, beauty salon, gift/logo shop, shopping, wedding chapel, and game arcade.

CAESARS PALACE, *3570 Las Vegas Blvd. South. Tel. 702/731-7110, Fax 702/731-7331. Toll free reservations 800/634-6001. Web site: www.caesars.com. 2,471 Rooms. Rates: $89-279. Major credit cards accepted. Located at the northwest corner of Flamingo Road. For Attractions, see Chapter 12.*

The guest rooms have always been and remain among the biggest and best in Las Vegas, regardless of what else they keep building. While even the rooms in the older portion of the hotel are just dandy, the best are located among the 1,134 rooms in the new Palace Tower. Among features found in many rooms throughout the hotel are mirrored walls and ceilings, round beds, and marble European style baths. Standard rooms in the Palace Tower are one of five different floor plans and average about 650 square feet. They have nine-foot ceilings, wood trimmed cabinets and wall treatments that were inspired by the lavish murals uncovered in Pompeii. The panoramic views from the new tower easily surpass those in the original buildings. Also standard in the tower are whirlpool tubs, in-room safe, and mini-refrigerator.

Convenience amenities are quite numerous and include fine toiletries packaged in containers made to resemble ancient Ionic columns, iron/ironing board, and hair dryer. The closets even have automatic lights activated by sensors to detect when you open the door.

Not that you're likely to be one of the lucky ones staying at a Caesars suite, but just in case you're in the money (or even better, a guest of the casino), suites range from about a thousand square feet all the way up to a humongous 11,750 square feet. Choices include one of 11 Via Suites, each named for a city of the Roman Empire, and created in the atmosphere of a lush Italian garden; to one of ten four-bedroom, two-story Fantasy Suites, each themed in Roman, Egyptian or Pompeiian decor; or, finally, one of two Forum Tower Penthouses. To say the very least, the suites will dazzle even the most experienced connoisseur of fine travel.

Dining: Bacchanal* (Continental), Empress Court* (Chinese), Cafe Roma (24 hour), Hyakumi* (Japanese), Neros (American), Palace Court* (French), and Terrazza (Italian). Palatium Buffet* and La Piazza Food Court*. Within the Forum Shops are Bertolini's (Italian). Chinois (Asian), La Salsa Fresh Mexican Grill & Cantina, The Palm (American), Spago (International) and several semi-fast food/sandwich places such as the Stage Deli, Cheesecake Factory and others.

Facilities: Casino, cocktail lounges, lounge/nightclub with entertainment, showroom, health spa and fitness center, swimming pools with outdoor whirlpool spa, tennis, beauty salon, gift/logo shop, shopping, game arcade and IMAX cinema.

MANDALAY BAY, *3950 Las Vegas Blvd. South. Tel. 702/632-7777, Fax 877/632-7100. Toll free reservations 877/632-7900. Web site: www.mandalaybay.com. 3,266 Rooms. Rates: $99-269. Major credit cards accepted. Located immediately to the north of the intersection of Russell Road. For Attractions, see Chapter 12.*

One of the newest of the fabulous latest wave of mega-resorts, the 60-acre Mandalay Bay takes its tropical and mystical theme all the way up to each guest room. The standard room averages a spacious 515 square feet and has been ornately appointed by an award-winning interior design team. Each room features, besides floor to ceiling windows for great views, a desk table with two chairs, his and her lighted closets, armoire with large screen TV, and iron/ironing board. Guests receive a robe and slippers. The oversized stone-floored bathrooms have separate tub and shower, twin vanities, telephone and hair dryer.

Mandalay Bay also has several hundred suites that range from just a little bit larger than the standard room, all the way up to a mansion-sized 6,670 square feet! Rooms on the 34th floor feature a House of Blues theme.

Dining: Among the 15 restaurants are Aureole* (American), Tratoria del Lupo* (Italian), Shanghai Lilly (Cantonese & Szechwan), China Grill* (Oriental/international), Red Square* (Russian/international); Rumjungle* (international), House of Blues* (Creole/Cajun), and. Raffle's Cafe (American). Bay Side Buffet*, and several snack bars.

Facilities: Casino, cocktail lounges, lounge with entertainment, House of Blues nightclub and entertainment complex, showroom, water recreation environment (including swimming pools, beach, river ride, jogging track, health spa, and exercise facility), gift/logo shop, and shopping.

MGM GRAND HOTEL & CASINO, *3799 Las Vegas Blvd. South. Tel. 702/891-1111, Fax 702/891-1030. Toll free-reservations 800/929-1111. Web site: www.mgmgrand.com. 5,005 Rooms. Rates: $69-329. Major credit cards accepted. Located at the northeast corner of Tropicana Avenue. For Attractions, see Chapter 12.*

The guest rooms are located in one of four separate 30-story high emerald green towers although, from the outside, the hotel appears as one huge building. Because of the size, some rooms seem like they're miles away from the casino and all the other action. While that's the case in quite a few of the larger Strip hotels, it's even more so at this Goliath. The standard rooms are comfortably sized and furnished. They feature elegant black and white marble bathrooms and plenty of closet space.

There are four themes among this class of rooms: Hollywood, Southern, Casablanca, and the Wizard of Oz. Since the MGM has all but done away with the W of O theme in public areas, we predict it won't be very long before the rooms with that theme are redone. All of the usual amenities are present. We like the spacious closets and luxurious towels.

There are hundreds of suites at the MGM varying a great deal in size and elegance. Starting with the Players Suites, which aren't that much bigger than the basic rooms, you can also choose from Spa, Vista, Lobby, Glamour, Patio, and Vista Parlor Suites, as well as one of 29 prvate villas in a wing called The Mansion. The largest range up to a staggering 6,000 square feet and have their own elevator and private butler!

Dining: Brown Derby (steakhouse), Coyote Cafe* (southwestern), Dragon Court* (Chinese), Emeril's* (seafood), Gatsby's* (Continental), La Scala (Italian), Rainforest Cafe* (American), Ricardo's (Mexican), Studio Cafe (24-hour) Tre Visi* (Italian), and Wolfgang Puck Cafe (American). Grand Buffet*, Stage Deli (sandwiches) and food court. Additional eating places (mainly fast food) in the Theme Park.

Facilities: Casino, cocktail lounges, lounges with entertainment/ nightclub, showroom, complete spa complex with health and fitness center, swimming pools, beauty salon, gift/logo shop, shopping, game arcade, theme park and MGM Grand Youth Activity Center..

THE MIRAGE, *3400 Las Vegas Blvd. South. Tel. 702/791-7111, Fax 702/791-7446. Toll free reservations 800/627-6667. Web site: www.themirage.com. 3,049 Rooms. Rates: $79-399. Major credit cards accepted. Located between Flamingo Road and Sands Avenue. For Attractions, see Chapter 12.*

Attention to detail is the hallmark of the finely appointed luxury rooms at the Mirage. Subtle colors like taupe, beige, and pink contrast with black accents. All of the carpeting, draperies, exquisite fabrics and wall coverings were custom designed for the Mirage and its tropical theme. Imported marble is generously used in entry ways and bathrooms. High quality art work graces each room. The hotel keeps its like-new appearance through one of the most ambitious programs of room remodeling in Las Vegas. It's almost a constant process at The Mirage.

Dining: Alex Stratta* (French), California Pizza Kitchen, Caribe Cafe (24 hour), Kokomo's (steak and seafood), Mikado* (Japanese), Moongate* (Chinese), Onda* (noveau Sicilian), and Samba* (Brazilian). Buffet* and snack bars.

Facilities: Casino, cocktail lounges, lounge with entertainment, showroom, health spa, swimming pool, golf (off-site) spa, beauty salon, gift/ logo shop, and shopping.

NEW YORK, NEW YORK, *3790 Las Vegas Blvd. South. Tel. 702/740-6969, Fax 702/740-6989. Toll free reservations 800/693-6763. Web site: www.nynyhotelcasino.com. 2,035 Rooms. Rates: $89-189. Major credit cards accepted. Located at the northwest corner of Tropicana Avenue. For Attractions, see Chapter 12.*

Many people who see New York, New York and don't stay there think that the towering skyscaper replicas are just a fancy facade. They're definitely more than that – they are the room towers, so you can tell people you stayed at the Chrysler Building or other famous New York City landmarks. The nicely designed rooms and suites are accented in classic art deco style and are generally of a nice size, even if some don't appear to be so. That's because many rooms have a rather unusual shape or odd corners to conform with the unusual exterior shape of the hotel. If you don't mind not staying in a traditional four-corner room, then you shouldn't have any complaints with the accommodations.

Dining: America Restaurant* (24 hour), Chin Chin (Chinese), Gallagher's (steakhouse), Il Fornaio (Italian), and the Motown Cafe* (American/International). In addition, the "Village Eateries" are the equivalent of a food court but are attractively arranged in an area that resembles the narrow streets of New York's lower east side. These places range from kosher style deli to cafe to fast food. There's also a Nathan's Famous on the arcade level.

Facilities: Casino, cocktail lounges, lounge with entertainment, showrom, swimming pool, gift/logo shop, shopping and game arcade.

PARIS, *3645 Las Vegas Blvd. South. Tel. 702/739-4612, Fax 702/739-4609. Toll free reservations 888/BON-JOUR. Web site: www.paris-lv.com. 2,914 Rooms. Rates: $129-239. Major credit cards accepted. Located adjacent to Bally's, just south of the intersection of Flamingo Road. For Attractions, see Chapter 12.*

The rooms in this newly opened resort have an elegance and style that is above par for most Vegas hotels. They all feature beautiful custom designed furnishings, crown molding, French fabrics, and stately armoires. The spacious marble bathrooms boast separate tub and shower with European style fixtures, and an oversized vanity with make-up mirror. Amenities include hair dryer, iron/ironing board and in-room safe.

Dining: The Eiffel Tower Restaurant* (French) is, naturally, located in the Eiffel Tower replica portion of the hotel, about a hundred feet above The Strip. Other restaurants are the Brasserie* (American/International), La Rotisserie* (French), Le Cafe (24 hour), and Le Provence (Italian). Le Village Buffet*, La Boulangerie, a bakery that also serves soups and salads, and Le Pool Cafe, a seasonal outdoor cafe specializing in sandwiches and salads.

Facilities: Casino, cocktail lounges, lounge with entertainment, showroom, complete European style spa and health club, swimming pool, tennis, beauty salon/barber shop, gift/logo shop, shopping and wedding chapel.

Moderate

BARBARY COAST HOTEL, 3595 *Las Vegas Blvd. South. Tel. 702/ 737-7111, Fax 702/737-6304. Toll free reservations 888/227-2279. 198 Rooms. Rates: $49-159. Major credit cards accepted. Located at the northeast corner of Flamingo Road.*

Named not for the North African pirates but rather the old San Francisco district noted for its bordellos and gambling houses before being destroyed in the 1906 earthquake, this smallest of the casino/hotels on The Strip has been a fixture for many years. It is reminiscent of a Victorian-era San Francisco hotel in the decor of its public areas as well as the adequate guest rooms. But the only pirates around are those you'll find at the gaming tables! The small casino is always crowded but the biggest attraction of the Barbary Coast (in addition to some of it's fine dining) is its location – right at one of the two most important Strip corners. In fact, big neighbor Flamingo Hilton would love to get its hands on this property.

Dining: Drai's (American), Michael's Gourmet Restaurant*, Victorian Room (24 hour, Chinese/American). Fast food outlets.

Facilities: Casino, cocktail lounge and gift shop.

FLAMINGO HILTON, 3555 *Las Vegas Blvd. South. Tel. 702/733-3111, Fax 702/733-3528. Toll free reservations 800/732-2111. 3,642 Rooms. Rates: $69-279. Major credit cards accepted. Located just north of the intersection of Flamingo Road. For Attractions, see Chapter 12.*

The extravagant but luxury tropical theme of this property is also reflected in the beautiful guest accommodations. Especially pleasing are the casual rattan furniture and the easy on the eye soft color scheme. The rooms range in size from about average to somewhat larger and there are, of course, numerous suite options to choose from. Rooms on the upper floors have excellent Strip and mountain views but we also like those that face the hotel's expansive grounds. Looking out your window on the latter will make you think that you're more in Florida or Hawaii than in the middle of the desert. You'll also find all of the usual amenities found in any Hilton property.

Dining: Alta Villa* (Italian), Conrad's* (steakhouse), Flamingo Room (American and Continental), Lindy's (24 hour), and Peking Market (Chinese). Paradise Garden Buffet* and deli.

Facilities: Casino, cocktail lounges, lounge with entertainment, showroom, health spa, swimming pool and aquatic park, beauty salon, gift/ logo shop, shopping, and wedding chapel.

HARRAH'S LAS VEGAS, *3475 Las Vegas Blvd. South. Tel. 702/369-5000, Fax 702/369-5008. Toll free reservations 800/634-6765. Web site: www.harahs.lv.com. 2,700 Rooms. Rates: $69-259. Major credit cards accepted. Located just south of the intersection of Sands Avenue. For Attractions, see Chapter 12.*

The carnival theme so obvious in the public areas doesn't extend to the guest rooms although they are quite colorful. With their white woods and bamboo, it is more tropical then carnival. However, they're quite nice and the rooms in the newer towers are fairly spacious. Who says that the rooms have to have the same theme as the casino anyway? Harrah's provides excellent accommodations and facilities at a reasonable price. Maybe it isn't quite in the "mega" class like some of its neighbors, but the location can't be beat and we don't have any significant complaints about this place.

Dining: Asia* (Oriental), Cafe Andreotti (Italian), Garden Cafe (24 hour), and The Range* (steakhouse). Fresh Market Buffet* and deli.

Facilities: Casino, cocktail lounges, lounge with entertainment, showroom, fitness center, swimming pool, gift/logo shop, shopping and game arcade.

HOLIDAY INN BOARDWALK, *3750 Las Vegas Blvd. South. Tel. 702/735-2400, Fax 702/730-3166. Toll free reservations 800/465-4329. Web site: www.hiboardwalk.com. 653 Rooms. Rates: $39-175. Major credit cards accepted. Located just south of the intersection of Harmon Avenue.*

The rooms at the Boardwalk are typical of what you would find in most any Holiday Inn hotel. They're a decent size and nicely decorated with all the standard amenities, but certainly nothing out of the ordinary. It is a reasonably priced place to stay given its location.

The atmosphere is casual and in keeping with the "funhouse" facade of the exterior. Recently acquired by the much more upscale Mirage Resorts, they are apparently (for now) going to leave things as is.

Dining: Coffee shop (24 hour), buffet, and fast food outlets.

Facilities: Casino, cocktail lounge, lounge with entertainment, swimming pool, gift shop, shopping, and game arcade.

IMPERIAL PALACE HOTEL & CASINO, *3535 Las Vegas Blvd. South. Tel. 702/731-3311, Fax 702/735-8578. Web site: www.imperialpalace.com. Toll free reservations 800/634-6441. 2,636 Rooms. Rates: $49-299. Major credit cards accepted. Located between the intersections of Flamingo Road and Sands Avenue. For Attractions, see Chapter 12.*

Dating back to the 1960's and catering to middle America rather than the high rollers, the Imperial Palace maintains its popularity in the face of increasingly luxurious competition. It does so by continuing to offer reasonable rates in an ideal location that's center Strip. The rooms aren't elegant but they're quite large and attractively decorated. However, they don't have a Far Eastern theme.

Dining: The Embers* (steakhouse), Ming Terrace (Chinese) Rib House, Seahouse (seafood), Tea House (American, also buffet). Imperial Buffet, Betty's Diner, and fast food outlets.

Facilities: Casino, cocktail lounge, showroom, health club, spa, swimming pool, gift/logo shop, showroom, shopping, and wedding chapel.

LUXOR HOTEL & CASINO, *3900 Las Vegas Blvd. South. Tel. 702/ 262-4000, Fax 702/262-4454. Toll free reservations 800/288-1000. Web site: www.luxor.com. 4,476 Rooms. Rates: $59-299. Major credit cards accepted. Located south of Tropicana Avenue at the intersection of Reno Avenue. For Attractions, see Chapter 12.*

Guest rooms are located either in the original 31 story high pyramid or in the more traditional step-pyramided East and West towers. The accommodations are first rate no matter which section you're in. All are nice sized rooms with an ancient Egyptian theme. The similarities, however, end there. Pyramid rooms (except for those on the fifth floor or lower) are reached by elevators that travel at a 39 degree tilt. They're called "inclinators" and you feel yourself move slightly forward as they come to a halt.

The rooms, which have slanted windows that may make you think you're a bit tipsy, all surround the magnificent atrium. The open corridors afford fantastic views of the huge inner space. The only shortcoming to staying in the pyramid is that the arrangement of the inclinators makes for a long walk to some of the rooms. Of course, that's a problem in many Vegas hotels because of their size. East and West Tower rooms are more traditional from an architectural standpoint. The decor, however, is even a little nicer than in the original rooms.

Dining: Isis* (Continental), Luxor Steak House, Papyrus* (Asian), Pyramid Cafe (24 hour), and Sacred Sea Room* (seafood). Pharaoh's Pheast* buffet, Nile Deli, Salsa Fresh (Mexican) and a food court.

Facilities: Casino, cocktail lounges, lounge with entertainment, nightclub, showroom, Oasis Spa (complete health club and swimming pool complex), gift/logo shop, shopping, game arcade and IMAX cinema..

MONTE CARLO HOTEL & CASINO, *3770 Las Vegas Blvd. South. Tel. 702/730-7777, Fax 702/730-7250. Toll free reservations 800/3111-8999. Web site: www.monte-carlo.com. 3,014 Rooms. Rates: $69-249. Major credit cards accepted. Located between the intersections of Tropicana and Harmon Avenues. For Attractions, see Chapter 12.*

The pleasant and comfortable rooms at Monte Carlo belie the generally low rates charged. The stated goal of this hotel is to provide luxury at affordable prices and they come very close to fulfilling that difficult promise. The decor is turn-of the-century and is highlighted by fancy accents and rich looking bathrooms with plenty of marble and brass. Although they're not the biggest standard rooms in town, the size is more than comfortable. It's a big place but has a smaller "feel" than many other hotels. Rooms are all arranged off of a Y-shaped tower, a common design technique in Las Vegas.

Dining: Andre's French Restaurant, Blackstone's Steak House, Cafe' (24 hour), Dragon Noodle Company (Oriental), Market City Cafe (American) and Monte Carlo Pub & Brewery. Buffet* and food court.

Facilities: Casino, cocktail lounge, lounge with entertainment, showroom, outdoor recreation facility with multiple pools and "river' ride, gift/logo shop, shopping, game arcade and wedding chapel.

NEW FRONTIER, *3120 Las Vegas Blvd. South. Tel. 702/794-8200, Fax 702/794-8326. Toll free reservations 800/634-6966. 986 Rooms. Rates: $39-199. Major credit cards accepted. Located between the intersections of Sands Avenue and Convention Center Drive.*

Certainly one of the less elaborate (and older) Strip properties, the "New" in Frontier primarily refers to new ownership that took over in 1998. The property had been open but on strike for more than four years before that time. It doesn't seem that the new ownership is going to invest a lot of money to bring this place up to standard, but for moderate rates you can get a clean and comfortable room that isn't too far from the heart of The Strip. The more attractive atrium tower houses spacious suite style accommodations, while the low rise that surrounds the pretty landscaped courtyard and pool area has more basic motor inn type rooms.

Dining: Gilley's Saloon & Barbeque*, Margarita's Mexican Cantina, Michelle's (24 hour coffee shop/buffet combination) and St. Thomas seafood Grotto.

Facilities: Casino, cocktail lounge, lounge with entertainment, swimming pool, gift/logo shop and game arcade.

RIVIERA HOTEL & CASINO, *2901 Las Vegas Blvd. South. Tel. 702/734-5110, Fax 702/794-9451. Toll free reservations 800/634-6753. 2,109 Rooms. Rates: $59-245. Major credit cards accepted. Located north of Convention Center Drive at the corner of Riviera Avenue. For Attractions, see Chapter 12.*

One of the oldest hotels on The Strip, the Riviera still has a popular following because of the reasonable rates and the value you get for your hard earned dollar. Many renovations have kept the rooms at a first class level. Among the common amenities are an in-room wet bar. The traditional but attractive decor is almost at a deluxe level, especially considering the price. Some low-rise units near the pool area, although attractive, are not of the same quality as in the hotel towers. The hotel is also well known for its extensive entertainment schedule.

Dining: Kady's (24 hour), Kristofer's Steak House, Rik' Shaw (Oriental), and Ristorante Italianio. World's Fare Buffet and food court.

Facilities: Casino, cocktail lounge, lounge with entertainment, showrooms, swimming pool, beauty salon, gift/logo shop, shopping and game arcade.

STARDUST RESORT & CASINO, *3000 Las Vegas Blvd. South. Tel. 702/732-6111, Fax 702/732-6296. Toll free reservations 800/634-6757. Web site: www.stardustlv.com. 2,335 Rooms. Rates: $36-150. Major credit cards accepted. Located opposite the intersection of Convention Center Drive.*

Most of the Stardust's rooms are in the modern and sleek tower that rises above The Strip. The accommodations in the tower are excellent and features generous use of attractive wicker in a modern and bright decor. In addition to the tower, the Stardust has a number of old motel style buildings in the rear of the property. Although they're less costly (downright cheap, to be more exact) we don't recommend them. They're showing their age quite a bit both inside and out and it doesn't seem that the management is inclined to do much about their budget rooms.

Dining: Ralph's Diner* (American), Tony Roma's (ribs/steak), Toucan Harry's (24 hour), Tres Lobos* (Mexican), and William B's* (steak/American/Continental). Warehouse Buffet* and snack bars.

Facilities: Casino, cocktail lounges, lounge with entertainment, showroom, swimming pool, gift/logo shop, shopping, and game arcade.

STRATOSPHERE HOTEL & CASINO, *2000 Las Vegas Blvd. South. Tel. 702/380-7777, Fax 702/383-4755. Toll free reservations 800/998-6937. 1,500 Rooms. Rates: $39-300. Major credit cards accepted. Located two blocks north of Sahara Avenue at the intersection of Main Street. For Attractions, see Chapter 12.*

Comfortable and nicely decorated rooms in a modern style that are a decent size and little more. They're a good value, however, as long as you don't mind being a little away from the most popular parts of The Strip. The hotel is in a mid-rise that is simply dwarfed by the adjacent tower. So, if you're expecting a great view from your room, forget it. In fact, the surrounding area (including the suspended construction on another hotel tower and the view of the garage) makes it better that you don't even bother looking out the window. On the other hand, the rooms are comfortable.

Dining: Montana Cafe & Grille (24 hour), Roxy's Diner (American), Top of the World* (Continental), and Tower of Pasta (Italian). Buffet and fast food outlets.

Facilities: Casino, cocktail lounge, lounge with entertainment, showroom, swimming pool, gift/logo shop, shopping and game arcade.

TREASURE ISLAND, *3300 Las Vegas Blvd. South. Tel. 702/894-7111, Fax 702/894-7414. Toll free reservations 800/944-7444. Web site: www.treasureisland.com. 2,900 Rooms. Rates: $59-359. Major credit cards accepted. Located at the southwest corner of Spring Mountain Road (Sands Avenue on the east side of The Strip). For Attractions, see Chapter 12.*

The "Adventure Resort" is the lowest priced of Mirage Resorts major Strip properties and, as a result, may actually be the best value from that company. That assumes, of course, that you're not seeking the highest level of luxury. The rooms are excellent but definitely a notch below either The Mirage or Bellagio. Soft earth tones, white-washed taupe woodworking, traditional furnishings, and European fabrics make for an attractive and comfortable room. Those on the upper stories have good views. If you face the front you can actually watch the pirate ship battle from your room (although it definitely loses something when you can't hear what's going on). In addition to standard rooms, Treasure Island offers a variety of suite accommodations.

Dining: Black Spot Grille* (American), Buccaneer Bay Club (Continental), Francesco's (Italian), Lookout Cafe (24 hour), Madame Ching's (Chinese), and The Plank* (seafood). Buffet*, deli and snack bar.

Facilities: Casino, cocktail lounges, lounge with entertainment, showroom, health spa and salon, swimming pool, beauty salon, gift/logo shop, shopping, game arcade and wedding chapels.

TROPICANA RESORT & CASINO, *3801 Las Vegas Blvd. South. Tel. 702/739-2222, Fax 702/739-2469. Toll free reservations 800/634-4000. 1,910 Rooms. Rates: $39-249. Major credit cards accepted. Located at the southeast corner of Tropicana Avenue. For Attractions, see Chapter 12.*

Another of the older properties in town, you have to distinguish between rooms in one of the two newer high rises versus the original low-rise motor inn style facilities. The former are quite good while the latter are more modest as to size and decor. Tower rooms are better than average and feature a colorful tropical motif. Many have excellent views. When it comes to the public areas, although there has been a considerable amount of refurbishing, some sections have a worn and rather tired looking appearance. If you can get a Tower location in the middle of the hotel's price range, then it's a good value. Its location at one of the two busiest Strip intersections makes it worth seeking out.

Dining: Calypso's (24 hour), Golden Dynasty (Chinese), Mizuno's Japanese Steak House, and Pietro (Continental). Island Buffet* and deli.

Facilities: Casino, cocktail lounge, lounge with entertainment, showroom, outdoor recreation environment with swimming pools, fitness center, gift/logo shop, shopping, and wedding chapel.

Inexpensive

CIRCUS CIRCUS, *2880 Las Vegas Blvd. South. Tel. 702/734-0410, Fax 702/734-5897. Toll free reservations 800/634-3450. Web site: www.circuscircus-lasvegas.com. 3,893 Rooms. Rates: $29-119. Major credit cards accepted. Located between Convention Center Drive and Sahara Avenue at the intersection of Circus Circus Drive. For Attractions, see Chapter 12.*

Given the prices at Circus Circus you can't really expect too much. Then again, you can be pleasantly surprised with what you get for your money. Large and cheerfully decorated rooms have always been the order of the day at Circus Circus. With their last expansion they also redid all of the older rooms and they are better than ever. While certainly not in the luxury category, you'll have all the comforts and amenities you need. Rooms in the newest tower are the best. A limited number of motel style units are available in a section of the hotel called The Manor. They're also not bad for the price.

Dining: Promenade Cafe and Pink Pony Cafe (both 24 hour), Stivali* (Italian), and The Steak House*. Circus Buffet* and many fast food outlets. Additional restaurants/snack bars in the Adventuredome theme park.

Facilities: Casino, cocktail lounges, swimming pools, gift/logo shop, shopping, wedding chapel, circus acts and midway games, and theme park.

EXCALIBUR HOTEL & CASINO, *3850 Las Vegas Blvd. South. Tel. 702/597-7777, Fax 702/597-7009. Toll free reservations 800/937-7777. Web site: www.excalibur-casino.com. 4,032 Rooms. Rates: $45-175. Major credit cards accepted. Located at the southwest corner of Tropicana Avenue. For Attractions, see Chapter 12.*

Considering that this is one of the biggest Strip hotels, the accommodations aren't among the best by any means. However, they're more than adequate for catching a few z's and, at the prices the Excalibur charges, what else can you expect? Our biggest complaint is the rather plain plastered walls, which are supposed to represent a "castle brick" motif. On the other hand, the wrought iron fixtures, dark wood furniture and some thoughtful colors do offer a medieval look. You won't see the pastels or southwestern earth tones that are so ubiquitous throughout Las Vegas.

Dining: Camelot* (Continental), Lance-A-Lotta Pasta (Italian), Nitro Grill (American), Sherwood Forest Cafe (24 hour), and Sir Gallahad's (steakhouse). Roundtable Buffet* and fast food outlets.

Facilities: Casino, cocktail lounge, lounge with entertainment, showroom, swimming pool, gift/logo shop, shopping, wedding chapel and game arcade.

KLONDIKE HOTEL & CASINO, *5191 Las Vegas Blvd. South. Tel. 702/739-9351, Fax 702/795-8710. Toll free reservations 888/272-8794. 150 Rooms. Rates: $29-129. Most major credit cards accepted. Located immediately to the south of the southern end of The Strip near Russell Road.*

One of the cheapest places on The Strip, the small Klondike would be your basic roadside motel in any other locality. But, since this is Vegas, they've added a casino. The rooms are clean and comfortable but are on the small side with just the ordinary amenities. Since you're likely to spend very little time in your Klondike room, those shortcomings may be of little consequence to you if you want to travel on a budget.

Dining: 24 hour restaurant.

Facilities: Casino and cocktail lounge.

SAHARA HOTEL & CASINO, *2535 Las Vegas Blvd. South. Tel. 702/737-2111, Fax 702/791-2027. Toll free reservations 888/696-2121. 1,750 Rooms. Rates: $29-159. Major credit cards accepted. Located at the southeast corner of Sahara Avenue.*

This venerable hotel dates from almost the origin of The Strip. It has recently undergone a thorough renovation in order to try and keep up with the ever increasing quantity and quality of the competition. The exterior has been refurbished as well and the new entrance is quite beautiful, especially at night. It is a round, rotunda like structure with an Arabian style top. The casino and most of the public areas have also received a facelift and are attractive or better. When it comes to accommodations, however, the Sahara is still a few notches below the better hotels. On the other hand, you can get a reasonably nice, comfortable room with a fresh, airy appearance for a bargain rate. Room sizes vary from on the small side to about average.

Dining: Caravan Coffee Shop (24 hour), Paco's Hideaway (Mexican), and Sahara Steak House (formerly House of Lords). Buffet* and fast food outlets.

Facilities: Casino, cocktail lounge, lounge with entertainment, showroom, swimming pool, gift/logo shop, shopping, and game arcade (featuring high-tech virtual reality equipment).

WESTWARD HO, *2900 Las Vegas Blvd. South. Tel. 702/731-2900, Fax 702/731-6154. Toll free reservations 800/634-6803. Web site: www.westwardho.com. 777 Rooms. Rates: $22-49. Major credit cards accepted. Located between the intersections of Convention Center and Circus Circus Drives.*

This is one of the world's largest motels. It isn't fancy or all that attractive – just basic four wall accommodations. However, considering that it's right on The Strip, the price is a real bargain. So, for travelers on the tightest of budgets who simply want to catch a few winks between gambling, seeing the sights and other activities, Westward Ho fits the bill. Unlike most big Vegas properties where you have to walk what seems like a mile to get to your car, all of the rooms at Westward Ho have parking right outside your door. On the other hand, the maze-like layout of the motel buildings can be a bit on the confusing side.

Outside on The Strip you'll usually see a sizable line waiting for a chance to get a free pull on what must be the world's biggest slot machine – not the machine itself, but the display. You see, the results of your "pull" will show up king size on the hotel's big electronic marquee. We've never won anything of great value but lots of people get free show tickets.

Dining: Coffee shop and buffet combination (24 hour) and deli.

Facilities: Casino, cocktail lounge, showroom, and seven swimming pools (each with Jacuzzi).

OFF-STRIP

Very Expensive

MARRIOTT SUITES, *325 Convention Center Drive. Tel. 702/650-2000, Fax 702/650-9466. Toll free reservations 800/244-3364. 287 Rooms. Rates: $159-300. Major credit cards accepted. Located a few blocks east of The Strip and one block west of Paradise Road and the Las Vegas Convention Center.*

Although the price seems unusually high at first glance, it's not all that bad when you consider that you get a spacious suite with separate bedroom and sitting areas. However, you can get similar style accommodations for considerably less, so this place is only for those who desire excellent accommodations but don't like, for whatever reason, to stay at a casino/hotel. The decor is modern and seems to be preferred by a business clientele. Amenities include refrigerator and coffee maker in every unit. The 17-story high tower is an attractive mix of modern architecture with hints of art deco.

Dining: Alley's Restaurant (American).

Facilities: Cocktail lounge, swimming pool and small exercise room.

Expensive

ALEXIS PARK RESORT, *375 E. Harmon Avenue. Tel. 702/796-3300, Fax 702/796-4334. Toll free reservations 800/223-0888. 500 Rooms. Rates: $105-375. Most major credit cards accepted. Located east of The Strip between Koval Lane and Paradise Road.*

One of the nicest hotels in town, the Alexis Park Resort features luxurious suites and mini-suites, each with a wet bar. Some have fireplaces. The Mediterranean style hotel also boasts nearly 20 acres of beautiful gardens, mini-waterfalls, gorgeous pool area, and general opulence oozing out of every pore.

The Alexis Park has plans to add additional rooms and a small casino. Although it won't be much of a gaming area by Las Vegas standards, this will probably come as a disappointment to many Alexis Park regulars who found the relaxed, refined, non-gaming atmosphere a plus.

Dining: Pegasus (Continental) and coffee shop

Facilities: Cocktail lounge, health spa and salon, swimming pools, putting green, tennis, and wedding chapel.

CROWNE PLAZA, *4255 Paradise Road. Tel. 702/369-4400, Fax 702/369-3770. Toll free reservations 800/227-8794. 201 Rooms. Rates: $125-145. Major credit cards accepted. Located between the intersections of Flamingo Road and Harmon Avenue.*

A typical example of Holiday Inn's "upscale" property, the Crowne Plaza has large, comfortable and attractive accommodations. The guest units are all suites so there's quite a bit of room to spread out if you're going to be staying more than a couple of days. The building and its public areas are a rather bland modern style, including the so-called atrium.

Dining: Atrium Bar & Grille.

Facilities: Swimming pool, whirlpool spa, sauna, exercise room and gift shop.

LAS VEGAS HILTON, *3000 Paradise Road. Tel. 702/732-5111, Fax 702/732-5805. Toll free reservations 800/732-7117. Web site: www.lv-hilton.com. 3,174 Rooms. Rates: $95-275. Major credit cards accepted. Located immediately to the north of the Las Vegas Convention Center. For Attractions, see Chapter 12.*

The guest rooms are large, comfortable, no-nonsense facilities that meet the high expectations of those used to staying at the Hilton chain. Rooms on upper floors that face The Strip have spectacular views.

There are a wide variety of guest room accommodations at the Hilton, ranging from standard rooms all the way up to three-bedroom suites. (There are even a few suites with more than 10,000 square feet that have a parlor area that can accommodate 60 people – that's just in case you want to have a few friends over for a drink!). But, back on a more realistic level, the standard rooms are comfortable, offering traditional or modern style furnishings with all of the amenities you would expect from a chain like the Hilton. On the other hand, we wouldn't characterize them as gorgeous or elaborate.

Dining: Andiamo* (Italian), Benihana Village* (Japanese), Garden of the Dragon (Chinese), Hilton Steakhouse*, Bistro Le Montrachet* (French), Margarita Grille (Mexican), Quark's Bar & Grille (American), and The Reef (seafood). Buffet*, Paradise Cafe (24-hour), and several snack bars.

Facilities: Casino, cocktail lounges, lounge with entertainment, night-club, showroom, complete health spa and fitness center, swimming pool, golf (off-site), beauty salon, gift/logo shop, shopping, and game arcade.

Moderate

FAIRFIELD INN BY MARRIOTT, *3850 Paradise Road. Tel. 702/791-0899, Fax 702/791-0899. Toll free reservations 800/348-6000.129 Rooms. Rates: $62-175, including Continental breakfast. Major credit cards accepted. Located south of the intersection of Twain Avenue, near the Convention Center.*

You'll find slightly better than the usual run of the mill motel rooms, as is the custom with this chain. The rooms are a good size.

Dining: Continental breakfast room. Restaurants nearby.

Facilities: Swimming pool.

HARD ROCK HOTEL & CASINO, *4455 Paradise Road. Tel. 702/693-5000, Fax 702/693-5010. Toll free reservations 800/473-7625. Web site: www.hardrockhotel.com. 688 Rooms. Rates: $70-225. Major credit cards accepted. Located at the intersection of Harmon Avenue. For Attractions, see Chapter 12.*

The surprisingly upscale rooms are done up in a 1950's rock theme. Why not – rock stars make lots of money. The French doors are attractive, even if they don't exactly fit with the theme. Generous use of bold colors greatly enhances the room appearance. The Hard Rock is proud to advertise that a portion of the revenue from slot machines goes to the Save the Rainforest Foundation. While not a big hotel by Las Vegas standards, the recent expansion (which added more than 300 rooms) takes the Hard Rock out of the "small, intimate and personalized" class of facility that the owners used to pride themselves on as distinguishing it from the rest of the pack.

Dining: Besides the famous Hard Rock Cafe (American), which is located outside of the hotel on the corner of Paradise and Harmon, you can dine at Morton's (Italian), Mr. Lucky's (24 hour), Nobu (Japanese/Asian), and a new steakhouse as well as a Mexican restaurant with a Tequila Bar.

Facilities: Casino, cocktail lounge, showroom/nightclub, "beach" environment with swimming pools, spa and salon, gift/logo shop and game arcade.

ORLEANS HOTEL & CASINO, *4500 W. Tropicana Avenue. Tel. 702/365-7111, Fax 702/365-7499. Toll free reservations 800/675-3267. Web site: www.orleanscasino.com. 800 Rooms. Rates: $49-225. Most major credit cards accepted. Located west of The Strip at the intersection of Arville Street.*

Oversized and cheerfully decorated New Orleans themed rooms in a high rise tower. Comfortable and attractively priced, the Orleans is a good place to stay if you're looking to save some money compared to most Strip properties. It is best, however, to have wheels if you're going to stay here. The decor of the public areas is beautiful and the party city atmosphere is well done. The colorful exterior facade resembles the architecture of the French Quarter. Inside the main entrance are three bigger than life alligators standing upright and playing musical instruments. They're led by none other than Al E. Gator himself. Surrounding the main gaming area is more French Quarter style architecture with its famous wrought iron fences and populated by life size figures of Orleans people – from musicians to ladies of the night.

Dining: Canal Street Grille* (American), Courtyard Cafe (24 hour), Don Miguel's (Mexican), and Vito's (Italian). French Market Buffet* and fast food outlets.

Facilities: Casino, cocktail lounge, lounge with entertainment, showroom, swimming pool, bowling alley, gift/logo shop, wedding chapel, game arcade, child care center, and cinema.

PALACE STATION HOTEL & CASINO, *2411 W. Sahara Avenue. Tel. 702/367-2411, Fax 702/367-2478. Toll free reservations 800/634-3101. Web site: www.stationcasinos.com. 1,028 Rooms. Rates: $39-149. Major credit cards accepted. Located west of The Strip adjacent to I-15.*

The rooms here are nice but nothing special. There has been some redecorating but maybe a little more is still in order – this is the oldest of the Station Casinos and it is beginning to show its age just a bit. The accommodations are of the standard hotel fare that is common in the lower priced Vegas hotels. Just missing out being walking distance from The Strip, it's generally a few bucks cheaper than hotels with a Strip address, which makes it a popular choice amongst the thrifty set.

Dining: The Broiler* (American), Guadalajara* (Mexican), Iron Horse Cafe (24 hour), and Pasta Palace* (Italian). Gourmet Buffet, deli and fast food outlets.

Facilities: Casino, cocktail lounge, lounge with entertainment, swimming pool, gift/logo shop, game arcade and child care center.

RIO SUITE HOTEL & CASINO, *3700 W. Flamingo Road. Tel. 702/ 252-7777; Fax 702/252-8909. Toll free reservations 800/752-9746. Web site: www.playrio.com. 2,563 Rooms. Rates: $95-149. Major credit cards accepted. Located west of The Strip between I-15 and Valley View Blvd. For Attractions, see Chapter 12.*

The "suites" of the Rio (except for some luxury units that are really multi-room affairs) are actually one oversized room with separate sitting and sleeping areas. That comes as a disappointment to some because of the name of the hotel, but the accommodations are beautiful and spacious, the minimum size being about 600 square feet. All have floor to ceiling windows and rooms on higher floors that face The Strip have absolutely fantastic views, especially at night. The mountain facing rooms aren't hard on the eyes either. The Rio's accommodations feature lots of nice little amenities, including an in-room safe to store all the loot you win at the tables.

The room prices at the Rio aren't bad considering what you get. However, although we love almost everything about this hotel – accommodations, dining, attractions, whatever – they have been taking advantage of their popularity when it comes to prices. Almost everything except the rooms are overpriced compared to Vegas in general. We're almost tempted to call it gouging. Yet, it still deserves the many awards it has received, including honors from Zagat Survey and the American Academy of Hospitality Sciences. As you can see, it gives us sort of a split personality.

Dining: All American Steak House, Antonio's* (Italian), Bamboleo (Mexican), Buzio's* (seafood), Fiore* (American), Fortune's (Chinese), Mama Marie's Cucina (Italian), Mask* (Oriental), Napa (Continental/American), Rio Beach Cafe* (24 hour), and Voo Doo Cafe* (Cajun and Creole). Carnival World Buffet*, Village Seafood Buffet*, Toscano's Deli & Market, and fast food outlets.

Facilities: Casino, cocktail lounges, lounge with entertainment, showroom and nightclub, complete health club and spa, outdoor recreation environment with sand "beach" and swimming pools, golf (off-site), gift/logo shop, shopping, and game arcade.

ST. TROPEZ SUITES, *455 E. Harmon Avenue. Tel. 702/369-5400, Fax 702/369-1150. Toll free reservations 800/666-5400. 149 Rooms. Rates: $115-125, including Continental breakfast. Most major credit cards accepted. Located east of The Strip between Koval Lane and Paradise Road.*

A very attractive all suite facility that is set around a pretty garden area. The two-story buildings are motel style in appearance but the accommodations are much better than that. They are tastefully furnished in a southwestern motif and are well appointed. Along with the free breakfast, evening refreshments are included in the room rate.

Dining: Several dining options are located within walking distance.

Facilities: Swimming pool and fitness center.

SAN REMO HOTEL, *115 E. Tropicana Avenue. Tel. 702/739-9000, Fax 702/736-1120. Toll free reservations 800/522-7366. 711 Rooms. Rates: $39-125. Most major credit cards accepted. Located immediately to the east of The Strip and the Tropicana Hotel.*

The guest rooms are located either in the original motor inn section or a newer tower section. Try to get a room in the latter since they are more plush and well appointed. The motor inn type units are adequate but nothing more. The San Remo is walking distance from The Strip.

Dining: Paparazzi (Steak and seafood), Pasta Remo, Ristorante dei Fiori (both Italian), and Sushi Bar San Remo. Deli.

Facilities: Casino, cocktail lounge, lounge with entertainment, showroom, swimming pool, gift shop and game arcade.

Inexpensive

BOURBON STREET HOTEL & CASINO, *120 E. Flamingo Road. Tel. 702/737-7200, Fax 702/794-9155. Toll free reservations 800/634-6956. 166 Rooms. Rates: $39-59. Most major credit cards accepted. Located immediately east of The Strip at Audrie Lane.*

A place for the budget conscious traveler to stay. The price is right considering that this hotel is only a couple of blocks away from one of the two busiest Strip intersections. The accommodations are decent, especially for the price, and consist of rooms with king or double beds or executive and full suites with Jacuzzi. The public areas are small and aren't anything special to look at.

Dining: French Market Restaurant & Bar (24 hour).

Facilities: Casino (no live gaming), cocktail lounge.

GOLD COAST HOTEL & CASINO, *4000 W. Flamingo Road. Tel. 702/367-7111, Fax 702/367-8575. Toll free reservations 800/402-6278. 750 Rooms. Rates: $39-175. Major credit cards accepted. Located about a mile west of The Strip at Valley View Blvd.*

Rooms at the Gold Coast feature a pleasant southwestern style decor and are quite comfortable, especially considering the price. There are also a small number of suites featuring more luxurious decor, wet bar and refrigerator. It's a little too far from The Strip to walk but the location (across the street from the Rio) is still quite good.

Dining: Cortez Room (steakhouse), Mediterranean Room (Italian) and Monterey Room (American/Chinese). Buffet and fast food outlets.

Facilities: Casino, cocktail lounge, lounge with entertainment, showroom, nightclub/dance hall, swimming pool, bowling alley, gift shop, game arcade, child care center and cinema.

HOWARD JOHNSON'S AT THE AIRPORT, *5100 Paradise Road. Tel. 702/798-2777, Fax 702/736-8295. Toll free reservations 800/634-6439. 327 Rooms. Rates: $45-145. Major credit cards accepted. Located just north of McCarran International Airport and south of Tropicana Avenue.*

Standard fare rooms that are in keeping with what you would expect from this moderately priced chain. It's not far from The Strip and they have a free shuttle service if you don't have a car. HoJo is also convenient to the airport for quick arrivals and get-aways. Otherwise, there isn't that much else to recommend it but some Las Vegas visitors prefer the ordinary motel stay rather than dealing with the big hotels.

Dining: Mini-mart and deli on premises. Restaurants in close proximity.

Facilities: Cocktail lounge and swimming pool.

LA QUINTA INN CONVENTION CENTER, *3970 Paradise Road. Tel. 702/796-9000, Fax 702/796-3537. Toll free reservations 800/531-5900. 228 Rooms. Rates: $89-99, including Continental breakfast. Major credit cards accepted. Located 3/4 mile south of the Convention Center near Twain Avenue.*
We listed the LaQuinta for the same reasons as we did HoJo. Some people prefer this type of accommodation, although the rooms at the LaQuinta are nicer as well as a little larger. Many have microwave oven or refrigerator; all have coffee makers. About a quarter of the units are multi-room suites with private Jacuzzi.

Dining: Restaurants located nearby but it helps to have a car if you want a better choice.

Facilities: Whirlpool.

MAXIM HOTEL & CASINO, *160 E. Flamingo Road. Tel. 702/731-4300, Fax 702/733-3928. Toll free reservations 800/634-6987. Web site: www.maximhotel.com. 800 Rooms. Rates: $35-55. Major credit cards accepted. Located east of The Strip at Koval Lane.*
We used to like the silver-foiled walls of Maxim's because, chintzy as it was, it had "Vegas" written all over it. But, the rooms were due for a good overhaul and they've finally gotten it. The decor and furnishings are more traditional now, nothing special but mildly attractive and comfortable. At the rates charged and considering its close Strip proximity, Maxim is a good value. The rather bland exterior is matched by public areas that are ho-hum at best.

Dining: DaVinci's (Italian/International), The Grill Room (American). Palm Beach Cafe (24 hour) and Buffet.

Facilities: Casino, cocktail lounge, lounge with entertainment, showroom, swimming pool, gift shop, and game arcade.

McCARRAN INN (Best Western), *4970 Paradise Road. Tel. 702/798-5530, Fax 702/798-7627. Toll free reservations 800/626-7575. 99 Rooms. Rates: $49-139, including Continental breakfast. Major credit cards accepted. Located a half block south of the intersection of Tropicana Avenue.*
There are several Best Western's throughout the Las Vegas area but we feel that this one has the best overall quality, location and value. The comfortable and nicely furnished units all have coffee makes.

Dining: Breakfast room. Restaurants are close by but a car is helpful to reach them.

Facilities: Swimming pool.

VACATION VILLAGE HOTEL & CASINO, *6711 Las Vegas Blvd. South. Tel. 702/897-1700, Fax 702/896-4353. Toll free reservations 800/338-0608. 313 Rooms. Rates: $20-65. Most major credit cards accepted. Located about a mile south of the beginning of The Strip at the intersection of Sunset Road.*
Slightly better than basic accommodations that feature a mildly attractive southwestern decor and plenty of light. The southwest desert

feel is capped by a fake saguaro cactus in each room. While this hotel isn't that far away from the beginning of The Strip, you don't need a car to get there because The Strip bus begins its route right outside the hotel's entrance.

Dining: Coffe shop (24-hour) and Chinese buffet.

Facilities: Casino, cocktail lounge, lounge with entertainment, swimming pool and game arcade.

WILD WILD WEST GAMBLING HALL & HOTEL, *3300 Tropicana Avenue. Tel. 702/740-0000, Fax 702/736-7106. Toll free reservations 800/777-1514. 300 Rooms. Rates: $39-59. Most major credit cards accepted. Located west of The Strip at Industrial Road.*

Popular with the California budget set for many years as the King 8 Hotel, they've spruced up the place a bit and sort of given it an old west theme, although you certainly won't mistake it for a Strip property. Accommodations are basic but clean and comfortable and the location is quite convenient. Still, having a car helps because the walk to The Strip isn't that short.

Dining: Gambler's Grill (American).

Facilities: Casino, cocktail lounge, swimming pool and spa.

DOWNTOWN

(The "attractions" aspect of all hotels in the downtown corridor are contained in the general downtown section in Chapter 12.)

Expensive

GOLDEN NUGGET HOTEL, *129 E. Fremont Street. Tel. 702/385-1906, Fax 702/386-8362. Toll free reservations 800/634-3454. Web site: www.goldennugget.com. 1,907 Rooms. Rates: $59-299. Major credit cards accepted. Located in the Casino Center area between First Street and Casino Center Blvd.*

The most luxurious hotel in Downtown Las Vegas, the Golden Nugget features a beautiful casino and other public areas highlighted by generous use of crystal chandeliers, Grecian marble and a general feel and look of European elegance. The guest rooms are equally inviting. Almost all (except for a few in the oldest section of the hotel) are oversized and all are attractively furnished.

Dining: California Pizza Kitchen, Carson Street Cafe (Continental), Lillie Langtry's* (Chinese), and Stefano's* (Italian). Buffet.

Facilities: Casino, cocktail lounge, lounge with entertainment, showroom, swimming pool, beauty salon, gift/logo shop, and shopping.

Moderate

CALIFORNIA HOTEL & CASINO, *12 Ogden Avenue. Tel. 702/385-1222, Fax 702/386-4463. Toll free reservations 800/634-6255. 650 Rooms. Rates: $40-80. Major credit cards accepted. Located in the Casino Center area between Main and 1st Streets, one block north of Fremont.*

Why a place called the California has a Pacific island theme (as in Hawaii or Polynesia), we really don't know. Despite this, the results are pretty good. The rooms are colorful and comfortable.

Dining: Pasta Pirate Restaurant (Italian), Redwood Bar & Grille (American), and Market Street Cafe (24-hour). Snack bar.

Facilities: Casino, cocktail lounge, gift shop, shopping and game arcade.

FITZGERALD'S CASINO HOTEL, *301 E. Fremont Street. Tel. 702/382-6111, Fax 702/388-2230. Toll free reservations 800/274-5825. Web site: www.fitzgeralds.com. 650 Rooms. Rates: $42-95. Major credit cards accepted. Located in the Casino Center area between 3rd and 4th Streets.*

Now a Holiday Inn franchise, Fitzgerald's offers modern and comfortable rooms with pleasant furnishings. Rooms on the upper floors have excellent views.

Dining: Limericks Steak House, Vincenzo's Italian Cafe, and Molly's (combination 24-hour cafe and buffet).

Facilities: Casino, cocktail lounge, lounge with entertainment, swimming pool, and gift shop.

FREMONT HOTEL, *200 E. Fremont Street. Tel. 702/385-3232, Fax 702/386-4463. Toll free reservations 800/634-6182. Web site: www.fremontcasino.com. 452 Rooms. Rates: $30-80. Major credit cards accepted. Located in the Casino Center area between Casino Center Blvd. and 3rd Street.*

The Fremont is similar to many other downtown hotels – older and more basic accommodations, although all of the rooms have been remodeled and are mildly attractive and comfortable. Likewise, the public areas and casino also follow the general downtown mold: darker, more crowded, and on the plain and old fashioned side, as well as considerably more smoke-filled than on The Strip.

Dining: Lanai Cafe (24 hour), Second Street Grille (American), and Tony Roma's (ribs & steak). Paradise Buffet*.

Facilities: Casino, cocktail lounge, and gift shop.

MAIN STREET STATION, *200 N. Main Street. Tel. 702/387-1896, Fax 386-4466. Toll free reservations 800/713-8933. Web site: www.mainstreetcasino.com. 406 Rooms. Rates: $50-125. Major credit cards accepted. Located in the Casino Center area at the intersection of Stewart Avenue, two blocks north of Fremont Street.*

Victorian themed throughout, Main Street has the best rooms downtown after the Golden Nugget. Considering that the prices are lower, it may well represent the best combination of value and quality to be found in the downtown Casino Center. The rooms, like the public areas, are filled with interesting and often beautiful antiques. The Victorian decor accentuates the hotel's extensive antique collection quite well and gives it a warm and inviting feeling.

Dining: Pullman Grille Steakhouse, Triple-7 Brew Pub, and coffee shop. Garden Court Buffet*.

Facilities: Casino, cocktail lounge and gift shop.

Inexpensive

BINION'S HORSESHOE HOTEL, *128 Fremont Street. Tel. 702/382-1600, Fax 702/382-5750. Toll free reservations 800/237-6537. 367 Rooms. Rates: $30-60. Major credit cards accepted. Located in the Casino Center area between First Street and Casino Center Blvd.*

About a quarter of the rooms constitute the original Binion's Hotel. All of the remainder were added when Binion's took over the old Mint Hotel. Although the former Mint rooms are somewhat bigger and more modern, we prefer the charm that comes with the Victorian decor of the older units.

Dining: Binion's Ranch Steak House*, Gee Joon (Chinese), and coffee shop (24 hour). Buffet, snack bars and deli.

Facilities: Casino, cocktail lounge, lounge with entertainment, rooftop swimming pool and gift shop.

FOUR QUEEN'S HOTEL & CASINO, *202 E. Fremont Street. Tel. 702/385-4011, Fax 702/387-5123. Toll free reservations 800/634-6045. 700 Rooms. Rates: $49-149. Major credit cards accepted. Located in the Casino Center area between Casino Center Blvd. and 3rd Street.*

Another hotel with Victorian decor in the guest rooms, the twin towers of the Four Queens house comfortable rooms that are decently sized and attractively furnished. Their best feature is the four-poster bed.

Dining: Hugo's Cellar* (Continental), Magnolia's (American/International), and French Quarter (Continental). Coffee shop and fast food.

Facilities: Casino, cocktail lounge and gift shop.

JACKIE GAUGHAN'S PLAZA HOTEL, *1 Main Street. Tel. 702/386-2110, Fax 702/382-8281. Toll free reservations 800/634-6575. 1,037 Rooms. Rates: $20-40. Major credit cards accepted. Located in the Casino Center area at the foot of Fremont Street.*

The good part about the accommodations at the Plaza (aside from the almost ridiculously low price) are that they are oversized. Unfortunately, the furnishings are rather drab and this venerable establishment can use a good refurbishing. The distant views from the upper floors are alright but if you face the railroad tracks don't even bother looking out your window.

Dining: Center Stage Restaurant* (American), coffee shop (24 hour).

Facilities: Casino, cocktail lounge, lounge with entertainment, show-room, swimming pool and tennis.

LADY LUCK CASINO HOTEL, *206 N. 3rd Street. Tel. 702/477-3000, Fax 702/384-2832. Toll free reservations 800/523-9582. 791 Rooms. Rates: $40-125. Major credit cards accepted. Located in the Casino Center area between 3rd and 4th Streets, a block north of Fremont Street.*

The brightly colored and spacious rooms in the modern 25-story high tower are comfortably furnished and all boast refrigerators. There are also some poolside garden units. "Junior suites" have Jacuzzi tubs. Considering the prices charged, this is an excellent value. The rooms, however, are more attractive than the public areas, which are mediocre.

Dining: Burgundy Room* (Continental), Marco Polo (Italian), and Winner's Cafe (24-hour). Buffet.

Facilities: Casino, cocktail lounge, showroom, swimming pool and gift shop.

LAS VEGAS CLUB, *18 E. Fremont Street. Tel. 702/385-1664, Fax 702/387-6071. Toll free reservations 800/634-6532. 410 Rooms. Rates: $30-45. Major credit cards accepted. Located at the west end of Fremont Street, corner of Main Street.*

One of the older hotels in an area of older establishments, the Las Vegas Club consists of a small original building with small rooms and a newer tower with somewhat bigger accommodations. None are anything to write home about but you will get clean and comfortable facilities for a very low price. The hotel has a sports theme, especially in the newer wing where a part of the casino is made to look something like the inside of a stadium. Well, sort of – they didn't spend as much money as a Strip hotel would have so it isn't nearly as realistic. Their main claim to fame is a collection of sports (mainly baseball) memorabilia.

Dining: Great Moments Room (Continental), coffee shop (24 hour).

Facilities: Casino and cocktail lounge.

AROUND LAS VEGAS

Very Expensive

THE RESORT AT SUMMERLIN, *221 N. Rampart Boulevard. Tel. 702/869-7777, Fax 702/869-7771. Toll free reservations 877/869-8777. 541 Rooms. Rates: $195-500. Major credit cards accepted. Located in Summerlin, west of Summerlin Parkway. Take US 95 north from Strip/Downtown to reach Summerlin Parkway.*

Part of the sprawling master-planned community of Summerlin in Las Vegas' rapidly growing northwest, the Resort consists of two separate but connected properties of the upscale Regent chain, which up to now has mainly been confined to Asia. It opened in July of 1999. Like it's soon-to-be competition at Lake Las Vegas, the Resort is catering to the *Conde Naste* crowd and will be attempting to lure travelers who usually go to Palms Springs or Scottsdale. The **Regent Grand Spa** (287 rooms) and the **Regent Grand Palms** (254 rooms) are each six story structures that are linked together by a low rise structure that houses all of the hotel's restaurants and other public facilities. Spanish revival architecture is the overall theme of the buildings, although each hotel has its own distinctive interior style. The lobbies and other public areas boasts a simple elegance and tranquility. There are 11 acres of lovely grounds and gardens with more than 800 palm trees and several waterfalls. This area is only open to the hotel's guests. The property is within a five minute drive of no fewer than five different golf courses. The Paseo de Vida houses some of the property's restaurants as well as a small but pretty shopping arcade.

Standard guest rooms measure a spacious 560 square feet and feature walk-in closet, bar, separate sitting area with sofa, and writing desk. Marble bathrooms boast double vanities, whirlpool tub and separate shower. Some units feature French doors. Approximately 80 suites range from just a tad better than the basic rooms to extravagant facilities with more than 2,000 square feet of space. One super suite measures over 6,000 square feet.

Dining: Ceres and Parian (both American/International), and the Putting Green (lighter fare). Buffet. Both Ceres and the Buffet feature patio dining. The Paseo de Vida houses Nevada Nick's (steakhouse), Hamada of Japan, Cafe Napolean (24-hour), Europa (Continental), and Spiedines (Italian). There is also a wine tasting shop. At press time we hadn't had the opportunity to personally review any of the Resort's dining establishments, but we believe they'll all be first rate.

Facilities: Casino, cocktail lounge, putting green, swimming pool, gift/logo shop, and shopping. The *Aquate Sulis* is a full service luxury health spa that bears the original Roman name of the public bath that would later become the English town of Bath. Massage, facials, aromatherapy, body wraps, scrubs, yoga and thalassotherapy are among the many treatments offered. It also has a salon and boutique. A smaller spa facility is located in the Regent Grand Spa.

Moderate

BOULDER STATION HOTEL & CASINO, *4111 Boulder Highway. Tel. 702/432-7777, Fax 702/432-7730. Toll free reservations 800/683-7777. Web site: www.stationcasinos.com. 268 Rooms. Rates: $59-109. Major credit cards accepted. Located just to the south of the Boulder Highway exit of I-515, between Desert Inn Road and Sahara Avenue.*

Colorful decor and modern furnishings highlight these nice sized and comfortable rooms at a great price. It isn't that far from the action of The

Strip as long as you have transportation. The casino is quite attractive, especially the live gaming area with its high ceiling and stained glass depictions of famous old trains. We also like the polished wooden floors (almost all casinos have carpeting in their public areas) and the lively atmosphere that the place has.

Dining: The Broiler* (American), Guadalajara* (Mexican), Iron Horse Cafe (24 hour), and Pasta Palace* (Italian). Feast Buffet* and fast food outlets.

Facilities: Casino, cocktail lounge, lounge with entertainment/nightclub, swimming pool, gift/logo shop, game arcade, child care center and cinema.

CLUB HOTEL BY DOUBLETREE, *7250 Pollock Drive. Tel. 702/948-4000; Fax 702/948-4100. Toll free reservations 888/444-CLUB. 190 Rooms. Rates: $89-99. Major credit cards accepted. Located immediately to the east of the Warm Springs Road exit of I-215.*

This hotel is actually designed for the business traveler (their Club Room has many business services including a CopyMax self-service business center), but the prices are comparable to other high quality non-casino hotels, so there's no reason you can't use it for a Vegas vacation. It's conveniently located to the airport as well as The Strip. Each spacious room features a work desk, coffeemaker, iron/ironing board and hair dryer, among other conveniences and amenities. The decor is modern and attractive. And, since this is a Doubletree family member, you get those delicious chocolate chip cookies upon check-in.

Dining: Au Bon Pain Bakery Cafe on premises is good for breakfast, snacks and light meals. Applebee's Neighborhood Bar & Grille immediately adjacent to property.

Facilities: Swimming pool and fully equipped exercise room.

SAM'S TOWN, *5111 Boulder Highway. Tel. 702/456-7777, Fax 702/454-8014. Toll free reservations 800/634-6371. 650 Rooms. Rates: $50-155. Major credit cards accepted. Located where Harmon Avenue and Nellis Boulevard intersect Boulder Highway. For Attractions, see Chapter 12.*

The rooms at Sam's Town have a definite western flair when it comes to decor. They're spacious, comfortable and very attractive. All units overlook the beautiful 25,000 square foot atrium lobby that goes by the name of Mystic Falls Park.

Dining: Billy Bob's Steak House & Saloon*, Diamond Lil's (Continental), Mary's Diner (American), Papamio's* (Italian), Smokey Joe's Cafe (American), and Willy & Jose's Cantina (Mexican), Great Buffet and Chuckwagon food court.

Facilities: Casino, cocktail lounge, lounge with entertainment, nightclub/dance hall, swimming pool, bowling alley, gift/logo shop, shopping, and game arcade.

SANTA FE HOTEL & CASINO, *4949 N. Rancho Drive. Tel. 702/658-4900, Fax 702/658-4919. Toll free reservations 800/872-6823. 200 Rooms. Rates: $38-99. Most major credit cards accepted. Located at the intersection of US 95.*

The southwestern furnishings and decor in the bright and cheerful rooms of the Santa Fe make it a delightful place to stay if you don't mind being a little bit further away from the main centers of action in Las Vegas. To some people, of course, the relative peace and quiet is a big plus. On the other hand, we don't think too many people come to Vegas for a rest cure. The mountain view from some rooms are pretty decent. All of the public areas at the Santa Fe have a genuine southwestern flavor and there's an air of elegance. Considering the prices and everything else, we think this hotel is an excellent value.

Dining: Kodiak Lodge (steakhouse), Pablo's Cafe (24 hour), Suzette's (French), and Ti Amo (Italian). Lone Mountain Buffet.

Facilities: Casino, cocktail lounge, lounge with entertainment, swimming pool, bowling alley, and ice skating rink.

TEXAS STATION HOTEL & GAMBLING HALL, *2101 Texas Star Lane, N. Las Vegas. Tel. 702/631-1000, Fax 702/631-8120. Toll free reservations 800/654-8888. Web site: www.stationcasinos.com. 200 Rooms. Rates: $59-129. Most major credit cards accepted. Located at the intersection of Rancho Road and Lake Mead Blvd.*

Although the number of rooms is quite small by Las Vegas standards (especially considering the big casino), they more than make up for the lack of quantity with their high quality. The rooms are big and comfortable, featuring wrought iron fixtures and genuine oak wood furniture. The rich and warm brocade upholstery adds a final nice touch.

The public areas have a few pretty features as well. Outside is an heroic statue of three horses. An even more beautiful piece is the standing white stallion that's located in the center of one of the casino bars. Most of the hotel's restaurants are attractively situated along a "river" walkway to one side of the casino.

Dining: Laredo del Mar (Mexican), San Lorenzo (Italian), Stockyard Steak House, and Yellow Rose Cafe (24-hour). Feast Around the World Buffet* and food court.

Facilities: Casino, cocktail lounge, lounge with entertainment, swimming pool, gift/logo shop, shopping, game arcade, "Kids Quest" child care center, and multi-screen cinema.

Inexpensive

ARIZONA CHARLIE'S, *740 S. Decatur Blvd. Tel. 702/258-5200, Fax 702/258-5192. Toll free reservations 800/342-2695. Web site: www.azcharlies.com. 257 Rooms. Rates: $48-69. Major credit cards accepted. Located a half mile south of the Decatur Blvd. exit of US 95.*

Clean and comfortable rooms that are attractively decorated and are almost a steal as long as you have a car to get to other places. (There isn't anything to see or do in the area where this hotel is located.) The public facilities aren't particularly attractive but are almost always crowded with local residents from the area who like to try their luck at the casino.

Dining: Chin's (Chinese), Yukon Grille (American), and Sourdough Cafe (24 hour). Wild West Buffet and several outlts in a small food court..

Facilities: Casino, cocktail lounge, lounge with entertainment/nightclub, showroom, swimming pool, gift/logo shop, and game arcade.

FIESTA HOTEL & CASINO, *2400 N. Rancho Drive. Tel. 702/631-7000, Fax 702/631-7070. Toll free reservations 800/731-7333. 100 Rooms. Rates: $45-99. Most major credit cards accepted. Located at the intersection of Lake Mead Blvd.*

With budget priced average to slightly better accommodations in a motor-inn type facility, this is another hotel that's located on the fringe and requires transportation, unless you're coming to Las Vegas just to gamble and any place with a casino and restaurant will do. The Fiesta was recently renovated and the public areas have an attractive, lively atmosphere.

Dining: Garduno's (Mexican), Old San Francisco Steak House, and Mr. G'z (24-hour). Festival Buffet*, fast food outlets and deli.

Facilities: Casino, cocktail lounge, lounge with entertainment, and game arcade.

NEVADA PALACE HOTEL & CASINO, *5255 Boulder Highway. Tel. 702/458-8810, Fax 702/458-3361. Toll free reservations 800/634-6283. 220 Rooms. Rates: $25-35. Most major credit cards accepted. Located between Tropicana and Harmon Avenues.*

Motel style accommodations that are quite basic. It's not high on our recommended list as a place to stay but will do in a pinch when rooms are hard to come by as well as for those on a tight budget. It is highly advisable to have a car if you're going to be staying here.

Dining: La Pasta Bella Steak & Seafood, Herman's Deli, and 24 hour coffee shop/buffet combination.

Facilities: Casino and cocktail lounge.

SHOWBOAT HOTEL & CASINO, *2800 E. Fremont Street. Tel. 702/ 385-9123, Fax 702/385-9123. Web: www.showboat-lv.com. Toll free reservations 800/826-2800. 468 Rooms. Rates: $29-69. Major credit cards accepted.*

Located where Fremont Street becomes Boulder Highway (corner of Charleston Blvd.).

A Mardi Gras themed hotel (we've heard that one before) that is quite attractive since a major renovation a couple of years ago. At least on the inside. The exterior is drab and doesn't have a very good showboat style facade. The rooms in the tower section are clean and comfortable. Although pretty much standard fare in every way, you definitely get your money's worth compared to many other places. However, we can't be too enthusiastic about units located in the older motel section. They look decrepit on the outside and are only slightly better on the inside.

Dining: Di Napoli (Italian), Plantation Room (American/Continental), and coffee shop. Captain's Buffet and fast food outlets.

Facilities: Casino, cocktail lounge, lounge with entertainment, swimming pool, bowling alley, and gift/logo shop.

SILVERTON HOTEL, *3333 Blue Diamond Road. Tel. 702/263-7777, Fax 702/896-5635. Toll free reservations 800/558-7711. 304 Rooms. Rates: $49-70. Major credit cards accepted. Located about a half-mile west of Las Vegas Blvd. at Industrial Road and the Blue Diamond Road exit of I-15.*

This hotel was formerly called Boomtown, a name which we liked a whole lot better given the old west mining town appearance of the exterior. The rooms aren't anything special (semi-western decor and not overly big), but at the price they're a real bargain. You can be on The Strip in five minutes. The place has a warm and friendly atmosphere.

Dining: Comstock Cafe (24-hour), Blue Diamond Buffet* and deli.

Facilities: Casino, cocktail lounge, lounge with entertainment, and showroom.

HENDERSON
Moderate
SUNSET STATION HOTEL & CASINO, *1301 W. Sunset Road. Tel. 702/547-7777, Fax 702/547-7606. Toll free reservations 888/786-7389. Web site: www.stationcasinos.com. 456 Rooms. Rates: $49-159. Major credit cards accepted. Located two blocks west of the Sunset Road exit of I-515. For Attractions, see Chapter 12.*

This hotel has only been open a couple of years but it has been so successful that they've just about finished the first phase of a major $45 million expansion. It is one of the few "local" casino/hotels that is glamorous enough to be compared with its bigger Strip competition. The beautiful decor isn't limited to the public areas. All of the oversized guest rooms are comfortably furnished and decorated in pleasing light shades with a hint of southwest or Mediterranean colors and style. There are also more luxurious petite and king suites available at slightly higher rates.

Dining: Capri Ristorante (Italian), Costa del Sol* (seafood), Rosalita's* (Mexican), Sonoma Cellar* (steakhouse), Sunset Brewing Company (micro-brewery/American; pizza), and Sunset Cafe (24 hour). Feast Around the World Buffet* and several fast-food eateries.

Facilities: Casino, cocktail lounge, lounge with entertainment, night-club/showroom, swimming pool, ice hockey/skating center, gift/logo shop, game arcade, child care center, and cinema.

Inexpensive

THE RESERVE HOTEL & CASINO, *777 W. Lake Mead Drive. Tel. 702/558-7000, Fax 702/558-7008. Toll free reservations 888/899-7770. 224 Rooms. Rates: $39-79. Major credit cards accepted. Located at the Lake Mead Drive exit of I-515. For Attractions, see Chapter 12.*

The safari theme that enlivens the public areas is continued all the way to the attractive and spacious guest rooms. Don't worry about all the jungle decor – it's safe to turn the lights out at night. One possible disadvantage of this hotel (if you don't have a car) is its location – not only is it a considerable distance from The Strip, but it isn't in the part of Henderson where you're surrounded by many restaurants and shopping opportunities.

Dining: Congo Jack's Cafe (24-hour), Serengeti Spaghetti Co., (Italian), Tusk's Wood-fire Grille (Steakhouse), and the Grand Safari Buffet* (Fast Food).

Facilities: Casino, cocktail lounge, lounge with entertainment, swimming pool, and gift/logo shop.

CAMPING & RV SITES

Las Vegas is one of the few big cities where you can hook up your RV right in the middle of town. While there aren't that many RV campsites on The Strip, there are plenty within a ten or fifteen minute drive. All places below have full RV facilities. Several are located on the property of major hotels. If you can pitch your tent there as well it will be so noted.

- **American Campgrounds**, *13440 N. Las Vegas Blvd. Tel. 702/643-1222.* Tent sites.
- **Circusland RV Park**, *2880 S. Las Vegas Blvd., part of Circus Circus Hotel. Tel. 702/794-3757*
- **Covered Wagon RV Park**, *6635 Boulder Highway. Tel. 702/454-7090*
- **KOA Kampground**, *4315 Boulder Highway. Tel. 702/451-5527.* Tent sites.
- **Oasis Las Vegas RV Resort**, *2711 Windmill Lane. Tel. 702/260-2020*
- **Sam's Town Hotel RV Park**, *5225 Boulder Highway. Tel. 702/454-8055*
- **Showboat Hotel RV Park**, *2800 Fremont Street. Tel. 702/385-9164*
- **Silverton Hotel RV Resort**, *3333 Blue Diamond Road. Tel. 702/263-7777*

TIME SHARES & EXTENDED STAY ACCOMMODATIONS

If you like to visit Las Vegas every year or even several times a year (and many people do), you might want to consider a time share unit. Most are apartment style facilities and you have a guaranteed place to stay at a definite time. Costs run from modest to extremely expensive (almost as much as buying a small vacation home) depending upon how big and how luxurious the facilities are. Here's a quick rundown on some popular Las Vegas time sharing places:

*   ***Carriage House**, 105 E. Harmon Ave., Tel. 702/798-1020 or 800/ 221-2301. Located a few blocks from The Strip near the MGM Grand. Also has some hotel units.*

*   ***Hilton Grand Vacations Club Flamingo**, at the Flamingo Hilton, Tel. 702/697-2900 or 800/799-4482. Occupying a luxurious art-deco style building behind the gardens of the Flamingo Hotel, this is the most luxurious facility of its type. It will soon be joined by a similar property on the grounds of the Las Vegas Hilton.*

*   ***Polo Towers**, 3745 Las Vegas Blvd. South, Tel. 702/261-1000 or 800/935-2233. A nice property located in the middle of the action. The Polo Towers also has some regular hotel units.*

*   ***Ramada Vacation Suites**, 100 Winnick Ave., Tel. 702/731-6100. More for the budget time share buyer, this slightly off-Strip property isn't in the same level of luxury as the preceding places.*

*   *And if you come to Vegas less often but spend a longer period of time (over a week), you'll probably find it is more economical to put your baggage down in an extended stay hotel. Among the many places of this type are **Budget Suites of America**, with seven locations (nearest property to Strip is on Paradise, Tel. 702/699-7000); **Extended Stay America**, two locations, Tel. 800/398-7829; and Marriott's **Residence Inn**, two locations, Tel. 800/331-3131.*

10. WHERE TO EAT

Up until recently gourmet folks looked down upon Las Vegas as a sort of culinary wasteland. All that has changed in practically the blink of an eye as scores of excellent restaurants have opened up all over the city, but especially in Strip hotels. The casino moguls have attracted some of the nation's premier chefs to work here and the result is a selection of first class restaurants that rival New York or San Francisco. And the dining Renaissance shows no signs of a slowdown as new places open on a regular basis.

The sheer number and variety of restaurants makes choosing which ones to recommend to you a daunting yet enjoyable task. Whether you dine at a major hotel, in one of the many independent restaurants along The Strip, or elsewhere around town, you're sure to find something to your taste and budget.

Major hotels generally have anywhere from three to eight restaurants. There are many larger hotels with ten or even 15 eateries. Buffets will be treated separately in the section following the restaurant listings. Most hotels have at least one gourmet restaurant as well as several specialty places. A common feature is the hotel coffee shop. These 24-hour restaurants serve family style meals that are quite good at reasonable prices. To use the term "coffee shop" would often be demeaning to their quality, however, we'll use it as a means of distinguishing them from other restaurants. We won't review them here (see the sidebar later in this chapter for information on some of the better ones) but you won't go wrong by dining in most of them.

RESTAURANT PRICE CATEGORIES

Prices are for entree and are exclusive of beverage, tax and gratuity. The price ranges apply only for restaurants and not buffets.
- **Very Expensive** – More than $30
- **Expensive** – $21–30
- **Moderate** – $11-20
- **Inexpensive** – $10 or less

RESTAURANTS

THE STRIP
Very Expensive

ALEX STRATTA RESTAURANT, *The Mirage. Tel. 702/791-7223. Major credit cards accepted. Dinner served nightly except Wednesday. Reservation are required.*

Haute French cuisine at its most elegant. The small and intimate dining room is a cheerful country French and is staffed by a professional group of servers who will attend to your every need. The food is sophisticated and distinguished by its use of richly seasoned sauces. There is a large wine list.

AUREOLE, *Mandalay Bay. Tel. 702/632-7401. Major credit cards accepted. Dinner served nightly. Reservations are suggested.*

Chef Charlie Palmer of New York has opened shop in Las Vegas. The much honored Palmer has received numerous awards, including the best restaurant in the Big Apple. As we went to press there wasn't a long track record for this new place but a first look was most impressive. Seasonal American and Italian dishes are prepared by Joe and Megan Romano, who have been Palmer disciples for more than ten years. Only the freshest ingredients are used. The luxurious interior is highlighted by something we've never seen – a four story high wine tower! The stewards don harnesses and are hoisted up the tower to retrieve bottles from the "Cellar in the Sky." The wine list, of course, is top-notch. The service at Aureole is impeccable, as should be the case in a fine restaurant, but sometimes doesn't happen in restaurants as large as this one is (383 seats).

BACCHANAL, *Caesars Palace. Tel. 702/731-7731. Major credit cards accepted. Dinner served Tuesday through Saturday with seatings between 6-6:30 pm or 9-9:30 pm. (Allow 2-1/2 hours). Reservations are required.*

Much more than a restaurant, Bacchanal epitomizes the glorious excess that is Las Vegas. You'll enter a beautiful sunken dining room guarded by gold lions to find a large marble pool in the center. Gorgeous wine goddesses will pour the liquid nectar all night long (unlimited wine or champagne is included in the price), feed the men grapes and also offer a soothing massage. The ladies, upon request, can receive a massage from a burly Roman slave. Since this is supposed to be an ancient Roman villa, it should come as no surprise that Caesar and Cleopatra show up to mingle with the guests.

The six course Continental dinner, which changes according to the season, is excellent – definitely gourmet, although not the best in town. Dancers entertain periodically during the feast, which lasts about 2-1/2 hours. Including tax and gratuity the Bacchanal will set you back about a hundred bucks a person but, assuming you can afford to spend it, is well worth the money for the unique and unforgettable experience. It's gourmet dining where you can let loose and have a great time!

DELMONICO STEAKHOUSE, *The Venetian. Tel. 702/733-5000. Major credit cards accepted. Dinner served nightly. Reservations are required. Dress code.*

Emeril Lagasse is one of America's best known chefs and, from the way he's been opening up restaurants, most successful. He now brings his outstanding New Orleans Creole style steakhouse to The Strip and our first look was positive. The succulent beef was prepared to perfection and served with flair in outstanding surroundings. Here, you can sit back and relax in leather booths with exquisite detail and savor what is definitely among the top steak places in town, and with all the great steakhouses in Las Vegas, that's saying a lot. They also have an excellent wine list.

ISIS, *Luxor. Tel. 702/262-4773. Major credit cards are accepted. Dinner served nightly. Reservations are suggested. Dress code.*

One of the most beautiful dining rooms in the city, it's almost worth a trip here just to experience the surroundings. There are the requisite (for the Luxor) Egyptian artifacts but the most beautiful feature is the colonnaded walkway surrounded by magnificent statues and generous amounts of glass embossed with the wings of Isis. Oh, yes, we might also mention that it has been declared to be one of the best restaurants in the nation by a number of "experts." The food is delicious and imaginative continental cuisine, served either in the traditional manner or with some twists conjured up by the acclaimed culinary staff of Isis. This is one of the restaurants worth spending extra on.

LE CIRQUE, *Bellagio. Tel. 702/693-8150. Major credit cards accepted. Dinner served nightly. Reservations are required. Dress code.*

Right off let's tell you that this isn't the restaurant for those on a limited budget. Seating only 80 guests, Le Cirque will set you back about $90 for a five course meal and a full seven courses runs $120, although you can get just the main course for under $40. Another New York City spinoff (which seems to be the latest trend in Las Vegas fine dining), it features excellent Continental cuisine. The appetizers are especially appealing, such as the foie gras saute or ravioli de truffe blanche. The intimate dining room allows the expert staff to offer careful and personalized service. Le Cirque has an outstanding wine list that includes more than 400 selections from all over the world. A knowledgeable sommelier will help you to select just the right one.

MONTE CARLO, *Desert Inn. Tel. 702/733-4400. Major credit cards accepted. Dinner served nightlu. Reservations are required. Dress code.*

First let's reemphasize the location – this is in the Desert Inn Hotel and not in the Monte Carlo Hotel. That will help explain the exclusive atmosphere and professional staff that is dedicated to ensuring that your dining experience is first class all the way. Overlooking the hotel's lovely gardens and pool area, Monte Carlo is an award winning French restaurant in the traditional style. The service is formal (a bit too stiff for us) but flawless if you like that sort of thing. They have an exceptional wine list that is big but emphasizes quality over quantity. We must advise you that dinner at Monte Carlo will likely run to more than $100 per person.

PALACE COURT, *Caesars Palace. Tel. 702/731-7731. Major credit cards are accepted. Dinner served nightly (seatings half-hourly). Reservations are required. Dress code.*

Caesars Palace has no shortage of excellent gourmet restaurants and the Palace Court fits in perfectly. The setting is magnificent and will remind you of being in an art museum, given all of the fine works on display. Reached by a private elevator, the room's domed stained glass ceiling is absolutely wonderful. This is "haute cuisine" all the way, although the traditional French cuisine is nicely supplemented by some imaginatively prepared American dishes. The deserts and pastries are delightful. Excellent wine list along with a user-friendly sommelier.

PICASSO, *Bellagio. Tel. 702/693-7223. Major credit cards accepted. Dinner served nightly except Wednesday. Reservations are suggested. Dress code.*

One of what is a seemingly unending list of great restaurants at Bellagio, the Picasso features an interesting cuisine that combines French with a Spanish influence. The result is superb. You'll find such wonderful dishes as poached oysters, shrimp and scallops, grilled lamb noisettes or roasted veal chop, to name just a few. Pastry chef Patrick Coston does an outstanding job with the desserts. Original works by Picasso, of course, adorn the walls of this beautiful restaurant. It's reported that Mirage Resorts chairman Steve Wynn likes to frequent this new restaurant.

PRIME, *Bellagio. Tel. 702/693-7223. Major credit cards accepted. Dinner served nightly. Reservations are suggested. Dress code.*

Bellagio's steakhouse includes, in addition to first cut beef, a nice selection of seafood and chops. However, every course is wonderful. Appetizers include dishes such as crab mango salad and garlic soup with frog legs. The sumptuous desserts make for a perfect ending to an outstanding meal, all exquisitely served by a knowledgeable and professional staff. The surroundings are elegant and although it's fairly big, it has the feel of a private dining salon.

SEASONS, *Bally's. Tel. 702/967-4651. Major credit cards are accepted. Dinner served Tuesday through Saturday. Reservations are suggested. Dress code.*

The name of the restaurant reflects their policy of changing the menu with the seasons of the year. No matter what time of year you visit, however, you'll encounter wonderful beef and seafood dishes as well as more unusual selections from around the world. The emphasis is on Continental cuisine. They have a large selection of fine wines including one of the biggest champagne choices in Las Vegas. The decor also changes according to the season and features generous amounts of colorful fresh flowers.

ZEFFIRINO, *The Venetian. Tel. 702/733-5000. Most major credit cards accepted. Lunch and dinner served daily. Sunday brunch. (Breakfast served during major conventions at the hotel.) Reservations are suggested.*

Long time Genoan chef extraordinaire Vincent Scotto has come to Las Vegas to personally supervise Zeffirino at the new Venetian. Mr. Scotto has earned a reputation that has enabled him to cook for such luminaries as the Pope and Frank Sinatra, among many others. The specialties of the house are Italian style seafood entrees prepared in wood fired ovens. Many of the ingredients are imported from Italy. The surroundings are elegant and the extensive wine list (more than 130 different selections) is superb. The service befits the decor and the notable status of the chef. Sure to take its place among the top restaurants in Las Vegas in no time at all.

Expensive

ALAN ALBERTS, *3763 Las Vegas Blvd. South. Tel. 702/740-4421. Major credit cards accepted. Dinner served nightly. Reservations are suggested.*

Not one of the city's older restaurants but already among the most respected, Alan Albert's has a well deserved reputation for fine dining. You'll be treated to delectable vintage steaks and superb prime rib. The attractive dining room contains interesting Las Vegas memorabilia. The service is first rate but friendly, much more like you would find in a local restaurant. They also serve excellent seafood, especially the fresh lobster.

CAMELOT, *Excalibur. Tel. 702/597-7449. Major credit cards accepted. Dinner served Thursday through Monday. Reservations are suggested.*

While the Excalibur isn't usually noted for its great dining, Camelot is a striking exception. The menu presents a nice variety of seafood (try the fresh Maine lobster), steak, rack of lamb and duck. While the food is excellent and the service is just fine, we're especially fond of Camelot's decor and atmosphere. It's an interesting combination of modern with medieval touches. Comfortable booth seating provides a view of the expansive exhibition kitchen. There are several entrees in the moderate price category. Acceptable wine list.

CONRAD'S, *Flamingo Hilton. Tel. 702/733-3111. Major credit cards accepted. Dinner served nightly except Tuesday and Wednesday.*

A beautiful room with rich, warm woods and plenty of brass trim give Conrad's the atmosphere of a private ranch club. The menu includes a good variety of gourmet steaks, chops and seafood that are all well prepared to your specifications and graciously served. Sophisticated elegance all the way.

COYOTE CAFE, *MGM Grand (Studio Walk). Tel. 702/891-7349. Major credit cards accepted. Lunch and dinner served nightly.*

Located on the busy promenade, the Coyote Cafe is the popular and usually quite crowded Las Vegas branch of the nationally famous restaurant of the same name that originated in Santa Fe, New Mexico. Acclaimed chef Mark Miller serves modern southwestern style cuisine in an attractive atmosphere. While it is an excellent dining experience we do think it is a bit on the overpriced side. However, if you have a few extra bucks from your gambling winnings, you won't go wrong investing them here.

DRAGON COURT, *MGM Grand (Studio Walk). Tel. 702/891-7380. Major credit cards accepted. Dinner served nightly. Reservations are suggested.*

Not your run of the mill Chinese restaurant, Dragon Court features a beautiful and romantically intimate atmosphere along with first class service and excellent traditional Mandarin and Cantonese cuisine. The menu selection is quite large and features beef, seafood, poultry, and vegetarian selections. The fan-tailed crispy fried shrimp is a great appetizer. We also like the pupu platter and the honey glazed barbecued pork.

EMERIL'S NEW ORLEANS FISH HOUSE, *MGM Grand (Studio Walk). Tel. 702/891-7374. Major credit cards accepted. Lunch and dinner served daily. Reservations are suggested.*

A great place for the seafood lover. Lobster and fresh fish are featured along with Emeril's unbeatable barbecued shrimp. Most dishes are served Creole or Cajun style. For lunch or a more casual dinner, we suggest having your meal in their adjoining seafood bar. To top off a wonderful meal, try one of Emeril's freshly baked pies, like the banana cream, which is almost as famous as celebrity chef and author Emiril Lagasse.

EMPRESS COURT, *Caesars Palace. Tel. 702/731-7731. Major credit cards accepted. Dinner served Thursday through Monday. Reservations are suggested. Dress code.*

A beautiful Asian restaurant with the typical glamorous surroundings you almost expect at Caesars Palace. Featuring delicious Chinese cuisine prepared by a chef imported directly from Hong Kong, you'll enjoy such wonderful dishes as shark-fin soup and abalone. The specialty teas are excellent. The elegance doesn't stop at the decor – the chinaware is equally impressive. Fine service.

GATSBY'S, *MGM Grand. Tel. 702/891-7777. Major credit cards are accepted. Dinner served nightly except Sunday. Reservations are suggested.*

The most gourmet dining experience among several that are available at the MGM, Gatsby's is an elegant room where the California style French cuisine is superb. Intimate surroundings and professional, highly personalized service make for an enjoyable evening. In addition to the excellent selection of beef and fish entrees, Gatsby's has a number of vegetarian dishes. Some of the specialties of the house include ostrich, pate de foie gras, and Dover rack of lamb. The wine list is one of the longest in Las Vegas. Three separate wine cellars, one each for white, red and champagnes, has more than 600 wines representing the entire world. Guests can see the wine cellar display inside the restaurant.

HYAKUMI, *Caesars Palace. Tel. 702/731-7731. Major credit cards accepted. Dinner served Tuesday through Saturday. Reservations are suggested.*

For elegance in Japanese dining, Hyakumi has few peers in Las Vegas or anywhere else. This is a completely remodeled version of the former Ah'So Japanese restaurant. Authenticity is important at Hyakumi (which translates into English as something like one hundred tastes), so there's *teppan yaki* style dining in a beautiful garden like atmosphere. The chefs expertly prepare sushi and sashimi as well as a good selection of other Japanese dishes. The choice of Japanese spirits, including sake, is also one of the best. In addition to the a la carte selections, you can opt for one of three prix-fixe *teppan yaki* four course feasts which run into the very expensive category.

JASMINE, *Bellagio. Tel. 702/693-7223. Major credit cards accepted. Dinner served nightly. Reservations are suggested.*

Perhaps the most upscale Chinese restaurant in town, Jasmine's gourmet chefs prepare the most delicious traditional Cantonese, Szechuan and Hunan style dishes. A typical meal might include the outstanding dim sum lobster dumplings for openers, followed by shark's fin and chicken served with sauteed sea cucumbers. There are also a few really unusual dishes, including Thai sashimi. While there is a decent selection of meats and poultry, the menu emphasizes a variety of fish and seafood dishes. Several entrees run into the very expensive category.

THE LOBSTER HOUSE, *3763 Las Vegas Blvd. South. Tel. 702/740-4431. Major credit cards are accepted. Dinner served nightly.*

This restaurant hasn't been around as long as the more famous Rosewood Grille, but in the few years it has been open, it has given the other place a good run for the money. Featured menu highlights are delicious fresh Main lobster, Alaskan King Crab and a nightly selection of fresh dishes. The chef is from Hawaii and he adds a little South Seas flair to several dishes. Some excellent steak entrees are available as well.

MICHAEL'S GOURMET RESTAURANT, *Barbary Coast Hotel. Tel. 702/737-7111. Major credit cards accepted. Dinner served nightly. Two seatings (between 6 and 6:30 pm or between 9 and 9:30 pm.)*

The Barbary Coast certainly isn't one of The Strip's more elaborate hotels, but Michael's, a Las Vegas tradition, ranks with the best of its restaurants. The Victorian styled room is beautiful and the continental cuisine is, to make it simple, absolutely delicious. The service is fabulous and the pace is tranquil, something not always the case in Las Vegas. Even though it is expensive, you could easily spend more in other places and wind up getting a lot less for your hard earned bucks.

MIKADO, *The Mirage. Tel. 702/791-7223. Major credit cards accepted. Dinner served nightly.*

The dining room is one of the most beautiful in town (and the best decor for Oriental cuisine) but despite the authentic Japanese style, the dining experience doesn't have the same feeling. The food is quite good and compares favorably with any Japanese restaurant in town. It's also one of the most expensive Japanese eateries in Las Vegas.

MORTON'S OF CHICAGO, *3200 Las Vegas Blvd. South, in the Fashion Show Mall. Tel. 702/893-0703. Most major credit cards accepted. Lunch and dinner served daily.*

Morton's is an exclusive chain located in major cities and their chefs certainly know how to do steak and roast beef right – thick and juicy and cooked just the way you order them. The atmosphere and service are only a little on the shy side of elegant. Worth the price if you really appreciate great beef.

OLIVES, *Bellagio (on the Via Bellagio). Tel. 702/693-7223. Major credit cards accepted. Lunch and dinner served daily..*

Famous Boston chef Todd English opens his first Las Vegas restaurant under the direction of executive chef Victor LaPlaca. The Mediterranean style cuisine is outstanding (although there's a hint of Boston – you can have cod cakes and lobster remoulade served with Boston baked beans). The delicious and unique salads are definitely worth trying. The lunch menu includes a number of American favorites (especially the side orders), but the a la carte pricing makes it too expensive for anything but dinner unless you've been very fortunate at the gaming tables.

ONDA, *The Mirage. Tel. 702/791-7223. Major credit cards accepted. Dinner is served nightly. Reservations are suggested.*

Onda opened in early 1999 and replaced another Italian eatery called *Ristorante Riva*. We're not trying to knock Onda, which is fine in just about every sense, but somehow we liked the more casual elegance of its predecessor more than we do this place, which tends a little toward the stuffy side. The prices are higher, too. But, if you're looking for excellent Northern Italian cuisine, then Onda certainly fits the bill.

OSTERIA DEL CIRCO, *Bellagio. Tel. 702/693-8150. Major credit cards accepted. Lunch and dinner served daily. Reservations are suggested.*

Alright, we know what you're probably saying – another Bellagio restaurant. We promise, this is the last. But, on the other hand, there's no debating the top quality of this hotel's restaurants. In this case you'll find outstanding Tuscan cuisine in a beautiful setting that, like most of the fine restaurants at Bellagio, overlooks the lake. The lobster, calamari and other delights from the sea are the best items on the menu and they're all served with a unique variety of vegetables. The service is excellent.

PINOT BRASSERIE, *The Venetian. Tel. 702/733-5000. Major credit cards accepted. Breakfast, lunch and dinner served daily. Reservations are suggested.*

California French style cuisine featuring grilled steaks, poultry, seafood and wild game as well as pasta, along with an extensive selection of European and American wines are on tap at Pinot. The beautiful dining room features many items imported from France in order to duplicate the feel of an authentic French brasserie. There's an exhibition style kitchen with a large rotisserie and an oyster bar. Dining *al fresco* overlooking the lagoon is a delightful option.

THE PLANK, *Treasure Island. Tel. 702/791-1111. Major credit cards accepted. Dinner served nightly. Reservations are suggested.*

What would a hotel that themes itself around seafaring pirates be without a good seafood restaurant? Probably just as good but it's nice that we can say that The Plank is an excellent place for fresh fish and popular seafood entrees. The surroundings are elegant (these are successful pirates) and are arranged in small, intimate dining rooms that look like a library (educated pirates, as well). The service is first rate. Good wine list. While the Treasure Island may well be one of the most child-friendly establishments in Las Vegas, the atmosphere at The Plank is much more grown-up.

POSTRIO, *The Venetian, in the Grand Canal Shoppes. Tel. 702/733-5000. Major credit cards accepted. Dinner served nightly. Reservations are suggested.*

Wolfgang Puck's Venetian entry features more California cuisine, this time with the influence of both Asia and the Mediterranean. The large menu changes daily and includes everything from gourmet pizzas to grilled quail, *foie gras terrine*, lamb chops and duck. This casual bistro has colorful decor and features a wood-burning pizza oven in the bar area along with an exhibition kitchen. The service is excellent.

THE RANGE, *Harrah's. Tel. 702/369-5084. Major credit cards accepted. Dinner served nightly. Reservations are suggested.*

You could easily pay a lot more at plenty of other restaurants in Las Vegas and not have nearly as excellent a dining experience as you can get at this outstanding eatery. The western decor and atmosphere create a casual atmosphere as you gaze out onto The Strip. The steak, seafood and chicken dishes are all expertly prepared and the portions are generous. You must, however, save some room for their wonderful desserts. The service is first rate and live music adds to the pleasing atmosphere. The Range's wine list is impressive.

ROSEWOOD GRILLE, *3339 Las Vegas Blvd. South. Tel. 702/792-5965. Major credit cards are accepted. Dinner served nightly. Reservations are suggested.*

Perhaps Las Vegas' most famous non-hotel seafood restaurant, and worthy of its reputation. Winner of more awards than you can count, the Rosewood Grille's European trained chef prepares jumbo steamed Maine lobster and wonderful scampi dishes among other delights of the sea. You also can't go wrong with their smaller selection of beef dishes. Excellent wine list (they've also won Wine Spectator Awards for many years running) and an attentive staff happy to answer any of your dining questions.

SAMBA, *The Mirage. Tel. 702/791-7223. Major credit cards accepted. Dinner served nightly. Reservations are suggested.*

The final member of the new trio of upscale restaurants at the Mirage (joining Alex Stratta and Onda), this is our favorite, not only of this group, but of all the Mirage eateries. Located off the casino, the colorful South American style decor is a delight and helps foster a casual and fun sort of atmosphere. Yet, the food is first class all the way. Delicious steaks and fresh seafood are the entrees of choice, all done up the Brazilian way, which means great taste and an almost perfect amount of seasoning. The service is friendly and efficient. There's a decent wine list although it isn't nearly as extensive as you'll find in most of the more formal high end restaurants.

SMITH & WOLLENSKY, *3767 Las Vegas Blvd. South. Tel. 702/862-4100. Most major credit cards accepted. Lunch and dinner served daily.*

Newly opened, S&W is a sure bet, in our opinion, to take its place amongst the better places to eat in Las Vegas. Smith & Wollensky originated on New York's Second Avenue back in 1977, a great place for fine restaurants (and where only the best survived). This one looks almost exactly like the original from the exterior's painted over tenement building look, to the old time interior with its wooden floors. The menu features superb steaks and prime rib along with a decent selection of seafood. The appetizers are superb. However, everything here is completely a la carte, so a full course meal will definitely run you into the very expensive category.

STAR CANYON, *The Venetian. Tel. 702/733-5000. Major credit cards accepted. Dinner served nightly. Reservations are suggested.*

New Texas cuisine at its best. No, this isn't your ordinary Tex-Mex joint. Star Canyon is a sophisticated restaurant in many ways, although the decor has some light cowboy touches to go with the elegant ranch look. The menu, too, is a complex combination of styles – southwestern with a bit of French culinary ideas thrown in, as well as other influences. Among the items that are absolutely delicious are the pinto bean-wild mushroom ragout, the red chile onion rings, chile relleno cooked with smoked chicken, and grilled sirloin with sweet potato enchiladas. Wow!

TOP OF THE WORLD, *Stratosphere. Tel. 702/380-7711. Major credit cards are accepted. Dinner served nightly. Reservations are suggested.*

You can't have a tall tower anywhere without having the obligatory revolving gourmet restaurant. We don't mean this as a knock in the subject case because the view from the 833-foot level is extraordinary. The menu features steaks, fresh fish, and seafood, including lobster. As the restaurant rotates completely in one hour you'll have more than enough time to take in the entire 360-degree panorama. The service is good and the food is certainly better than average, but the prices are justified only if you really must have that view while you eat.

TRATORIA DEL LUPO RESTAURANT, *Mandalay Bay. Tel. 702/ 632-7777. Major credit cards accepted. Lunch and dinner served nightly.*

The famous husband and wife team of Wolfgang Puck and Barbara Lazarof have found success at several restaurants in Las Vegas. This is their newest venture and it's a great Italian eatery. The authentic trattoria atmosphere is fun and casual as patrons watch from a piazza like setting as pasta and baking chores are handled by the outstanding kitchen staff. They even have a wood burning rotisserie and pizza oven for that real Italian taste. The cuisine features dishes from all parts of Italy – north, south and regional, so no matter what your taste in Italian is, you'll find it here. The center of this most attractive restaurant features a beautiful bar that contains the restaurant's wine room. And the wine selection is outstanding.

TRE VISI, *MGM Grand (Studio Walk). Tel. 702/891-7331. Major credit cards are accepted. Breakfast, lunch and dinner served daily.*

Patio style dining indoors, Tre Visi is a gracious Italian cafe with excellent food and very good service. The menu is representative of Northern, Southern, Tuscan and Milanese cuisines. Everything from the appetizers through dessert is well prepared, although portions are definitely on the scarce side. Despite the casual surroundings and pleasant service, Tre Visi has an elegant feel to it. Maybe it's because it's so easy to imagine that you're dining street side in Italy. Oh, yes, they have a different flavor of gelato every day of the year!

NEWS FLASH: POWER CHEFS OPEN NEW POWER RESTAURANTS

During the last year, but especially in the several months prior to this edition's preparation, there has literally been an explosion of upscale restaurants in Strip hotels featuring some of the most famous names in wold Chefdom. Among the outstanding names in gastronomy now on the Las Vegas scene are Todd English, Emeril Lagasse, Mark Miller, Charlie Palmer, Wolfgang Puck, Stephan Pyles, Piero Selvaggio, Joachim Splichal and last, but not least, James Beard Award winner Alex Stratta. That's a menu that New York or Paris would be hard pressed to top. And more are sure to join the parade as Las Vegas becomes synonymous with great dining.

We like to be able to personally report on restaurants before including them in our listings. This wasn't possible in the case of the new Paris Hotel. However, reports are that there will be several outstanding places to choose from. Accordingly, you probably wouldn't be going in the wrong direction if you headed to:

Brasserie: *Moderate/Expensive. The only restaurant in a Strip hotel that has actual outside seating. Sophisticated and imaginative menu. Breakfast, lunch and dinner.*

Eifel Tower: *Expensive. At the 100-foot level, this authentic gourmet French restaurant affords a great view of The Strip.*

La Rotisserie: *Expensive. Two-level dining room featuring distinctive French entrees wonderfully marinaded and prepared in rotisserie ovens in view of the diner.*

Names of restaurants were tentative at press time. Enjoy!

Moderate

AL DENTE, *Bally's. Tel. 702/967-4656. Major credit cards accepted. dinner served Saturday through Wednesday.*

Yes, you can get "gourmet" pizza here, but Al Dente is mainly for those looking for great Italian food, both traditional and unusual. The antipasto and pasta dishes are especially appetizing. The pasta is always right – "al dente." Ditto for the glorious deserts which could easily have come right out of a Rome cafe.

ALTA VILLA, *Flamingo Hilton. Tel. 702/733-3333. Major credit cards accepted. Dinner served Friday through Tuesday.*

Wow, another Italian restaurant! This is a casual and attractive place for good food. From the moment you enter the restaurant with it's lovely fountain, you're in for an enjoyable time. They have a nice selection of traditional Italian dishes at a reasonable price. The wine list is more than adequate.

ASIA, *Harrah's. Tel. 702/369-5084. Major credit cards accepted. Dinner served nightly. Reservations are suggested.*

As the name implies, this restaurant highlights food from throughout the Far East, although fine Chinese cuisine is predominant. The food is just about as good as at any Oriental restaurant in town so we consider this to be a better than average value for fine dining. The decor is absolutely stunning, featuring elegant Oriental themes in a colorful yet refined manner. The service is also well above average.

BLACK SPOT GRILLE, *Treasure Island. Tel. 702/791-7111. Major credit cards accepted. Lunch and dinner served daily.*

An "outdoor" style cafe in the indoors, the Black Spot is an attractive casual eatery that overlooks both the casino and the shopping promenade at Treasure Island. Menu staples are burgers, pasta dishes and excellent salads. Very friendly atmosphere. A few entrees are in the inexpensive category.

CANALETTO, *The Venetian, in the Grand Canal Shoppes. Tel. 702/733-5000. Major credit cards accepted. Lunch and dinner served daily.*

Bravo! Bravo! Bravo! Here's the Italian restaurant to satisfy the most demanding gourmet as well as the person looking for elegant surroundings. This two-story restaurant is the only restaurant in The Venetian that truly has a Venetian theme itself. You can dine "outside" on the patio overlooking the Grand Canal adjacent to a 40-foot high statue, or in the main dining room with its navy blue striped booths, polished hardwood floors and 16-foot high ceilings. (The upstairs consists of several small private dining rooms styled like a Venetian *palazzo*.) The exhibition style kitchen is a sight to behold. The service is exceptional. Both the food and wine concentrate on the cuisine of the Veneto region but there are also a good number of Northern Italian staples such as risotto, gnocchi and polenta. And, finally, although several entrees do edge into the expensive category, this is certainly an affordable restaurant. It's one of the few where we can say you get more than what you pay for.

CHIN'S, *3200 Las Vegas Blvd. South, in the Fashion Show Mall. Tel. 702/733-8899. Most major credit cards accepted. Lunch and dinner served daily.*

An award winning restaurant with some of the best Chinese food around. They've been in business since 1973 and feature a variety of Chinese cooking styles. There's also a branch at Arizona Charlies.

DIVE!, *3200 Las Vegas Blvd. South, outside the Fashion Show Mall. Tel. 702/369-3483. Most major credit cards accepted. Lunch and dinner served daily.*

Standard fare (burgers, chicken, etc.) along with pizza and pasta that is usually overpriced (although some dishes are in the inexpensive category), but in return you get a rather unique atmosphere unless you happen to be from Los Angeles where the original *Dive!* is located. The place, both inside and outside, is designed to resemble a submarine. *Dive!* logo merchandise is on sale in the gift shop.

THE EMBERS, *Imperial Palace. Tel. 702/794-3261. American express, Discover, MasterCard and Visa accepted. Dinner served Wednesday through Saturday. Reservations are suggested.*

It's hard not to highly recommend The Embers because it is a real bargain when you compare it to other fine steakhouses. The surroundings are elegant, like a private club, and the service is warm and attentive. The steak and prime rib, as well as lamb, veal and a smaller selection of seafood entrees, are among the tops in town. You'd be hard pressed to find better at any price. This is truly the style restaurant for the rich at prices the middle class will appreciate.

GILLEY'S SALOON, DANCE HALL & BAR-B-QUE, *New Frontier Hotel. Tel. 702/794-8200. Major credit cards accepted. Dinner served nightly; lunch only on Saturday and Sunday*'.

The latest branch of the now famous Texas honky-tonk, Gilley's combines good fun with good food – "real" food such as ribs, Texas style steaks and the like. The value is excellent; you'll even find quite a few entrees in the inexpensive category. Entertainment takes many forms at Gilley's, including live performers on a huge stage, dancing and line dancing, and the mechanical bull. We suggest you try the latter *before* you eat!

HARLEY DAVIDSON CAFE, *3725 Las Vegas Blvd. South. Tel. 702/740-4555. Major credit cards accepted. Lunch and dinner served daily.*

One of many "theme" restaurants popular throughout the country but which have developed a life of their own in Las Vegas, the H-D features popular American dishes like burgers, steak, ribs and such. The food is alright but certainly nothing special and the value is average at best. However, lots of people like to have an "experience" when they eat out and this place is that. The front of an oversized motorcycle protrudes from over the entrance and several Harley-Davidson cycles are on display. There's all sorts of celebrity memorabilia and the back wall of the restaurant is a giant American flag constructed of metal chains painted red, white and blue. It's unique. That isn't available for sale in their retail shop but just about everything else is.

HOUSE OF BLUES, *Mandalay Bay. Tel. 702/632-7777. Major credit cards accepted. Lunch and dinner served nightly.*

This huge restaurant has art and memorabilia from entertainers of the Deep South along with original Bas-relief portraits. Some of it looks like a church; other portions are decorated with bottle caps from beer! It's highly eclectic to say the least and lots of fun. It's part of the larger House of Blues entertainment complex within Mandalay Bay. In keeping with the theme, the menu features southern inspired regional cuisine. The catfish, barbecued ribs and "Blues" burgers are all good but we think you're better off spicing things up a bit with such delights as jambalaya, gumbo and ettoufee. If you're into Gospel music then you should definitely go for the live entertainment of the Gospel Brunch.

MOTOWN CAFE, *New York, New York. Tel. 702/740-6969. Major credit cards accepted. Lunch and dinner served daily.*

This place is practically decorated wall-to-wall with gold records as well as many life-like bronze statues of some of your favorite Motown entertainers, including one on the stage of the relatively small but colorful dining room. An enjoyable place for standard American fare (especially southern style dishes) and some international selections, accompanied by music videos and a fun, friendly atmosphere that's hard to beat. It's very popular so expect to wait at peak times.

PAPYRUS, *Luxor. Tel. 702/262-4774. Major credit cards are accepted. Dinner served Thursday through Monday. Reservations are suggested.*

Excellent but straight forward Chinese food is the feature at this casual but extremely attractive restaurant. We like the large selection and the friendly and efficient service. It may not be the best Chinese restaurant in town, but if you're looking for one on The Strip that gives you high quality at an affordable price, then Papyrus is a wise choice.

RAINFOREST CAFE, *MGM Grand. Tel. 702/891-8580. Major credit cards accepted. Breakfast, lunch and dinner served daily.*

There are other Rainforest Cafes scattered about the country but none are quite as elaborate as the Las Vegas version. What else would you expect? For those of you who aren't familiar with RFC's, the imaginative setting and fun that goes along with it is, perhaps, more important than the food. You'll dine inside a veritable jungle, complete with thick vegetation, rushing waterfalls, animals large and small (some moving and making noises), colorful birds and, of course, periodic downpours accompanied by thunder and lightning. We especially like the chairs at the bar, which have colorful animal tails! There's also a fascinating gift shop with more animals (including a ferocious looking alligator), butter-flies, tropical aquariums, and much, much more.

Oh, yes...the food. The Cafe boasts a big selection of popular dishes, especially American but with a smattering of just about anything. It isn't great but it is better than what you'll usually find in many of these theme restaurants. The prices are a bit on the high side considering what you get but someone has to pay for the great atmosphere.

RED SQUARE, *Mandalay Bay. Tel. 702/632-7777. Major credit cards accepted. Dinner served nightly. Reservations are suggested.*

After a successful debut in Miami's ritzy South Beach, Red Square opens a branch in Las Vegas with the elaborate Russian style decor that was such a hit in Florida. The dinner selections are a combination of traditional Russian cuisine along with Continental, Italian and American specialties. All in all, there's something for everyone on the menu. Red Square also boasts an elaborate frozen ice bar that includes more than a hundred different types of frozen vodkas and "Russian inspired" martini's. Fortunately, they don't serve Molotov cocktails. And in case you want them to keep a special bottle of vodka just for you – they'll be more than happy to do so. You see, Red Square has private vodka lockers that celebrities seem to go for. It's hard to miss Red Square – a larger than life statue of a headless Vladimir Lenin stands outside the entrance. We want to let you know that the rumor of Red Square's and other Mandalay Bay restaurant chefs meeting the same fate if guests complain about their dinners is definitely untrue.

RUMJUNGLE, *Mandalay Bay. Tel. 702/632-7777. Major credit cards accepted. Dinner served nightly.*

We really do like the selection of restaurants in the new Mandalay Bay and rumjungle (no capitalization and one word, please) is no exception. It's a whole lot more than just a restaurant – it's one of those places that makes dining an entertaining experience. It begins the moment you enter and encounter the dancing firewall that becomes a wall of water. Inside the rum and spirits rise over an illuminated bar and the open pit fire where the cooking is done is a backdrop for the "dueling congas" dance floor. It's just wild. So is the food, much of which is served by waiters carrying flaming skewers. The menu contains a good variety of chicken, meat and fish. In addition to the normal bar drinks, rumjungle has an almost endless list of the most exotic drinks you could imagine. On the dance floor you can sway to a variety of different rhythms, including Latin, Caribbean and African. For an evening to remember, rumjungle gets a definite thumbs up from us.

SACRED SEA ROOM, *Luxor. Tel. 702/262-4772. Major credit cards accepted. Dinner served nightly. Reservations are suggested.*

A beautiful dining room decorated with tile mosaics and hieroglyphic murals to keep in touch with the Luxor theme. Although the surroundings are elegant the atmosphere is much more casual. Sacred Seas serves a big variety of fresh and salt-water fish that includes favorites from America, Europe and the South Pacific. They also have a decent selection of non-fish entrees for the land lubbers in your group.

THE STEAK HOUSE, *Circus Circus. Tel. 702/794-3767. Major credit cards are accepted. Dinner served nightly. Sunday brunch. Reservations are accepted.*

In the same class as The Embers – great steaks perfectly done and served in an inviting atmosphere at almost bargain prices. The Steak House is an award winning establishment in a hotel that is otherwise not known for its fine dining. You'll see your dinner being grilled mesquite style in the restaurant's exhibition kitchen. The service is excellent. One of the most popular steakhouses in town.

STIVALI, *Circus Circus. Tel. 702/691-5820. Major credit cards accepted. Dinner served nightly.*

Part of Circus Circus' master plan to upgrade the dining facilities at what was previously a mostly undistinguished place for restaurants, Stivali is an elegant Italian eatery that has a good selection of traditional entrees. Their fresh home made pastas and savory sauces are truly excellent and make just about any item from the menu a delicious treat. Although the prices are already decent, you can do even better by skipping lunch and having an early dinner on weekdays. Get there between 3pm and 5pm and you can experience their "Taste of Stivali" – cocktails and appetizers are on the house.

WARNER BROTHERS' STAGE 16 RESTAURANT, *Venetian (in the Grand Canal Shoppes). Tel. 702/733-5000. Major credit cards accepted. Lunch and dinner served daily.*

The most reasonably priced eatery in the upscale Venetian (along with the coffee shop), this is also one of the most unusual restaurants in the place. It certainly is the most fun for the person who doesn't like stuffy dining. You'll eat on a "movie set" such as Casablanca, only to find that the set changes to another motion picture while you're dining. And so do the costumes of the staff, which always match the set you're on. The food is standard fare American but, like most themed restaurants, people seem to come in more for the light atmosphere than for the culinary experience.

WILLIAM B'S, *Stardust. Tel. 702/732-6111. Major credit cards accepted. Dinner served nightly. Reservations are suggested.*

Another great restaurant where you would expect the prices to be even higher, William B's has a pleasant and subdued turn-of-the-century atmosphere – casual but extremely attractive. The selection of entrees covers a wide range of American cuisine. Although it is best known for fine steaks and prime rib, diners can choose from a surprisingly large menu that includes veal, pork, poultry and fish. Excellent service without being overly stuffy.

Inexpensive

LA PIAZZA FOOD COURT, *Caesars Palace. Tel. 702/731-7731. Major caredit cards accepted. Lunch and dinner served daily. Limited breakfast selections are also available.*

This is not your ordinary food court with independent stores like the major national burger chains and similar eateries. Instead, you can choose from a wide selection of well prepared food (sandwiches as well as hot plates, salads, desserts and more) that run the gamut from American to

Oriental and from Mexican to Italian. Once you've made your selections and pass through the central check-out counter, you can take a seat in the large and comfortable dining area that overlooks the casino. There's even a full service bar. La Piazza is also the scene for live entertainment during the later evening hours.

RALPH'S DINER, *Stardust. Tel. 702/732-6111. Major credit cards accepted. Breakfast and lunch served daily.*

A throwback to the 1950's, this fun place features black and white floor and wall tiles, an authentic soda fountain, and jukebox selector at every table. The food is good and consists of burgers, salads, and the like. Try the daily "blue plate special."

TRES LOBOS, *Stardust. Tel. 702/732-6111. Major credit cards accepted. Dinner served Tuesday through Saturday.*

An extensive menu of good Mexican cuisine served in an attractive atmosphere. The fajitas and chimichangas are especially good. The adjacent Cantina is a nice, lively spot for drinks and chatter.

WHERE'S THAT RESAURANT WE ALWAYS LIKED?

*In a city where "out with the old and in with the new" is a way of life, even we have trouble keeping up with the changes in the hotel restaurant lineup. Just as an example, the long popular (including with us) **Wild Bill's Steakhouse** at the Excalibur closed down and was replaced with the wrestling themed **Nitro Grill**, just weeks before we went to press.*

The driving force behind the changes is two-fold. First, although the popularity of themed restaurants may have peaked nationwide, it is still an increasingly popular venue in this town. Second, and even more important, is the desire to upgrade hotel restaurants and solidify Las Vegas' position as a dining destination. Increasing sophistication is the name of the game.

So, return visitors shouldn't be surprised to find that someplace they used to eat at when visiting Las Vegas has been replaced. Try out something new!

OFF-STRIP
Expensive

HILTON STEAKHOUSE, *Las Vegas Hilton. Tel. 702/732-5755. Major credit cards accepted. Dinner served nightly. Reservations are suggested.*

This is one of the older steakhouses in Las Vegas and they've been doing it right for a long time. The beautiful decor is highlighted by rich dark wood booths surrounded by equally pleasing etched glass. The walls are adorned with works of art. The steaks are outstanding but the extensive menu also features a good variety of well prepared veal, lamb and fresh seafood in addition to poultry and pork. Careful, attentive service.

BISTRO LE MONTRACHET, *Las Vegas Hilton. Tel. 702/732-5755. Major credit cards accepted. Dinner served Thursday through Monday. Reservations are required. Dress code.*

If you're looking for a traditional gourmet restaurant serving excellent French cuisine, then Le Montrachet is your kind of place. Expertly prepared and beautifully served, the food will please the most difficult to please gourmet. This restaurant also has one of the biggest wine cellars in Las Vegas, with more than 400 varieties to select from. The wine steward will help you sort through that impressive list with expertise.

MASK, *Rio Hotel. Tel. 702/247-7923. Major credit cards accepted. Dinner served nightly.*

An outstanding selection of Far Eastern delights, all tastefully presented by an efficient and knowledgable staff. The surroundings are beautiful and elegant (the decor is that of a rain forest) although the atmosphere is fun and casual. Sushi dishes; *teppan yaki* style dining.

PAMPLEMOUSSE, *400 E. Sahara Ave. Tel. 702/733-2066. Major credit cards accepted. Dinner served nightly. Reservations are suggested.*

Located only a block off of The Strip behind the Sahara Hotel, Pamplemousse boasts a delightful country French cottage atmosphere with an enclosed patio. Very popular with locals looking for fine French cuisine at an affordable price, Pamplemousse has also been selected as one of the best restaurants in the country on several occasions by numerous sources. The menu features steak, seafood and veal but we especially like the duck. The service is attentive and the pace very relaxed - in fact, there are only four seatings each evening.

VOO DOO CAFE, *Rio Hotel. Tel. 702/247-7923. Major credit cards accepted. Dinner served nightly.*

While there aren't that many Cajun/Creole restaurants in Las Vegas, this one is, without any doubt in our mind, the best. For a variety of reasons. First and foremost is the excellent food. The efficient and friendly service is another reason. And last, but certainly not the least, is the location. Sitting atop the towering Rio, the view is the best in town – restaurant or otherwise. Even the Stratosphere's "Top of the World" doesn't match this one. The restaurant also has a separate lounge with live entertainment to make for an even more enjoyable evening.

Moderate

ANTONIO'S, *Rio Hotel. Tel. 702/247-7923. Major credit cards accepted. Dinner served nightly.*

First we have to tell you that the prices at this excellent restaurant almost put it into the expensive category. The traditional Italian fare in

HOTEL COFFEE SHOPS –
A TASTY AND INEXPENSIVE ALTERNATIVE

Disappointed that so many of the restaurants are expensive? Don't fret. As indicated at the outset of this chapter, the 24-hour hotel coffee shops are generally good places for a tasty meal at a good price (mostly in the inexpensive category but with some entrees going into the moderate range). You can choose from any meal at any time of the day, a real convenience in Las Vegas where normal hours are often thrown at the window. They're especially good for breakfast, especially since most of the fancier restaurants aren't open in the morning. Many of them have the word "cafe" in their names, an indication of the informal atmosphere that prevails. If you want a sit-down meal that isn't fancy but is well prepared, they're an excellent choice. That also applies if you have children since the little ones don't usually enjoy the fancy restaurants. So, here's a quick rundown on the restaurants in this category that we consider above average.

__AMERICA RESTAURANT (New York, New York).__ Fun atmosphere and good food. The selection is quite large and features American favorites along with a little of just about everything else. The huge map of the United States that's suspended from the ceiling is an eye-catcher. The American theme is carried out in many other ways, including the stars on the floor. This place, like the entry that follows, is a little bit higher priced than a lot of the hotel coffee shops, but it's still well within the moderate range.

__CAFE BELLAGIO (Bellagio).__ Adjoining the magnificent Conservatory, this is definitely the most elegant looking 24-hour restaurant of any Las Vegas hotel. The food is excellent and the service is efficient. If you ever wondered what an upscale coffee shop is, this is it.

__GRAND LUX CAFE (The Venetian).__ More than 200 items on the menu plus tons of great desserts. The Renaissance theme includes handpainted ceilings, wall mosaics, limestone tables and marble flooring. The brainchild of the founder of the yummy Cheesecake Factory, the Grand Lux is a little more expensive than many of the other coffee shops but is still family priced.

__LOOKOUT CAFE (Treasure Island).__ One of the best selections on The Strip. Good food and selection, served in a pleasant atmosphere (some tables have a good view of Treasure Island's pool area). Friendly staff.

__RIO BEACH (Rio Hotel).__ A pretty coffee shop with food good enough to take its place amongst Rio's fine restaurants. Wide selection of American, Mexican and other dishes, all nicely prepared and served. Outstanding desserts.

Some other good choices are __Roma Cafe (Caesars Palace), Garden Cafe (Harrahs), Studio Cafe (MGM Grand),__ and the __Sourdough Cafe (Arizona Charlies).__

this attractive dining room with exhibition style kitchen is excellent and worthy of the fine reputation that just about every Rio restaurant has earned. Antonio's also has a humongous wine list, with better than 300 selections available. Good service and nice atmosphere.

BATTISTA'S HOLE IN THE WALL, *4041 Audrie, off of Flamingo Road. Tel. 702/732-1424. American express, Diner's, MasterCard and Visa accepted. Dinner served nightly. Reservations are suggested.*

Located across the street from the Flamingo Road side of Bally's, this place has become something of a Las Vegas institution. The same chef has been cooking excellent pasta, veal piccata, steak, and seafood since 1973. A casual and fun atmosphere prevails and it attracts locals, tourists, and quite a few famous celebrities. You can get anything from pizza to a full dinner, the latter served with an unlimited amounts of an excellent house wine. They also make the best cappuccino in Nevada.

BENIHANA VILLAGE, *Las Vegas Hilton. Tel. 702/732-5755. Major credit cards accepted. dinner served nightly. Reservations are suggested.*

Consisting of several dining rooms around a garden-like setting, there are pools, plenty of statues, and sound effects such as chirping birds and a thunderstorm to enhance your dining pleasure. Don't forget, they had all of that well before the Rainforest Cafe! Getting back to the main topic, the Japanese food is quite good and features authentic table side Hibachi preparation.

BOISON'S, *4503 Paradise Road. Tel. 732-9993. Most major credit cards accepted. Dinner served nightly. Reservations are suggested.*

This restaurant has been rewarded on several occasions by readers of the local newspaper and it is deserving. A warm and inviting dining room that's well suited to the enjoyment of finely prepared cuisine, Boison's features Continental and French specialties along with some excellent Italian entrees. They have a first rate wine list and the service is also of a high quality. Several entrees are in the expensive category.

THE BROILER, *Boulder Station, Tel. 702/432-7777 and Palace Station, Tel. 702/367-2411. Major credit cards accepted. Dinner served nightly.*

Excellent selection of fish and seafood entries as well as steak. This isn't a fancy place, just large portions of good food at a reasonable and well affordable price. Either location is a solid choice, but the Palace Station Broiler has an advantage because it's the one that has an Oyster Bar – and it's outstanding!

BUZIO'S, *Rio Hotel. Tel. 702/247-7923. Major credit cards accepted. Lunch and dinner served daily.*

This is a great place for the freshest and finest seafood dishes. The room is casual elegant – lots of wood and brass and overlooking a corner of Rio's beautiful pool area. The service is excellent and the extensive menu will present you with a real problem deciding what you want.

Patrons can watch as their dinner is prepared in the open, exhibition style kitchen. Buzio's mussels and clam dishes are great. Try them and we're sure you won't be disappointed. The oyster bar is a local favorite. Several entrees move over into the expensive price range.

CANAL STREET GRILLE, *Orleans Hotel. Tel. 702/365-7111. Major credit cards accepted. Dinner served nightly. Reservations are suggested.*

This is a relatively new steakhouse that has made quite an impression. Understated elegance with no pretension of glitz – just comfortable surroundings that include a warm fireplace. Steaks, prime rib, and other selections are broiled to perfection.

FERRARO'S RESTAURANT, *5900 W. Flamingo Road. Tel. 702/364-5300. Most major credit cards accepted. Lunch and dinner served daily.*

Family owned and operated since 1985, Ferraro's is a good place for traditional Italian food. The specialties are fresh seafood and great osso buco. The place has won several awards, including one given out by the American Academy of Restaurants. For entertainment, Ferraro's features a piano bar. Wine cellar with excellent selection. There is also a branch of Ferraro's at the Stratosphere Hotel, but all of the locals will tell you that the original location is better. Also now in Henderson.

FIORE, *Rio Hotel. Tel. 702/247-7923. Major credit cards accepted. Dinner served nightly.*

Another of the Rio's many attractive restaurants that continue a tradition of warm surroundings, efficient and friendly service, and, most of all – outstanding food. From the name Fiore you would expect Italian cuisine. While there is some of that in several regional specialties representing the northern coastal style of preparation, Fiore also has entrees from the south of France and a big selection of American style cuisine. The rack of lamb is always excellent. For something a little more out of the ordinary we suggest the pheasant ravioli. Delicious desserts and extensive wine list.

KIEFER'S ATOP THE CARRIAGE HOUSE, *Carriage House Hotel. Tel. 702/739-8000. Major credit cards accepted. Dinner served nightly.*

Kiefer's serves a nice variety of well prepared seafood entrees (mostly done Cajun style) in one of the most romantic dining rooms in the city. The view of The Strip is partially obstructed but is, nevertheless, impressive. The service is refined.

QUARK'S BAR & RESTAURANT, *Las Vegas Hilton, Tel. 702/697-8725. Major credit cards accepted. Lunch and dinner served daily..*

If you follow Star Trek, you know that some of the food eaten by those alien species isn't always very appetizing to us "yu-mahns." Well, Quark's has a few of those outer space dishes but don't be alarmed – they're just slightly disguised American favorites like burgers and beef or chicken. The food at Quarks is alright. Don't expect gourmet. What people do come here for is the quirky atmosphere and decor. They do have some wild specialty drinks, too. Your order will be taken on a tricorder and Klingons and Ferengi are available to recommend some of the intergalactic specialties of the house. And if you need an explanation of that, you probably won't enjoy dining at Quark's – so don't ask.

THE TILLERMAN, *2245 E. Flamingo Road. Tel. 702/731-4036. Major credit cards accepted. Dinner served nightly.*

A well known restaurant with the locals, the Tillerman is a good place for seafood lovers if you're looking for reasonable prices and a nice, casual atmosphere. They also feature a more than adequate selection of steaks and other food for land lubbers. The service is efficient and friendly.

Inexpensive

FREDDIE G's DELI & DINER, *325 Hughes Center Drive. Tel. 702/892-9955. Major credit cards accepted. Breakfast, lunch and dinner served daily.*

A nice little place to either sit down and have a tasty meal at great prices, or to pick up something for on the go. Freddie G's is under the same ownership as another well known local restaurant, so the food here is a notch above the usual deli restaurant. They have a daily special (usually something simple and truly American, such as meatloaf or beef brisket) as well as a fresh catch of the day.

DOWNTOWN
Expensive

HUGO'S CELLAR, *Four Queens Hotel. Tel. 702/385-4011. Major credit cards accepted. Dinner served nightly.*

One of the most elegant restaurants in the Downtown area. Things start out on the right track upon entering when each female guest is presented with a fresh red rose. The atmosphere is right out of New Orleans. Prime rib and steak are excellent but Hugo's also serves a nice variety of fish and seafood. The cellar in the name comes from the fact that Hugo's has its own wine cellar with an extensive list to choose from. Wonderfully attentive service without being overbearing.

Moderate

BINION'S RANCH STEAK HOUSE, *Binion's Horseshoe Hotel. Tel. 702/382-1600. Major credit cards accepted. Dinner served nightly.*

Very good steak and prime rib at affordable prices along with good service and a nice atmosphere. The restaurant is located on the 24th floor of the hotel and affords a good view of Las Vegas.

BURGUNDY ROOM, *Lady Luck Hotel. Tel. 702/477-3000. American Express, MasterCard and Visa accepted. Dinner served nightly. Reservations are suggested.*

Gourmet dining and Downtown don't seem to go together, but there are several real classy joints to be found in this area. The Burgundy Room is, in our opinion, the best of the Downtown dining rooms, especially when you figure in price/value considerations. The decor is reminiscent of 19th century Paris and contains many fine original works of art (this room had "class" before Vegas decided that was a good idea). The menu features the usual selection of steaks and seafood along with a few other entrees, but they're all extremely well prepared and served very nicely.

CENTER STAGE, *Jackie Gaughan's Plaza Hotel. Tel. 702/386-2110. Major credit cards accepted. Breakfast, lunch and dinner served daily.*

Overlooking the glitter of Glitter Gulch, Center Stage is a good place to go if you want a nice restaurant at a reasonable price and don't want it to be too fancy. This one has been around forever and it still attracts a sizable crowd even with the increasing competition as time goes by. American cuisine is featured.

LILLIE LANGTRY, *Golden Nugget Hotel. Tel. 702/385-7111.Major credit cards accepted. Dinner served nightly.*

Don't let the name fool you – this is a first rate Chinese restaurant. The atmosphere is that of San Francisco's Chinatown at the turn of the century and is quite attractive. Excellent service and food are the hallmarks of Lillie Langtry, which has a reputation as one of the better places in Las Vegas to go to when you're looking for Chinese cuisine.

STEFANO'S, *Golden Nugget Hotel. Tel. 702/385-7111. Major credit cards accepted. Dinner served nightly. Reservations are suggested.*

If you're looking to have Italian food while downtown, then Stefano's is clearly the unequaled choice along Fremont Street. Traditional atmosphere and menu. Good wine list and fine service. Very popular.

AROUND LAS VEGAS
Expensive

RANCH HOUSE, *6250 Rio Vista (US 95 to Ann Road). Tel. 702/645-1399. Most major credit cards accepted. Dinner served nightly.*

Dating all the way back to 1955 (which is almost ancient for a Las Vegas restaurant), this place has an out-of-the-way location, although not as much as in the past when this part of town was nearly open sagebrush country. It still has a secluded atmosphere where you'll find first rate service and award winning cuisine. The menu features steaks, chicken and fresh seafood, all well prepared over an authentic mesquite grill and served in ample portions.

Moderate

BILLY BOB'S STEAK HOUSE & SALOON, *Sam's Town Hotel. Tel. 702/454-8031. Major credit cards accepted. Dinner served nightly. Reservations are suggested.*

Great place for those who like to have their thick, juicy steak in a casual and fun atmosphere. Located along the beautiful Mystic Falls Park in the hotel atrium, Billy Bob's is known for its 28-ounce rib-eye steak, but just about everything on the menu is excellent. It's a large place with five different dining rooms. They even have an old fashioned piano player. Great specialty drinks from the bar.

CELEBRITY DELI, *4055 S. Maryland Parkway. Tel. 702/733-7827. American Express, MasterCard and VISA accepted. Breakfast, lunch and dinner served daily, except breakfast and lunch only on Sunday.*

The deli serves both sandwiches and hot dinner plates. This Jewish eatery is kosher style, which means that the meat is kosher but that they don't adhere to strict orthodox religious regulations that prohibit, for example, a restaurant from mixing meat and dairy dishes. While some of the hot specials are quite tasty, we prefer the humongous deli sandwiches such as corned beef, pastrami, or combinations. Preceded by a cup of matzoh ball soup and accompanied by an order of oversized french fries, it's a meal!

COUNTRY INN, *2425 E. Desert Inn Road, Tel. 702/731-5035; 1401 S. Rainbow Blvd., Tel. 702/254-0520; and 1990 W. Sunset Road (Henderson), Tel. 702/898-8123. Most major credit cards accepted. Breakfast, lunch and dinner served daily.*

Very attractive country style decor with lots of plants as well as kitchen and dining room trinkets on shelves and hanging from the walls. Nice central fireplace. Dinner at Country Inn is tasty and features excellent turkey, pork, or roast beef. Generous tossed salad and delicious home made rolls with honey. The apple pie for dessert is tops. For solid family dining you can't possibly go wrong with any of the Country Inns – nothing fancy, just wholesome home style food. Some entrees are in the inexpensive category.-

HABIB'S PERSIAN CUISINE, *4750 W. Sahara Avenue. Tel. 702/870-0860. American Express, Discover, MasterCard and VISA accepted. Lunch and dinner served daily except Sunday.*

Habib's serves a nice selection of well prepared Middle Eastern dishes with an emphasis on lamb and vegetarian items. The multi-course fare includes many kebob items. Pleasant atmosphere and friendly service. Friday and Saturday nights are the best times to dine here because then you can be entertained by belly dancers. There are several other Middle Eastern restaurants in Las Vegas (including some that are closer to The Strip), but for good food and good value, none are better than this one.

MOUNT CHARLESTON RESTAURANT, *1300 Old Park Road (Kyle Canyon) at Mount Charleston Lodge. Tel. 702/872-5408. Most major credit cards accepted. Breakfast, lunch and dinner served daily.*

In a wonderful natural setting about 45 minutes north of Las Vegas, the Mount Charleston Restaurant serves excellent beef but is probably best known for fresh game dishes. While we don't necessarily advise you to take a trip all the way up here just for the restaurant, it will top off a nice day if you plan on taking in the scenery of the Mount Charleston area.

PAPAMIO'S ITALIAN KITCHEN, *Sam's Town Hotel. Tel. 702/454-8041. Major credit cards accepted. Dinner is served nightly; Sunday brunch.*

Overlooking the waterfall area of the Mystic Falls Park atrium, Papamio's an attractive restaurant featuring an exhibition style kitchen. You can choose from a wide range of traditional and contemporary Italian cuisine.

PASTA PALACE, *Boulder Station Hotel. Tel. 702/432-7777. Major credit cards accepted. Dinner served nightly.*

While there isn't anything wrong with Papamio's, the place to go for Italian on the Boulder Strip is right here. Start with an attractive dining room with true Mediterranean atmosphere, add excellent seafood, veal, and pasta dishes, attentive and friendly service and very reasonable prices – and what do you get? One of the best places for Italian dining in Las Vegas. Great Italian bread is served in huge baskets and the house wine (complimentary with some entrees) is excellent.

If we have one complaint it's that the dessert menu is somewhat limited (although tasty) and overpriced compared to the value you get for the bountiful entrees. Then again, after all that food you may not have room for desert. There's also a Pasta Palace at the Palace Station Hotel but we don't like it quite as much as we do the above location. Perhaps it's because the surroundings aren't quite as attractive.

Inexpensive

GUADALAJARA, *Boulder Station Hotel, Tel. 702/432-7777; Palace Station, Tel. 702/367-2411. Major credit cards accepted. Lunch and dinner served daily.*

Although some entrees are priced in the moderate category, this is definitely an excellent value. Authentic and Mexican food is served in great quantities by a friendly and efficient wait staff in colorful and casual atmosphere. It sure is a great formula for success. Good Margaritas and good times!

PIZZERIA UNO CHICAGO BAR & GRILL, *2540 S. Decatur Blvd. Tel. 702/876-8667. Lunch and dinner served daily.*

Here's where to go when you're looking for pizza that comes as close as you can get to the real thing. They serve delicious original Chicago style deep dish pizza along with stuffed hero sandwiches and a decent selection of hot dishes among the more than two dozen menu items. It's a great spot for lunch but you wouldn't be making a mistake coming here for dinner either.

RESTAURANT ROW...ORIENTAL STYLE

*While Las Vegas has a small Chinatown with a number of good restaurants, why not try an even more exotic culinary journey into the Far East? The **Commercial Center** is located just off The Strip at 953 E. Sahara Avenue and has four good Asian restaurants. For Thai food go to **Lotus of Siam**, Tel. 702/735-3033 or **Komol**, Tel. 702731-6542. The first one is moderately priced and the second is inexpensive. Korean fare is on the menu at **Seoul BBQ**, Tel. 702/369-4123 a moderately priced place for those who like life on the spicy side. Japanese cuisine can be found at the moderately priced **Tokyo**, Tel. 702/735-7070. In the expensive category and located across the street from the Commercial Center is the Japanese restaurant **Ginza**, 1000 E. Sahara Ave., Tel. 702/732-3080. Ginza features a great sushi bar.*

HENDERSON
Expensive
CARVER'S, *2061 W. Sunset Rd. Tel. 702/433-5801. Most major credit cards accepted. Dinner served nightly.*

Specializing in excellent steaks and chops, Carver's features a pleasant and dignified atmosphere with well attentive, highly professional service. This is a traditional style restaurant with no gimmicks of any kind – which may well be just the type of place you might be looking for after several nights of sampling the far more unusual dining opportunities that the Las Vegas area has to offer.

SONOMA CELLAR STEAK HOUSE, *Sunset Station Hotel. Tel. 702/547-7777. Major credit cards accepted. Dinner served nightly.*

Because Station Casinos has built a good portion of its reputation and success among locals and visitors through high quality, moderate priced restaurants, Sonoma represents a major departure from that concept. Not in quality, but in price and style. This upscale restaurant is designed around a wine cellar theme and even gives the impression of being underground. Consisting of two separate beautifully appointed, tapestry covered dining rooms, Sonoma emphasizes fresh ingredients, expert preparation and personalized service. As befits a restaurant with this name, there is a huge list featuring the wines of Sonoma county.

Moderate

COSTA DEL SOL, *Sunset Station Hotel. Tel. 702/547-7777. Major credit cards accepted. Dinner served nightly in the main dining room; lunch and dinner daily at the Oyster Bar.*

A very attractive restaurant that serves excellent fresh fish and seafood, mostly Mediterranean style. The atmosphere is casual but especially so at their popular Oyster Bar. The whole place has the appearance of a rocky grotto. The service is friendly and efficient.

HOUSE OF JOY, *7380 S. Eastern Ave. Tel. 702/896-4648. Most major credit cards accepted. Lunch and dinner served daily.*

The best local Chinese restaurant around. Casual and unpretentious, the House of Joy serves huge portions of delicious food. Most of it is on the mild side so if you like things hotter, then be sure to ask for it. The service is quick and amazingly efficient and the prices are just right. The hot and sour soup is superb.

RENATA'S, *4451 E. Sunset Road. Tel. 702/435-4000. Most major credit cards accepted. Dinner served Tuesday through Saturday.*

Consisting of a warm and inviting dining room as well as a more casual bistro, Renata's offers fine dining that features Continental dishes along with Chinese and a good selection of steaks and fresh seafood. The Bistro allows you to create your own dinner specialities from a list of available items. Both rooms are attractive. The service is good.

ROSALITA'S, *Sunset Station Hotel. Tel. 702/547-7777. Major credit cards accepted. Dinner served nightly.*

For the best in Mexican food you don't have to look any further than Rosalita's. The decor is warm and inviting, the service excellent, and the food colorfully prepared and delicious. There's plenty to eat at Rosalita's and no one leaves hungry. This is Sunset Station's version of the Guadalajara Mexican restaurant found at some of their other locations. While those are fine, this one is much better, even though the prices are a little bit higher.

BUFFETS

The Las Vegas buffet is in a class all by itself. It's almost an institution in this city. Every major Strip hotel (with the exception of New York, New York and the Venetian) has one, an indication of its acceptance and importance. Buffets used to be places for the budget conscious traveler to go to, or the person without very active taste buds. There was plenty of food at ridiculously low prices although the quality wasn't high. In fact, a lot of savvy eaters felt that it wasn't much better than hospital or school cafeteria food. Not very appetizing sounding to say the least.

Although there are some buffets that still fit the old description, they're fewer and fewer as the years go by. The culinary renaissance that has hit Las Vegas restaurants in general also applies to the buffet. Food quality has been increased immeasurably (although you can't call it gourmet food) and so is the availability of freshly prepared dishes. Chefs now routinely prepare orders to your specifications at so called cooking or action stations. Of course, the prices of the buffets has also increased, but they're still a big bargain by comparison with most restaurants. For the price of an entree at a moderate priced restaurant you can get all you can eat soup, salad, main course, vegetables, dessert and beverage. How can you go wrong? We often wonder why visitors to Las Vegas sometimes stop into a fast-food place. For a couple of dollars more (and sometimes even for the same price) you can choose from a vast selection of much better food. Remember to leave a tip for the person who clears the table and brings your beverage.

The buffet is the ultimate paradise for gluttons but even if you don't have the humongous appetite, it's still an excellent choice. It's tempting to try a little of everything but people who are able to control themselves will walk out satisfied without feeling like they're going to explode. We suggest not filling yourself up on a lot of breads. Do have a salad since that's good for you and it will take up a little room so you don't overdo the heavier foods. Since many buffets are known for their outstanding desserts make sure you leave some room for the finale. People watching at buffets is entertaining and desserts are the best part of the show. You'll often see someone walking back to their table with one tiny piece of cake on their plate, accompanied by their partner juggling six plates with assorted cakes, pies and pastries.

Las Vegas has literally hundreds of regular restaurants, but because of space limitations it's impossible to list all of them here. On the other hand, there are a limited enough number of buffets to include all of the worthy choices. Therefore, while we have no doubt that you could find a good restaurant that wasn't included in the previous section, the omission of a buffet on this list is purposeful. If it isn't here – don't try it. In our opinion it fits the old time buffet description we mentioned at the outset. (Those are the ones you'll most often see free coupons for – that's telling you something.)

Here's a money saving tip courtesy of your favorite travel authors – most buffets have the same menu for lunch as they do for dinner. At most they add a couple of things for dinner, maybe some shrimp or the like. Lunch is always several dollars cheaper. So, unless you have to have that extra item or two, use lunch as an early dinner and save yourself some money. For a family the savings can amount to more than $10. Not bad for the same food, huh?

The prices (rounded up to next dollar) in the individual listings are as follows: **B**=Breakfast; **BR**=Brunch; **L**=Lunch, and **D**=Dinner. All buffet prices include as much as you can eat including beverage. Some buffets have special nights where the charge is a couple of dollars higher (usually for seafood; sometimes steak). These places will be indicated by a range of prices for dinner. Otherwise, the only additional costs are gratuities and acholic beverages (where available). Inquire about children's prices as quite a few do have lower prices for little appetites. All buffets are open daily.

THE STRIP

BALLY'S (Big Kitchen Buffet), B=$9; L=$10, D=$14.

One of the more elaborate buffet spreads in a city known for all-you-can-eat eating, the Big Kitchen offers a wide selection of nicely prepared dishes in an attractive setting upstairs from the casino. Shrimp is a specialty for which this buffet has become well known. While we don't have any complaints, there are buffets of equal or even better quality that don't charge quite as much.

BELLAGIO (The Buffet). B=$10; BR=$19 (Saturday/Sunday); L=$13; D=$20.

Who says that upscale hotels can't have a buffet to entice the gourmet crowd? This buffet is a wonderful culinary experience. The selection is better than average as far as the variety of dishes is concerned. What separates it from the competition is the large number of items that are not part of most buffets, things like pheasant, venison, mussels and much more. There are many seafood dishes (dinner is so much more expensive because of additional items like crab leg). Everything is freshly prepared and of high quality. Scrumptious desserts complete the picture. The surroundings are attractive but not overly fancy considering what the rest of Bellagio looks like. If you don't want to fork over an Alexander Hamilton for a buffet dinner, we suggest making lunch your main meal of the day. At that price it's a relative bargain for what you get.

CAESARS PALACE (Palatium Buffet), B=$8; BR=$13 (Saturday), $15 (Sunday); L=$9-14, D=$14-23.

Large napkins, lots of glass and brass, and a general ritzy atmosphere is what the Palatium has to offer dining patrons. The food selection is only average (although they do have several items not found at most of the lower priced buffets). Moreover, we don't find any special quality for your extra dollars. The higher price for dinner is the seafood buffet where each person is entitled to one full lobster.

CIRCUS CIRCUS (Circus Circus Buffet), B=$5; L=$6; D=$7.

For a long time, this was a popular place with the budget set and was known for a big selection of food at unheard of prices. It didn't have much more but the school cafeteria quality and surroundings didn't seem to bother the people who chose to eat here. We're glad to announce that a recent refurbishing has significantly improved the dining room's decor and you no longer have to get all of your food on one long, continuous line that made it inconvenient to go back for seconds. The food is still a bit below average but something has to give for the price.

EXCALIBUR (Roundtable Buffet), B=$5; L=$6; D=$8.

Everything that was said about the preceding entry also applies to this establishment, including the recent refurbishment and improvement. Even the menu's are virtually identical. So, unless you're really into "budget" eating, we wouldn't suggest eating at both of these places in the same trip.

FLAMINGO HILTON (Paradise Garden Buffet), B=$7; L=$8; D=$11-13.

Simply one of the best buffets in town. The room is the most elaborate of any buffet – three separate circular dining areas overlooking the Flamingo's beautiful waterfalls and grounds. The rooms have a big tree in the center. The elaborate and spacious food serving areas are equally impressive as they feature fancy statues and multi-tiered niches filled with plants. The food selection is excellent – from salad bar all the way to dessert, with quality well above average. There's a different international theme each night. We also like the little extras at the Paradise Garden, such as more than one fork (so you don't have to eat each course with the same utensil) and a friendly staff that is generally several notches more attentive than at most buffets. Given all that and the fact that it is a Hilton, we think the price is a big bargain.

HARRAH'S (Fresh Market Buffet), B=$8; BR=$13 (Saturday/Sunday); L=$9; D=$13.

Colorful decor and a festive atmosphere highlight the Fresh Market Buffet. There are people-sized pieces of fruit and vegetables all over the place (which may even inspire the kids to eat their veggies!). The selection is a bit above average and the food quality is quite high. We could recommend it even more highly if it were a couple of bucks cheaper. After all, this is Harrah's, not Caesars Palace. On the other hand, it's a better buffet than at Caesars!

LUXOR (Pharaoh's Pheast), B=$6; L=$8; D=$10.

Located on the hotel's lower level, this is one of the most unusual looking buffets in Las Vegas. It's designed to resemble an archaeological site and you're surrounded by ladders, partially unearthed ancient ruins, gold coins, and much more. Eclectic, to say the least, but the result is attractive and fun. Unfortunately, things go downhill after that. The selection is barely average and the same can be said for the food. Overall, for the price, it isn't a bad buy if you're simply looking for a lot to eat at a low price.

MANDALAY BAY (Bay Side Buffet), B=$9; BR=$15; L=$10; D=$14. Like most of the newer and better buffets, this one features "live action stations" and good quality food. The attractive room accommodates 500 diners but is sectioned off nicely and has a much cozier feel. If you sit by the windows that overlook Mandalay Bay's 11-acre tropical lagoon, the tropical atmosphere is even more inviting. Our major complaint is that the selection isn't that large. Overall, a good place to eat but, considering all the factors, not one of the better price values for a Las Vegas buffet.

MGM GRAND (Grand Buffet), BR=$8; D=$13. The Grand Buffet recently replaced the hotel's original Oz Buffet. It's fancier looking and more adult oriented than its predecessor. The food quality has been upgraded (along with the price) but our biggest objection is that the selection isn't on a par with the better buffets.

THE MIRAGE (The Buffet), B=$9; BR=$15 (Sunday); L=$10; D=$14. Colorful, pleasant surroundings, good food, and a decent selection. Absolutely nothing wrong with this buffet but there isn't anything to distinguish it either. It's in the middle of the pack on just about every score. So why is it so high priced by comparison? Well, this is the Mirage, after all. If you want to pay extra for the privilege of saying you ate here, fine. We don't think it's worth the extra cost. You're better off paying a little more and going to the Bellagio.

MONTE CARLO (Monte Carlo Buffet), B=$7; BR=$11 (Sunday/ holidays); L=$7; D=$10. A very attractive buffet that features Casbah-like Moorish architecture and dining areas broken into smaller sections for a feel of privacy. Even the food service area is pretty. The food selection is somewhat below average and the quality is middle of the road as well. The overall value, however, is decent.

PARIS (Le Village Buffet), Pricing not available at press time, but we can tell you that it won't be one of the cheaper places in town. Although unreviewed by us, we feel this buffet is worthy of mention because of what it is going to feature. It is the only Las Vegas buffet where the food will be themed to the hotel – in this case French cuisine. The quality is reportedly going to be high. On the atmosphere side, the attractive dining rooms will give patrons the choice of munching either in a quaint town square or in a French country home.

STARDUST (Warehouse Buffet), B=$6; L=$7; D=$9.

Run-of-the-mill food selection, quality and appearance but at a good price for those who call pate chopped liver. Don't take this as a knock any more than similar statements we've already made about several buffets. You have to eat. And if you're looking for value and quantity rather than gourmet food, there's nothing wrong with the lower tier of buffets in this list.

STRATOSPHERE (Stratosphere Buffet), B=$6; L=$7; D=$9-12.

Given the price, a surprisingly good dining experience. The pleasantly attractive surroundings contain an average selection of well prepared food. We're especially fond of some of the unusual desserts that you can prepare yourself.

TREASURE ISLAND (The Buffet), B=$7; BR=$10 (Sunday); L=$8; D=$10.

The biggest shortcoming at TI's buffet is the relatively small selection, not that we've ever had any problem filling our plate. That's because the quality of the food at this buffet is among the top echelon, even though lack of space doesn't allow for the increasingly common action stations. There are two dining rooms, each with their own identical food service area. The decor is in keeping with the hotel's pirate theme and is quite attractive, although both rooms are small and you can feel a bit cramped when it's crowded.

TROPICANA (Island Buffet), BR=$8; D=$12-15.

Located at the very end of the Wildlife Walk, the Island Buffet is a colorful affair that blends nicely with the tropical theme. It overlooks the pool area and attractive grounds. The food selection and quality are both good but you won't find anything too unusual on the menu. It would be a much better value at a couple of dollars less.

OFF-STRIP

LAS VEGAS HILTON (The Buffet), B=$8; BR=$12 (Saturday/Sunday); L=$9; D=$11-13.

Excellent food and a good selection combine with a pleasant atmosphere and a friendly, helpful staff to make this a fine buffet dining experience. It doesn't quite make the top five and, if you're not in the neighborhood, isn't worth making a special trip for. But if you're staying at the Hilton or are here for some other reason, go for it.

THE ORLEANS (French Market Buffet), B=$4; BR=$8 (Sunday); L=$5; D=$8-12.

Completely redone in 1999, this buffet now features a large selection of well prepared food in seven different action stations. A good value for the budget-minded.

THE RIO (Carnival World Buffet), B=$8; BR=$12 (Saturday/Sunday); L=$10; D=$12.

This is the place that brought buffets out of the industrial food category and into an art form in their own right. For many years, Carnival World had the biggest selection, the best food and one of the most attractive atmospheres of any buffet in the city. And it was enormously popular for those reasons. Ever increasing prices and competition on the same level now make several other buffets a better choice, but this one is still in the top echelon. There's a separate area for each type of cuisine (including American, Italian, Mexican and Chinese, among others). Live cooking is done at the Amazon Grill or you can select your own meats at the butcher counter and have them cook up a juicy steak just for you. Kids will enjoy the section that features burgers, hot dogs and shakes. That's something you don't see at any other buffet. The dessert selection is outstanding and delicious.

THE RIO (Village Seafood Buffet), BR=$22 (Saturday/Sunday); L=$18; D=$24.

The only buffet in Las Vegas that is devoted entirely to delicacies of the sea at all times. This is a small room (especially when you compare it to the Carnival World Buffet), and the selection isn't as large as at most buffets. However, because of the narrow nature of the menu, you're likely to find quite a few seafood items that you don't often see. Crab, shrimp, mussels, and many other popular dishes are always available. The food quality is excellent. But we still feel that it is somewhat overpriced. Unfortunately, that's something that's increasingly less surprising at the Rio.

DOWNTOWN

FREMONT HOTEL (Paradise Buffet), B=$5; BR=$8 (Sunday); L=$7; D=$10-15.

The second best downtown buffet. The setting is very attractive, from the colorful aquarium at the entrance, to the foliage filled dining room. Extravagant chandeliers and comfortable booths give this room the feel of a nightclub and help to enhance your enjoyment. The food selection is a bit beyond average and the quality is first rate.

MAIN STREET STATION (Garden Court Buffet), B=$5; BR=$8 (Saturday/Sunday); L=$7; D=$10-14.

This is the only downtown buffet that surpasses the one at the Fremont. And this one is on a par with any in town. It has everything going for it. The beautiful, almost idyllic looking dining room features a high ceiling with intricate wood lattice-work, graceful palms and many interesting antiques. The humongous food selection is grouped by type of cuisine and includes Chinese, Mexican, Italian (they have pizza!), treasures from the sea, and several others. The food is among the best tasting of any Vegas buffet and every section is eye appealing. The dessert bar may be the biggest in town and we have yet to try any piece of cake or pie that wasn't anything but delicious.

AROUND LAS VEGAS

ARIZONA CHARLIES (Wild West Buffet), B=$4; L=$5; D=$7.

This doesn't have the size, selection or glamour of many of the better Strip or even local buffets, but it has proven popular because you get good food at good prices.

FIESTA HOTEL (Festival Buffet), B=$4; BR=$8 (Saturday/Sunday); L=$7; D=$9-13.

While this may be a few dollars higher than the preceding entry, we'd rather travel the couple of extra miles to here because everything is a notch or two higher up the quality ladder. The selection is one of the more extensive ones that you can find. The espresso bar serves up excellent specialty coffees and other beverages (at a slight additional charge). We also like the festive Mexican "outdoor" cafe atmosphere and the colorful serving stations.

SILVERTON (Blue Diamond Buffet), B=$4; BR=$6 (Sunday); L=$5; D=$8-11.

They can change the hotel's name all they want (it used to be Boomtown), but their buffet is still among our favorites. The atmosphere is as informal as you can get – the food service area consists chiefly of chuckwagons and the several dining rooms reflect various mercantile establishments in an old western town. It's quaint and attractive. The food is real good and the selection is better than average, especially given the prices. Even their higher priced seafood and prime rib evenings are an excellent value. Leave some room for dessert, of course – you might want to build your own strawberry short cake, a perennial favorite at the Blue Diamond.

TEXAS STATION (Feast Around the World Buffet), B=$4; BR=$8 (Saturday/Sunday); L=$7; D=$9-11.

One of two Station Casinos with a Feast Around the World Buffet (see below), this is far superior to the so-called Gourmet Feast available at the same company's Palace Station. Featuring several live action stations, the selection is excellent and all of the food is tasty and well prepared. The old-west style Texas atmosphere is attractive.

HENDERSON

THE RESERVE (Grand Safari Buffet), BR=$6; D=$8-12.

When this place opened in February of 1998 we said to ourselves, "oh, goodness, another local buffet to go check out." Were we surprised! This is one of the very best buffets in the Las Vegas Valley regardless of price or location. At the above prices it almost feels like we're robbing the joint. No wonder the locals don't want to cook. Action stations include Italian, American, Chinese, and a Mongolian Barbecue along with a separate seafood station. Then again, you'll find an unusual amount of fresh fish and seafood at almost all of the stations even though the Grand Safari doesn't have a special seafood night. The vast selection is surpassed only by how good the food is. It's hard to have room for dessert but do your best because the freshly baked cakes are superb.

SUNSET STATION (Feast Around the World Buffet), B=$4; BR=$8 (Saturday/Sunday); L=$7; D=$9.

Much of what can be said about Texas Station's Feast applies here, except for one thing – we think this one is even better. Choose from Country Barbeque, Chinese, Italian, and several other separate food areas. You'll enjoy the food from whichever stations you select. The central dessert bar is a sight to be seen – the decor as well as the sinful collection of delicious delights. You can even make your own "root beer float." The entire buffet is very attractive and is highlighted by a zodiac themed ceiling in the central rotunda along with a statue of Atlas holding up the world. You'll probably feel like you're holding up something heavy after you finish your meal – namely, your full stomach.

THE BEST BUFFETS IN TOWN

We've taken into consideration the selection, food quality and price/value in making our choices for the best buffets in Las Vegas. The best places to pig-out are:

Garden Court Buffet *(Main Street Station)*
Paradise Buffet *(Flamingo Hilton)*
The Bellagio Buffet
Grand Safari Buffet *(The Reserve)*
Carnival World Buffet *(The Rio)*

Honorable mention goes to the Big Kitchen Buffet (Bally's), Blue Diamond Buffet (Silverton), and the Feast Around the World Buffet (Sunset Station).

11. GAMBLING IN VEGAS

CASINO BASICS

In this chapter we'll get you oriented to the casino gambling environment and show you the all-important techniques of money management. **Avery Cardoza**, the best-selling writer of more than a dozen gambling books and strategies and the foremost gambling publisher in the world, has prepared the following chapter with visitors to Las Vegas specifically in mind. No other living gambler/author has as much experience teaching the basics of the games, and as much experience winning!

Converting Traveler's Checks & Money Orders to Cash

The dealers accept only cash or chips at the table, so if you bring traveler's checks, money orders or the like, you must go to the area of the casino marked **Casino Cashier** to get these converted to cash. Be sure to bring proper identification to ensure a smooth transaction.

Casino Chips

Chip denominations run in $1, $5, $25, $100 and $500 units. If you're a big stakes player, you may even find $1,000, $2,500, $5,000 and $10,000 chips available!

The usual color scheme of chips is as follows: $1 chips are silver dollars, $5 chips will be red, $25 - green, and $100 - black. Chips of larger deniminations, such as $500 or $1,000, may be white, pink or other colors.

In casino parlance, $1 chips are generally referred to as *silver*, $5 chips as *nickels*, $25 chips as *quarters*, and $100 chips as *dollars*. Unless playing at a 25¢ minimum craps table, $1 chips are the minimum currency used.

Betting

Casinos prefer that the player uses chips for betting purposes, for the handling of money at the tables is cumbersome and slows the game. However, cash can be used to bet with, though all payoffs will be in chips.

House Limits

The house limits will be posted on placards located on each corner of the table. They will indicate the minimum bet required to play and also the maximum bet allowed.

Minimum bets range from $1 and $5 per bet, to a maximum of $500, $1000 or $2,000 a bet. Occasionally, 25¢ tables may be found as well, but don't count on it. If special arrangements are made, a player can bet as much as he can muster in certain casinos. The Horseshoe Casino in Las Vegas is known to book any bet no matter the size.

In 1981, a man walked into the Horseshoe and placed a bet for $777,777. He bet the *don't pass* in craps, and walked out two rolls later with one and a half million dollars in cash!

Converting Chips into Cash

Dealers do not convert your chips into cash. Once you've bought your chips at the table, that cash is dropped into a dropbox, and thereafter is unobtainable. When you are ready to convert your chips back to cash, take them to the cashier's cage where the transaction will be done.

Free Drinks and Cigarettes

Casinos offer their customers unlimited free drinking while gambling at the tables or slot machines. In addition to alcoholic beverages, a player can order milk, soft drinks, juices or any other beverages available. This is ordered through and served by a cocktail waitress.

Cigarettes and cigars are also complimentary and can be ordered from the same cocktail waitress.

Tipping

Tipping, or **toking**, as it is called in casino parlance, should be viewed as a gratuitous gesture by the player to the dealer or crew of dealers he feels has given him good service. Tipping is totally at the player's discretion, and in no way should be considered an obligation.

If you toke, toke only when you're winning, and only if the crew is friendly and helpful to you. Do not toke dealers that you don't like or ones that try to make you feel guilty about not tipping. Dealers that make playing an unpleasant experience for you deserve nothing.

MONEY MANAGEMENT

Your trip to Las Vegas can be a great one, but only if you don't lose your shirt at the tables. Don't be one of those gamblers who, as the saying used to go, drives into town in a $20,000 Cadillac and leaves in a $150,000 Greyhound bus.

To be a winner at gambling, you must exercise sound money management principles and keep your emotions under control. The temptation to ride a winning streak too hard in the hopes of a big killing, to bet wildly during a losing streak, or to try for a quick comeback, can spell doom. Wins can turn into losses, and moderate losses can turn into a nightmare.

Instead, one must plan ahead and prepare for the game. It's important to understand the nature of the gamble. In any gambling pursuit where luck plays a role, fluctuations in one's fortunes are common. It is the ability of the player to successfully deal with the ups and downs inherent in the gamble that separate the smart gamblers from the losers.

Here are the three important principles of money management:

1. Never gamble with money you cannot afford to lose either financially or emotionally.

Do not gamble with needed funds no matter how "sure" any bet seems. The possibility of losing is real, and if that loss will hurt, you're playing the fool.

2. Bankroll yourself properly.

Undercapitalization leaves a player vulnerable in two ways. First, a normal downward trend can wipe out a limited money supply (sometimes very quickly). Next, and more important, the bettor may feel pressured by the shortage of capital and play less powerfully than smart play dictates.

If the amount staked on a bet is above your head, you're playing in the wrong game. Play only at levels of betting you feel comfortable with.

3. Know when to quit – set stop-loss limits.

What often separates the winners from the losers is that the winners, when winning, leave the table a winner, and when losing, restrict their losses to affordable amounts. Smart gamblers never allow themselves to get destroyed at the gamble.

Minimizing losses is the key. You can't always win. If you're losing, keep the losses affordable - take a break. You only want to play with a clear head.

When you're winning big, put a good chunk of these winnings in a "don't touch" pile, and play with the rest. You never want to hand all your winnings back to the casino. Should a losing streak occur, you're out of there – a winner!!!

EYE IN THE SKY

Look above the playing area in any casino and you'll see dark, half-circle globes that look like light fixtures. What you're seeing is casino security in action, the ubiquitous "Eye in the Sky." The device is a one-way surveillance camera, used by security to ensure that no cheating occurs, either by players or dealers. Cameras are also located in other key spots in the casino, usually behind glass doors or walls. Considering that every conceivable kind of cheating has at one time or another been attempted in Las Vegas, the casinos have become pretty expert in spotting ne'er-do-wells.

But what you and I consider cheating sometimes differ from what the casino considers cheating. The biggest difference between the casinos and the players is over card counting in blackjack. Most players and experts argue that card counting is merely a way of regaining the edge the house has given itself in every hand. Gamblers argue that not counting is akin to a major league baseball player holding back on his slugging advantage, or not bagging a ball easily within reach. To the casino operators, card counting is cheating, pure and simple - so be careful if you're going to count!

A QUICK GUIDE TO CASINO ACTION

Every casino/hotel as well as just about every other casino in town will have a variety of slot machines and other electronic gaming options. You can apply the rule of thumb that the larger the casino, the more machines there will be and the greater the chance of finding more unusual machines. Table games are another matter. Some of the smallest casinos are essentially slot clubs and you'll find no table games or only a limited number (usually blackjack). Larger casinos (and that includes every major Strip property) will have plenty of live gaming options for you to choose from, including blackjack, craps, roulette and poker (against the house). Keno and Big Six are also staples.

Poker rooms are where you play against other individuals and not the casino. However, the house takes a percentage. These are less common and are listed in the accompanying table along with some betting options that aren't always found. We've listed over 30 of the largest casinos as well as some others that are popular with visitors. Besides baccarat, you can find mini-bacarrat. It's the same game except that the stakes are lower and is found in most hotel/casinos with table games.

GAMING AVAILABILITY BY HOTEL/CASINO

	Bacarrat	Bingo	Poker Room	Race/Sports Book
Bally's	X			X
Barbary Coast	X			X
Bellagio	X		X	X
Binion's	X	X	X	X
Caesars Palace	X			X
Circus Circus	X		X	X
Desert Inn	X			X
Excalibur	X		X	X
Fitzgerald's			X	
Flamingo Hilton	X		X	X
Four Queens		X		Sports only
Gold Coast	X	X		X
Golden Nugget	X			X
Hard Rock	X			X
Harrah's	X		X	X
Imperial Palace				X
Las Vegas Hilton	X			X
Luxor	X		X	X
Main Street Station				
Mandalay Bay	X		X	X
MGM Grand	X		X	X
Mirage	X		X	X
Monte Carlo	X		X	X
New York, New York	X			X
Orleans	X		X	X
Palace Station	X	X	X	X
Paris	X			X
Rio	X			X
Riviera	X	X	X	X
Sahara	X		X	X
Sam's Town	X	X	X	X
Stardust	X		X	X
Stratosphere	X		X	X
Treasure Island	X			X
Tropicana	X			Sports only
Venetian	X			X

WINNING STRATEGIES FOR THE MAIN GAMES

You can win in Vegas! – sometimes with luck, sometimes with skill, but it is the smart player, the one who learns the skills necessary to win, that has the best chances of beating the house. In this chapter, we'll give you those basic skills and show you how to be a winner!

In **blackjack**, we'll show you the winning strategies that actually give you an edge over the casino; in **craps**, we show you the best bets to make, some of which give the casino no edge at all; in **keno**, you'll learn how to go for a $50,000 win; in **poker**, you'll learn to play and win at five variations; in **video poker**, how to get the edge over the machines; in **roulette**; how to make over 150 wagers; and in **slots**, we'll show you a few inside strategies for winning jackpots.

While no one can guarantee whether you'll win or lose you'll have the best chances to come home with money if you read this section carefully. Pay attention and good luck!

For your information: The legal gambling age is 21. And casinos do enforce the law!

BLACKJACK

You can win at blackjack! With proper play, you can actually have the edge over the casino, and thus, the expectation to win money every time you play! In this section, we'll show you how to do just that – be a winner.

Object of the Game

The object of blackjack is to beat the dealer. This can be done by having a higher total than the dealer without exceeding 21 points, or if the dealer's total exceeds 21 (this is called **busting**, assuming the player hasn't busted first).

Decks of Cards - The Basics

Las Vegas casinos use one, two, four, six and sometimes as many as eight decks of cards in their blackjack games. Each deck used in blackjack is a standard pack of 52 cards. Suits have no relevance; only the numerical value of the cards count. Cards are counted at face value, 2 = 2 points, 3 = 3 points, except for the ace, which is valued at 1 or 11 points at the player's discretion, and the **picture cards,** the J, Q, K, all of which count as 10.

THE BLACKJACK LAYOUT

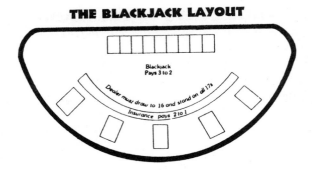

Blackjack
Pays 3 to 2

Dealer must draw to 16 and stand on all 17s

Insurance pays 2 to 1

Entering a Game

To enter a blackjack game, sit down at any unoccupied seat at the blackjack table, and place the money you wish to gamble with near the betting box in front of you. The dealer will exchange your money for chips.

SINGLE DECK - HITTING AND STANDING

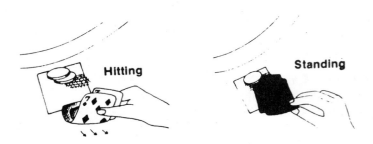

Hitting

Standing

MULTIPLE DECK - HITTING AND STANDING

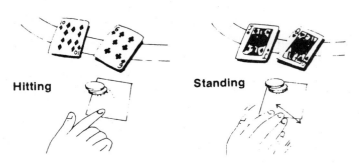

Hitting   Standing

The Player's Options

Each player is dealt two cards, as is the dealer. The player receives both cards face down; the dealer receives one card face down, the other face up. After examining your cards and the dealer's exposed (face-up) card, the player has several options.

He can **stand**, take no more cards; **hit** or **draw**, take an additional card or cards; **double down**, double his bet and take one more card only; **split**, take cards of equal value and split them into two separate hands; or if offered, **surrender**, forfeit the hand along with half the bet.

A player may draw cards until he is satisfied with his total; however, once his total exceeds 21, his hand is **busted**, and he's a loser, regardless of what subsequently happens to the dealer's hand.

The Dealer's Rules

The dealer, however, has no such options, and must play by prescribed rules. Once the players have played out their hands, it's the dealer's turn. He turns over his hidden card for all to see, and must draw to any hand 16 or below and stand on any total 17-21. The dealer has no options and cannot deviate from these rules.

In some casinos the dealer must draw to a **soft** 17 – a total reached when the Ace is valued at 11 points.

Payoffs

The bettors only play against the dealer and must have a higher point total without exceeding 21 to win. Winning bets are paid at even money. When both hold the same total, it is a **push**, a tie, and nobody wins.

If the dealer busts, all remaining players (those who have not already busted) win and are paid out at **even money**, $1 paid for every $1 bet.

Players who get dealt a **blackjack**, an ace and any 10-value card (10, J, Q or K), get paid 3-2 ($3 for every $2 bet) unless the dealer gets a blackjack also, where it's a push. If the dealer gets a blackjack, he wins only what the player has bet.

Insurance

When the dealer shows an Ace as the exposed card, the player is offered an option called **Insurance**. It's a bet that the dealer has a 10-value card underneath for a blackjack. The player is allowed to bet up to one half of his original bet, and gets paid 2 to 1 if he is correct. This is always a bad bet and should not be made unless you're a card counter.

Winning Strategies

Dealer Pat Hands: 7-Ace as Upcard – When the dealer shows a 7, 8, 9, 10 or Ace, hit all hard totals of 16 or less.

Dealer Stiffs: 2-6 as Upcard – When the dealer shows a 2, 3, 4, 5 or 6, he will frequently bust. The player should stand on all hard totals of 12 or more. Exception - Hit 12 vs. dealer upcard of 2 or 3.

Player Totals of 11 or Less – On point totals of 11 or less, always draw (if you do not double down or split).

Player Totals of Hard 17 or More – On point totals of hard 17 or more, stand.

Doubling and Splitting – Play aggressively, taking full advantage of doubling and splitting options, as presented in the master strategy chart on the following page.

THE MASTER STRATEGY CHART

The **Master Strategy Chart** on the following page gives you an extremely accurate game against both single and multiple deck games in Las Vegas. For single deck games, make the plays as shown. For multiple deck games, where there is an asterisk, hit only – do not double down or split.

BLACKJACK: MASTER STRATEGY CHART

– Dealer's Upcard –

	2	3	4	5	6	7	8	9	10	A
7/less	H	H	H	H	H	H	H	H	H	H
8	H	H	H	H	H	H	H	H	H	H
9	D*	D	D	D	D	H	H	H	H	H
10	D	D	D	D	D	D	D	D	H	H
11	D	D	D	D	D	D	D	D	D	D*
12	H	H	S	S	S	H	H	H	H	H
13	S	S	S	S	S	H	H	H	H	H
14	S	S	S	S	S	H	H	H	H	H
15	S	S	S	S	S	H	H	H	H	H
16	S	S	S	S	S	H	H	H	H	H
A2	H	H	D*	D	D	H	H	H	H	H
A3	H	H	D*	D	D	H	H	H	H	H
A4	H	H	D	D	D	H	H	H	H	H
A5	H	H	D	D	D	H	H	H	H	H
A6	D*	D	D	D	D	H	H	H	H	H
A7	S	D	D	D	D	S	S	H	H	H
A8	S	S	S	S	S	S	S	S	S	S
A9	S	S	S	S	S	S	S	S	S	S
22	H	spl*	spl	spl	spl	spl	H	H	H	H
33	H	H	spl	spl	spl	spl	H	H	H	H
44	H	H	H	H	H	H	H	H	H	H
55	D	D	D	D	D	D	D	D	H	H
66	spl	spl	spl	spl	spl	H	H	H	H	H
77	spl	spl	spl	spl	spl	spl	H	H	H	H
88	spl	spl	spl	spl	spl	spl	spl	spl	spl	spl
99	spl	spl	spl	spl	spl	S	spl	spl	S	S
1010	S	S	S	S	S	S	S	S	S	S
AA	spl	spl	spl	spl	spl	spl	spl	spl	spl	spl

H = Hit   **S** = Stand   **D** = Double   **spl** = Split
*In multiple deck games, hit only - do not double or split.

CRAPS

Craps is the most exciting of the casino games. The action is fast, and a player catching a good roll can win large sums of money quickly. In this section we'll show you the basics of play and how to be a winner at the game of casino craps.

The Basics of Play

The game of craps centers around the craps **layout**, made of green felt covering listing the bets available. On this layout wagers are made and the dice are rolled. In this very popular and action-packed game, the players make bets against the house, which books these bets, and receives paybacks ranging from even-money to payoffs as high as 30 to 1, depending on your bet.

The equipment of the game is simple; a craps layout and table, two standard six-sided dice, numbered from 1 to 6, the chips or cash used by the players, and a few accessories used by the house to mark and move the action along. Casino craps is run by two **dealers** who collect and pay off bets; a **stickman**, who calls the game and passes the dice to the player; and a **boxman**, who sits in the middle of the action, lording over the chips, and supervising the proceedings.

To enter a game, simply find a space at the craps table. Exchange your cash for chips from one of the dealers working the table, or if you already have chips or want to play cash, you're ready to go.

The Basics

Play starts when one of the players, known as the **shooter**, chooses two dice from the dozen or so offered to him by the stickman, shakes them up and rolls them the length of the table. This first roll by the shooter, called the **come-out roll**, can determine immediate winners or losers if it is a 2, 3, 7, 11, or 12, or it will establish a **point**, any of the other throws possible - 4, 5, 6, 8, 9, or 10. Here's how it works.

Players making **pass line** wagers, betting that the shooter will "pass," or win, are hoping that the come-out roll is a 7 or an 11, an automatic winner for them. If the roll instead is a 2, 3 or 12, the shooter is said to have **crapped-out**, and that's an automatic loser for pass line bettors. These wagers are made by placing bets in the area marked *Pass Line*.

Players making **don't pass** wagers, betting against the dice, are hoping for just the opposite. A 7 or 11 thrown on the come-out roll is an automatic loser for them, while the 2 and 3 are automatic winners. The 12, if rolled, is a tie for don't pass bettors (In some casinos it's the 2 instead that's a tie and the 12 is a winner.) These wagers are made by placing bets in the area marked *Don't Pass*.

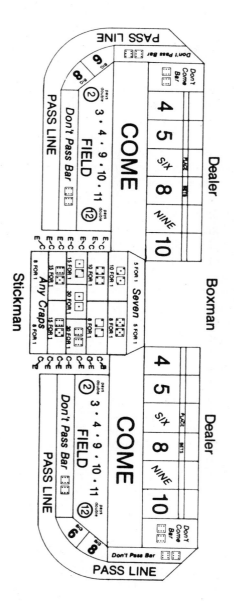

NEVADA CRAPS LAYOUT

Any other number thrown on the come-out roll, the 4, 5, 6, 8, 9, and 10, becomes the **point**. Once a point is established, there are only two numbers that matter to pass or don't pass bettors - the 7 and the point. If the 7 is thrown before the point is thrown a second time, pass line bettors lose and don't pass bettors win. And if the point repeats before the 7, then the opposite is true; the pass line bettors win, and the don't pass bettors lose. All other throws are immaterial. For example, if the point is a 6, rolls of 12, 3, 8, and 10 are completely inconsequential. It's only the 7 or the point, the 6, that affects these wagers.

The **shoot**, as this progression of rolls is called, will continue until the point repeats, a winner for pass line bettors, or until a 7 is rolled, called **sevening-out**, a loser on the pass line but a winner for don't pass bettors. The very next roll will be a new come-out roll, and a new shoot will begin.

The shooter will continue to roll the dice until he either sevens out or voluntarily gives up the dice. And then, in a clockwise direction, each successive player gets a chance to be the shooter, or that player may decline and pass the privilege to the next player. There is no benefit (nor downside) to being a shooter. The only requirement a shooter has, other than throwing the dice, is to make either a pass or don't pass bet.

Winning pass and don't pass bets pay even-money. For every dollar wagered, a dollar is won.

The Bets

In addition to the pass and don't pass bets discussed above, the player has a wide choice of bets available. We'll look at these below.

Come and Don't Come Bets

Come and don't come bets work exactly like the pass and don't pass except that these bets can be made only *after* the come-out roll, when a point is already established. (Pass and don't pass bets can be made only on a *come-out roll*.)

The throw of a 7 or 11 on the first roll is an automatic winner for come bets while the throw of a 2, 3, or 12 is an automatic loser. Don't come bets work the opposite way; a 7 or 11 on the first throw is an automatic loser, and the 2 or 3 is a winner. The 12, or in some casinos the 2 instead, is a tie for don't come bettors, just like on the don't pass.

Any other throw, the 4, 5, 6, 8, 9, or 10 establishes a *come point*. Once that occurs, only the 7 and the point are consequential rolls for come and don't come bettors. Come bettors win when the point repeats before the 7 is thrown, and lose if the 7 occurs first, while don't come bettors win if the 7 is thrown before the point repeats.

For example, if the first throw after the placing of a come bet was a 5, throws of 11, 2, 9 and 8 have no effect on this bet. Should the next roll be a 7, the come bettor will now lose that point, while don't come bettors with established points will win. (Incidentally, the 7 will make losers on all *established* pass and come points, and winners on *established* don't pass and don't come points.) Newly placed come bets though, before a point is established, would be winners on that throw of a 7.

These bets are made by placing the wagers in the area marked *Come* or *Don't Come*, and pay even-money on winners.

Free-Odds Bets

Free-odds bets, so named because the casino enjoys no edge on them, are the best bets available to the player, and should be a part of every player's winning strategy. To make a free-odds bet, the player must first have placed a pass, don't pass, come or don't come wager, since the free-odds are made in conjunction with these bets.

Free-Odds: Pass Line

After a point is established (a 4, 5, 6, 8, 9, or 10), the pass line bettor is allowed to make an additional wager, called a **free odds** or **single odds** bet, that his point will repeat before a 7 is thrown. He may bet up to the amount wagered on his pass line bet and does so by placing the chips behind that wager. For example, if $10 is bet on the pass line, the player may bet $10 as the free-odds wager.

On points of 4 or 10, the casino will pay 2 to 1 on a free-odds win, on points of 5 or 9, it will pay 3 to 2 and on points of 6 or 8, it will pay 6 to 5. Notice that these are the exact odds of winning. For example, if the point is a 6, there are five ways to win (5 ways to roll a 6) and six ways to lose (six ways to roll a 7) - 6 to 5 odds. So if the player bet $10 on a free-odds point of 8, he would win $12 on that bet, getting paid the true odds of 6-5.

Free Odds: Don't Pass Line

Works the other way. Free-odds bettors wager that the 7 will be thrown before the point repeats. Since the odds favor the bettor once the point is established, there being more ways to roll a 7 than any other number, the don't pass free-odds bettor must **lay odds**, that is, put more money on the free-odds bet than he will win.

The allowable free-odds bet is determined by the *payoff*, not the original bet. The bettor is allowed to win only up to the amount bet on the don't pass line.

We'll assume a $10 don't pass bet, which means the player can win only up to $10 on the free odds bet. On points of 4 or 10, the player must lay $20 to win $10; on points 5 and 9, he must lay $15; and on points 6 and 8, he must lay $12 to win that $10.

To sum up, the player must give 1 to 2 odds on points of 4 and 10, 2 to 3 odds on points of 5 and 9, and 5 to 6 odds on points 6 and 8.

Don't pass free odds bets are made by placing the wager next to the don't pass wager in the don't pass box.

Free Odds: Come and Don't Come Bets

These bets work the same as the free odds on the pass (corresponds to the come bet) and don't pass line (corresponds to the don't come) except they can only be made *after* the come point is established.

The only other difference is that the free-odds bet is not in play on the come-out roll, though the come bet itself is. (The free odds on the don't come, pass and don't pass bets are always in play.)

You make these wagers by giving your chips to the dealer - they'll place the bets for you.

Double Odds

Some casinos offer double odds as an inducement to the bettor. These work just like the odds bets described above except that even more money can be bet on the free odds wager. In the case of double odds, double the money could be wagered on the bet.

Place Bets

These are bets that a particular point number, the 4, 5, 6, 8, 9 or 10, whichever is bet on, will be rolled before a 7 is thrown. The player can make as many place bets as he wants, and bet them at any time before a roll. Place bets of 4 or 10 are paid at 9 to 5, on 5 or 9 are paid at 7 to 5 and 6 or 8 are paid at 6 to 5. These bets are not in play on the come-out roll.

Big 6 and Big 8

These are bets that the 6 (Big 6) or 8 (Big 8) are rolled before the 7. Winning bets are paid off at even money.

Field Bet

This is a one roll bet that the next roll of the dice will be a number listed in the field box - a 2, 3, 4, 9, 10, 11 or 12. Rolls of 2 and 12 pay double, all others in the box pay even money. Rolls of 5, 6, 7 and 8 are losers. This bet can be made anytime. (In some casinos, the 2 or 12 may pay triple.)

One Roll Bets

These bets are about the worst you can find in a casino. They're found in the center of the layout and are made by giving the chips to the dealer.

The **Any 7** is a bet that the following roll will be a 7 and pays the winner 4 to 1; **Any Craps** is a bet that the following roll will be a 2, 3 or 12, pays 7 to 1; **2 or 12** is a bet that the next roll will be a 2 (or 12). You can bet either or both, pays 30 to 1. **3 or 11** is a bet that the 3 or the 11, whichever is chosen, will come up next. Pays 15-1.

The **Horn Bet** is a four-way bet that the next roll will be a 2, 3, 11 or 12. Pays off 15-1 on the 3 or 11 and 30-1 on the 2 or 12. The other three losing chips are deducted from the payoff.

Whenever the numbers 4, 6, 8 and 10 are rolled as doubles, the roll is said to be thrown **hardways**. Betting *hardways* is a wager that the doubled number chosen comes up before a 7 is thrown, or before the number is thrown *easy* (not as a double). Bets on hardways 6 or 8 pay 9 to 1, and on hardways 4 or 10, pay 7 to 1.

Right and Wrong Betting

Betting with the dice, pass line, and come betting, is called *right betting*. Betting against the dice, making don't pass and don't come bets, is called *wrong betting*.

Betting right or wrong are equally valid methods of winning, with equivalent odds.

Winning Strategy

To get the best chances of beating the casino, you must make only the bets that give the casino the least possible edge.

You can see from the chart that bets vary in house edge from the combined pass line: double odds wager where the house has but a 0.6% edge to the horn bet where the house edge can be as high as 16.67%!

To win at craps, make only pass and come bets backed up by free-odds wagers or don't pass and don't come bets, and back these wagers up with free-odds bets.

These bets reduce the house edge to the absolute minimum, a mere 0.8% in a single odds game or 0.6% in a double odds game if this strategy is followed.

By concentrating our bets this way, we're making only the best bets available at craps, and in fact, will place the majority of our bets on wagers the casino has absolutely no edge on whatsoever! This is the best way to give yourself every chance of beating the casino when the dice are hot and you've got bets riding on winners.

Try to keep two or three points going at one time by making pass and come bets if you're a right bettor, or don't pass and don't come bets if you're a wrong bettor and back all these bets with the full free odds available.

Money management is very important in craps, for money can be won or lost rapidly. However, try to catch that one good hot streak, and if you do, make sure you walk away a winner.

HOUSE EDGE IN CRAPS CHART

Bet	Payoff	House Edge
Pass or Come	1 to 1	1.41%
Don't Pass, Don't Come	1 to 1	1.40%
Free Odds Bets*	***	0.00%
Single Odds**	***	0.8%
Double Odds**	***	0.6%
Place 4 or 10	9 to 5	6.67%
Place 5 or 9	7 to 5	4.00%
Place 6 or 8	7 to 6	1.52%
Field	2 to 1 on 12	
	1 to 1 other #s	5.56%
Field	3 to 1 on 12	
	1 to 1 other #s	2.78%
Any Craps	7 to 1	11.11%
Any 7	4 to 1	16.67%
2 or 12	30 for 1	16.67%
	30 to 1	13.89%
3 or 11	15 for 1	16.67%
	15 to 1	11.11%
Hardways 4 or 10	8 for 1	11.11%
6 or 8	10 for 1	9.09%

*The free odds bet by itself
**The free odds bet combined with pass, don't pass,
   come and don't come wagers
***The payoffs on the free odds portion of the bets vary. See
   discussion under free odds for payoffs.

SLOTS

The allure of slot machine play has hooked millions of players looking to reap the rewards of a big jackpot!

There are basically two types of slot machines. The first type, the **Straight Slots**, pays winning combinations according to the schedule listed on the machine itself. These payoffs never vary.

The second type of machine is called **Progressive Slots.** These too have a standard set of payoffs listed on the machine, but in addition, and what sometimes makes for exciting play, it has a big jackpot which progressively gets larger and larger as each coin is put in. The jackpot total is posted above the machine and can accumulate to enormous sums of money!

SLOT CLUBS

There's hardly a hotel/casino in Las Vegas that doesn't have a slot club. You sign up at their casino club desk and get a card that looks like a credit card. Each time you play at slots or video poker you put the card in the machine and earn points for as long as you play. The points can be redeemed for free meals, gift items, room discounts and, increasingly, for cold cash. Different hotels have different ways of awarding points but the general rule is that you add up points quicker on the higher denomination machines. Some of the more upscale hotels only allow slot club card use on $1 machines, although that is still the exception to the rule.

Is this a great deal or what? Well, yes and no. A one-time visitor will have to play an incredible amount in order to earn enough points to get something. On the other hand, if you come to Vegas regularly (once a year to eighteen months is the typical use requirement to keep your point total active) and you like to gamble at the same place, then it makes sense to sign up for a card. There is no cost to join so you don't lose anything by having the card. Some hotels even give out little trinkets just for signing up. They also frequently award bonus points at the time you join.

The Basics

Slots are easy to play. Machines generally take anywhere from 1 to 5 coins. Insert the coins into the machine, pull the handle, and see what Lady Luck brings.

There are many types of slot machine configurations but all work according to the same principle - put the money in and pull! Some machines will pay just the middle horizontal line, while others pay on winning combinations from left to right, diagonally, and other combinations .

Often, the number of lines the machine will pay on depends on the amount deposited. One coin may pay the middle line, a second coin will pay the top line as well, a third coin - the bottom line, a fourth - the diagonal and a fifth - the other diagonal.

SLOTS CITY

Slots are huge money-makers for the casinos. On average, the typical Vegas slot machine pulls in more than $100,000 a year. At The Mirage and others, one cushy slot area allows you the pleasure of plunking $100 tokens into the one-armed bandits. And if that's too puny, several machines let you deposit $500 a throw!

With computer advances, many slot machines have gone electronic. You can now push a spin button instead of pulling the lever. And many of the machines are tied together either in citywide or statewide networks, so the jackpots keep growing and growing.

*Operated by IGT (International Game Technology), five networks are now in operation. **Nevada Nickels Network** requires three nickels to win a statewide jackpot; **Quartermania** requires two quarters to win; **Fabulous Fifties** requires two half-dollar coins to win; **High Rollers** demands two $5 tokens to win big; and the most widespread of the networks, **Megabucks**, mandates a wager of three dollars to hit the huge enchilada. Megabucks jackpots start at $5 million. The record so far is a bewildering $27 million.*

In case you were planning on winning one of the outsized slots jackpots, casinos pay off over time in regular payments. But several casinos now pay some jackpots on the spot: the Boyd Group, operator of the California, Sam's Town, Fremont, and Stardust, offers a 25¢ slots network paying out $250,000 jackpots immediately. And Mandalay Resort Group's eight casinos in the state pay out $500,000!

More winning rows do not necessarily equate to better odds of winning. The odds are built into the machine and no amount of lines played will change them. The most important factor is how loose or tight the machines are set by the casino. That is what determines the odds facing a slots player.

Winning Strategy

The most important concept in slots is to locate the machines with the loosest setting, or with progressive machines, to play only the machines with the highest jackpot.

Some casinos advertise slots with returns as high as 97% to the player, others, even as high as 99%! Obviously, the player stands a much better chance of winning at these places than others where a standard return of only 84% might be the norm. On some machines, players may not even get an 84% return.

In general, the poorer paying machines will be located in areas where the casino hopes to grab a few of the bettor's coins as he passes through an area or waits on a line.

Airport terminals, restaurants, show lines, bathrooms and the like tend to have smaller returns.

On the other hand, casinos that specialize in slots and serious slots areas within a casino will have better payoffs. These casinos view slots as an important income, and in order to keep regular slots customers, bettors must hear those jackpot bells ringing - after all, winning is contagious!

Some machines are set to pay better than others, and these slots will be mixed in with poorer paying ones, so it's always a good idea to look for the hot machine. Better yet, ask the change girls. They spend all day and night near the slots and know which machines tend to return the most money. When you hit a jackpot, don't give the money back – make sure you walk away a winner!

KENO

There are 80 numbered squares on a keno ticket which correspond exactly to the 80 numbered balls in the keno cage. A player may choose anywhere from one number to fifteen numbers to play and does so by marking an "x" on the keno ticket for each number or numbers he or she so chooses.

The Basics

Twenty balls will be drawn each game and will appear as lighted numbers on the keno screens. Winnings are determined by consulting the payoff chart each casino provides. If enough numbers are correctly **caught**, you have a winner, and the chart will show the payoff. The more numbers caught, the greater the winnings.

Bets are usually made in 70¢ or $1 multiples, though other standard bets may apply, and a player may bet as many multiples of this bet as he desires as long as the bet is within the casino limits.

Marking the Ticket

The amount being wagered on a game should be placed in the box marked *Mark Price Here* in the upper right hand corner of the ticket.

Leave out dollar or cents signs though. $1 would be indicated by simply writing 1- and 70¢ by .70. Of course, any amount up to the house limit can be wagered. Underneath this box is a column of white space. The number of spots selected for the game is put here. If six spots were selected on the ticket, mark the number 6, if fifteen numbers, mark 15.

This type of ticket, which is the most commonly bet, is called a **straight ticket**.

5 SPOT STRAIGHT TICKET

1	2	3	4	✕	6	7	8	9	10
11	✕	13	14	15	16	17	18	19	20
21	22	23	24	25	26	27	✕	29	30
31	32	33	34	35	36	37	38	39	40

KENO LIMIT **$50,000.00** TO AGGREGATE PLAYERS EACH GAME

41	42	43	44	45	46	47	48	49	50
51	52	53	54	✕	56	57	58	59	60
61	✕	63	64	65	66	67	68	69	70
71	72	73	74	75	76	77	78	79	80

Split Tickets

A player may also play as many combinations as he chooses. **Split tickets** allow a player to bet two or more combinations in one game. This is done by marking two sets (or more) of numbers from 1-15 on a ticket and separating them by either a line, or by circling the separate groups. Numbers may not be duplicated between the two sets.

On split tickets in which several games are being played in one, the keno ticket should be marked as follows. In addition to the x's indicating the numbers, and the lines or circles showing the groups, the ticket should clearly indicate the number of games being played.

For example, a split ticket playing two groups of six spots each would be marked 2/6 in the column of white space. The 2 shows that two combinations are being played, and the 6 shows that six numbers are being chosen per game. If $1 is bet per combination, we would put a 1- and circle it underneath the slashed numbers to show this, and in the *Mark Price Here* box, we would enter 2, to show $2 is being bet – $1 per combo.

Winning Strategy

Keno is a game that should not be played seriously, because the odds are prohibitively against the player. The house edge is typically 20% and higher - daunting odds if one wants to win in the long run.

One thing to look out for are casinos that offer better payoffs on the big win, so a little shopping might get you closer to a bigger payoff. For example, some casinos will pay $50,000 if you catch all the numbers while another pays just $25,000. Why not play for the $50,000?

Keno is a great game to test out your lucky numbers. Picking birth dates, anniversaries, license plate numbers, and the like offer a big pool of possibilities to see which ones will really pay off. If you know your lucky numbers, you may just give them a whirl and see if you can't walk away with a $50,000 bonanza!

POKER

Poker is played with a 52 card deck and can support anywhere from two to usually a maximum of eight or nine players. There are many variations of this great game, the most popular being seven card high stud, high-low stud, lowball, draw poker, seven card stud, hold'em, and of course, jacks or better and anything opens.

Let's go over the ranks of the hands in ascending order, from the lowest ranking to the highest. We'll employ the following commonly used symbols: ace = A, king = K, queen = Q, Jack = J, and all others by their numerical symbol, such as nine = 9 and so on.

RANKS OF POKER HANDS

One Pair - *Two cards of equal value, such as 7-7 or K-K.*

Two Pair - *Two sets of paired cards, such as 3-3 and 10-10.*

Three of a Kind - *Three cards of equal value, such as 9-9-9.*

Straight - *Five cards in numerical sequence, such as 3-4-5-6-7 or 10-J-Q-K-A.*

Flush - *Any five cards of the same suit, such as five hearts.*

Full House - *Three of a kind and a pair, such as 2-2-2-J-J.*

Four of a kind - *Four cards of equal value, such as K-K-K-K.*

Straight Flush - *A straight all in the same suit, such as 7-8-9-10-J, all in spades.*

Royal Flush - *10-J-Q-K-A, all in the same suit.*

Low Poker Rankings

In low poker, the ranking of hands are the opposite to that of high poker, with the lowest hand being the most powerful. The ace is considered the lowest and therefore the most powerful card, with the hand 5 4 3 2 A being the best low total possible.

Play of the Game

Many games use a **blind**, a mandatory bet that must be made by the first player to act in the opening round of play, regardless of cards. Some games require an **ante**, a uniform bet placed by all players into the pot before the cards are dealt.

Except for the times when a bet is mandatory, as is usually the case in the initial round of play, the first player to act in a betting round has three options: He can **bet** and does so by placing money in the pot, he can **check** or **pass**, make no bet at all and pass play on to the next player; or he can **fold** or **go out**, throw away his cards and forfeit play in the hand.

Once a bet is placed, a player no longer has the option of checking his turn. To remain an active player, he must either **call the bet**, place an amount of money into the pot equal to the bet; or he can **raise (call and raise)**, call the bet and make an additional bet. If a player doesn't want to call the bets and raises that have preceded him, then he must fold and go out of play. Each succeeding player, clockwise and in turn, is faced with the same options: calling, folding or raising.

When play swings around to the original bettor, he or she must call any previous raises to continue as an active player as must any subsequent players who have raises due, or he must fold. A player may raise again if the raise limit has not been reached.

The number of raises permitted vary with the game, but generally, casino games limit the raises to three or five total in any one round, except when only two players are left, when unlimited raising is allowed. A player may only raise another player's bet or raise, not his own bet.

Play continues until the last bet or raise is called by all active players, and no more bets or raises are due any player. The betting round is now completed and over.

Check and raise, a player's raising of a bet after already checking in a round, is usually allowed.

Betting Limits (Limit Poker)

Betting in poker is often two-tiered, such as $1-$2, $1-$3, $5-$10, $10-$20 and $30-$60. When the lower limit of betting is in effect, for example in a $5-$10 game, all bets and raises must be in $5 increments, and when the upper range is in effect, all bets and raises must be in $10 increments. We'll show when these are in effect for the individual games.

Table stakes is the rule in casino poker games, and states that a player's bet or call of a bet may not exceed the amount of money he has in front of him.

A *tapped-out* player can still receive cards until the showdown and play for the original pot, but can no longer take part in the betting, and has no part in the **side pot** in which all future monies in this hand are placed by the remaining players.

The **showdown** is the final act in a poker game, after all betting rounds are concluded, when remaining players reveal their hands to determine the winner of the pot. The player with the best hand at the showdown wins all the money in the pot, or in the unlikely event of a tie, then the pot is split evenly among the winners.

If only one player remains in the game at any time, there is no showdown and the remaining player automatically collects the pot.

The biggest differences between casino poker and private poker games is that the dealer in a casino game is not a player as he would be in a private game, and that the casino dealer receives a **rake**, a small cut of the action for his services.

Understanding the Rules of the Game

Though poker is basically the same game played anywhere, rules vary from game to game. Before playing, know the answers to the following questions:
1. What are the betting limits?
2. Is "check and raise" allowed?
3. Are antes and blinds used, and if so, how much?
4. What are the maximum number of raises allowed?
5. When playing a casino game, the additional question, "How much is the rake? should be asked.

Draw Poker Variations

All bets before the draw in draw poker games, high or low, are in the lower tier of the betting limits when a two-tiered structure such as $1-$2 or $5-$10 are being used, and in the upper limit after the draw is completed.

Draw Poker: Jacks or Better

Each player is dealt five cards face down, and their identity is known only to the player. There are two betting rounds. The first occurs before the **draw**, when players have an opportunity to exchange up to three unwanted cards for new ones, or up to four cards, if the remaining card is an ace. (Casinos allow players to exchange all five cards if desired.)

The draw occurs after the first betting round is completed with each remaining player, proceeding clockwise, drawing in turn. The second round of betting follows the draw, and once completed, the showdown occurs.

Draw Poker: Anything Opens

This variation is played exactly the same as in jacks or better except that any hand, regardless of the strength, may open the betting.

Lowball: Draw Poker

In this game, the lowest hand wins. The ace being the lowest value is the best card, and the hand 5 4 3 2 A, called a **wheel** or **bicycle**, is the best hand.

In lowball, the high card counts in determining the value of a hand: the lower the high card, the better the hand. When the high cards of competing hands are equivalent, the next highest cards are matched up, and the lowest value of these matched cards determines the winner. The hand 8 6 4 3 2 beats 8 7 3 2 A, because the former has a 6 as its high card versus a 7 in the latter (both hands have 8 so it's discounted).

When competing hands are the same, the hand is a tie and the pot is split. Straights and flushes are not relevant in lowball and do not count.

Players may draw as many cards as they want at the draw, exchanging all five cards if so desired.

There are two betting rounds, one before the draw and one after, and then there is the showdown, where the lowest hand collects the plot.

Seven Card Stud Poker Variations

In each variation, players form their best five card combination out of the seven dealt to produce their best hand. In seven card high stud, the highest ranking hand remaining wins the pot. In seven card low, the lowest hand wins.

In high-low stud, players vie for either the highest ranking or lowest ranking hand, with the best of each claiming half the pot.

In each variation, players receive three initial cards, two face down and one face up. This marks the beginning of the first betting round. The next three cards are dealt face up, one at a time, with a betting round accompanying each card. The last card, the seventh, comes **down and dirty**, and is the third and last closed card received by the players.

At the showdown, remaining players now hold three **hole cards** (hidden from the other players' view) and four open cards. These are their final cards. One more round of betting ensues and then the showdown occurs.

Hold 'Em

This is the game best associated with free-wheeling poker. Players receive two down cards and combine these with five face-up community cards that are pooled in the middle to form their best five card hand.

Altogether, hold 'em has four betting rounds, beginning with the initial deal where all players receive two face down hole cards. The player to the left of the dealer must make a mandatory opening bet in the opening round. Subsequent players must either call (or raise) to play, or they must fold.

Once the initial betting round is over, it is time for the **flop**. Three cards are turned face up in the center of the table and this is followed by the second round of betting.

Two more open cards, one at a time, will be dealt face up in the center of the table, with a round of betting following each. This is followed by the showdown, where the highest ranking hand wins, or, if all opponents have folded, then the last remaining player takes the pot.

BACCARAT

Baccarat is a game that combines the allure and glamour of European tradition with relatively low house odds, 1.17% betting Banker and 1.36% betting Player.

Baccarat can be played by anyone. There's no need to bet mini-fortunes or even to play at high stakes. It is a leisurely game, and there are only two decisions you need to make: how much you want to bet and which position, Player or Banker, you decide to wager.

If you're still intimidated by the big tables, the mini-baccarat tables, now found in most casinos alongside the blackjack tables, can be a good place to begin play and become accustomed to the game.

The low casino edge makes baccarat a perfect place to try your favorite betting system, and at the same time, it's a game you can play in style!

The Basics of Play

Baccarat is a simple game to play. The **dealer** or **croupier** directs all the action according to fixed rules.

Baccarat is played with six to eight decks of cards dealt out of a shoe. Bets must be placed before the cards are dealt and are made by placing the chips in the appropriate box, **Banker** or **Player**, located in front of the bettor on the layout.

No matter how many players are betting in a game, only two hands will be dealt; one for the Banker position and one for the Player position.

Cards numbered 2 to 9 are counted according to their face value: a 2 equals 2 points, a 7 equals 7 points. An Ace equals one point. The 10, Jack, Queen, and King have a value of 0 points and have no effect when adding up the points in a hand.

Points are counted by adding up the value of the cards. However, hands totaling 10 or more points have the first digit dropped so that no hand contains a total greater than 9 points. For example, two nines (18) is a hand of 8 points and a 7 5 (12) is a hand of 2 points.

The hand with the closest total to 9 is the winner, while the worst score is zero, called **baccarat**. A tie is a standoff or **push**, and neither hand wins.

There are two opposing sides, the **Player** and the **Banker**, and initially, after the betting is done, each side will receive two cards. Bettors may wager on either hand.

A dealt total of 8 or 9 points is called a **natural**, and no additional cards will be drawn. It is an automatic win unless the opposing hand has a higher natural (a 9 vs. an 8), or the hand is a tie.

On all other totals, the drawing of an additional card depends strictly on established rules of play and will be handled by the croupier. There is never more than one card drawn to a hand.

The Player's hand will be acted upon first, and then the Banker's hand.

Let's sum up the rules for drawing a third card and than we'll show the rules in chart form for both the Banker and Player positions.

Situation 1 – Either the Player or the Banker position has a natural 8 or 9. It is an automatic win for the hand with the natural. If both hands are naturals, the higher natural wins. (A natural 9 beats a natural 8.)
If the naturals are equal, the hand is a tie.

Situation 2 – If the Player position has a 0-5, Player must draw another card; if a 6-7, the Player must stand.

Situation 3 – If Player stands, than the Banker hand follows the same rules as the Player – it must draw on totals of 0-5 and stand on 6-7.

Situation 4 – If Player draws, Banker must draw or stand according to the value of the third card dealt as show below in the Banker Rules chart.

BANKER RULES

Banker Two Card Total	Banker Draws When Giving Player This Card	Banker Stands When Giving Player This Card
0 - 2	0-9	
3	0-7, 9	8
4	2-7	0-1, 8-9
5	4-7	0-3, 8-9
6	6-7	0-5, 8-9
7	*Banker Always Stands*	
8-9	*A Natural – Player Can't Draw*	

Note that unless the Player has a Natural, the Banker always draws with a total of 0-2.

PLAYER RULES

Two Card Total	Player's Action
0-5	Draw a Card
6 or 7	Stand
8 or 9	Natural. Banker cannot draw.

The winning hand in baccarat is paid at 1 to 1, **even money**, except in the case of the Banker's position where a 5% commission is charged on a winning hand. Commission is charged because of the inherent edge the Banker position has over the Player position.

With the commission, the Banker edge over the bettor is only 1.17%, quite low by casino standards. The house edge over the Player position is only slightly more, 1.36%.

During actual play, this commission is kept track of on the side by use of chips, and bets won in the Banker position are paid off at even money. This avoids the cumbersome 5% change-giving on every hand. The commission will be collected later; at the end of every shoe, and of course, before the player parts from the game.

Mini-Baccarat

This is the same game as regular baccarat except that it's played on a miniature blackjack-type table, and the bettors do not deal the cards.

ROULETTE

Roulette offers the player a multitude of possible bets, more than any other casino table game. All in all, there are over 150 possible combinations to bet. While roulette still gets some table action in Las Vegas, it is not nearly as popular as the *single zero* European game which offers the player much better odds than the American double zero game.

THE AMERICAN WHEEL

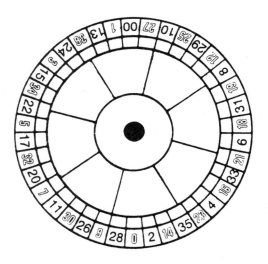

The Basics

Roulette is played with a circular wheel containing 36 numbers from 1 to 36 and a betting layout where players can place their wagers.

The Play of the Game

Play begins in roulette with the bettors placing their bets on the layout. The wheel is spun by the dealer who will also throw the ball in the opposite direction from which the wheel is spinning. When the ball is about to leave the track, the dealer will announce that bets are no longer permitted.

When the ball has stopped in a slot, the outcome is announced, and the dealer settles bets.

Let's now look at the bets available at roulette:

THE BETS

Single Number Bet - A single number bet can be made on any number on the layout including the 0 and 00. To do so, place your chip within the lines of the number chosen, being careful not to touch the lines. Otherwise you may have another bet altogether. Payoff is 35 to 1.

Split Bet - Place the chip on the line adjoining two numbers. If either number comes up, the payoff is 17 to 1.

Trio Bet - The chip is placed on the outside vertical line alongside any line of numbers. If any of the three numbers chosen are hit, the payoff is 11 to 1.

4-Number Bet - Also called a **square** or **corner** bet. Place the chip on the spot marking the intersection of four numbers. If any come in, it is an 8-1 payoff.

5-Number Bet - Place the chip at the intersection of the 0, 00 and 2 to cover those numbers plus the 1 and 3. If any of these five land, the payoff is 6-1. It is the only bet not giving the house an edge of 5.26%. It's worse - 7.89%!

6-Number Bet - Also called a **block** bet. Wagers are placed on the outside intersecting line that separates the two sets of three numbers chosen. The payoff is 5-1.

Columns Bet - A chip placed at the head of a column, on the far side from the zero or zeros, covers all 12 numbers in the column and has a winning payoff of 2-1. The 0 and 00 are not included in this bet.

Dozens Bet - A bet on 1-12, 13-24 or 25-36. They're called the first, second and third dozen respectively. The winning payoff as in the column bet is 2 to 1.

THE EVEN MONEY BETS

You can also bet:

- **Red-Black** - There are 18 black and eighteen red numbers. A player may bet either the red or the black and is paid off at 1 to 1 on a winning spin. Bets are placed on the black or white diamond.
- **High-Low** - Numbers 1-18 may be bet (low) or 19-36 (high). Bets are paid off at 1 to 1. Bets are placed in these particular boxes.
- **Odd-Even** - There are 18 even numbers and 18 odd numbers. Winning bets are paid at 1 to 1. Bets are placed in the odd or even box on the table.

THE ROULETTE LAYOUT

			0	00	
1to18	1st 12		1	2	3
			4	5	6
EVEN			7	8	9
			10	11	12
◇	2nd 12		13	14	15
			16	17	18
◆			19	20	21
			22	23	24
ODD	3rd 12		25	26	27
			28	29	30
19to36			31	32	33
			34	35	36
			2-1	2-1	2-1

Winning Strategy

It must be stated clearly: the casino has the mathematical edge over the player in roulette. No betting strategy or playing system can overcome those odds. Except for the five number bet which is at 7.89%, all bets at roulette give the house a 5.26% advantage.

You can have fun at roulette and come home a winner if you catch a good streak. Money management is all-important - protect your losses and quit when ahead. Betting strategies can work - in the short run - and provide the player with a fun, working approach to winning. And really, that's what the game is all about.

ROULETTE PAYOFF CHART

Roulette Bets	#	Payoff
Single Number	1	35-1
Split Bet	2	17-1
Trio	3	11-1
4-Number (Corner)	4	8-1
5-Number	5	6-1
6-Number or Block	6	5-1
Columns Bet	12	2-1
Dozens Bet	12	2-1
Red or Black	18	1-1
High or Low	18	1-1
Odd or Even	18	1-1

 # column is the amount of numbers covered by the bet.

VIDEO POKER

This game is rapidly becoming the most popular machine game in the casinos. Decision-making and skill is involved, and proper play can make you a winner!

Video poker is basically played as draw poker. To play, anywhere from one to five coins are inserted into the machine. Press the button marked **DRAW/DEAL** (Sometimes the cards will be dealt automatically. In these cases there's no need to press the draw/deal button.)

The Draw/Deal Button

Five cards are dealt. Players may keep some or all the cards and do so by pressing the button marked hold underneath the corresponding card they wish to keep. **HELD** will appear on the screen underneath each card chosen.

The DRAW/DEAL button is now pressed and those cards not chosen to be held will be replaced with new ones. This set of cards is the final hand.

A player may keep all five original cards and does so by pushing the hold button under each card; or he or she may discard all five original cards if so desired. This is done by pressing the DRAW/DEAL button without having pressed any of the hold buttons.

If your hand is a winner, the machine will flash "WINNER" at the bottom of the screen. Winning hands are automatically paid according to the payoffs shown on the machine.

Deuces Wild and Jokers Wild

Besides the Jacks or Better machine discussed above, some video poker machines are played as **deuces wild** or **jokers wild**. Wild cards can be given any value or suit and the machine will interpret wild cards in the most advantageous way for the player.

For example, the hand 2 2 5 6 8 in deuces wild would be a straight: one 2 would be used as a 7 and the other as either a 9 or 4. The 2s could also be used as eights to give three of a kind, but since the straight is more valuable to the player the machine will see it as a straight.

Wild card machines have different payoff schedules than the jacks or better machines, and these payoffs will give credit only on a 3 of a kind hand or better.

Jacks or Better Payoffs

The following chart shows typical payoffs for video poker on a Jacks or Better machine. This machine is known as an **8-5 machine**, so named for the payoffs given on the full house and flush respectively.

PAYOFFS: JACKS OR BETTER: 8-5 MACHINE

Coins Played	1	2	3	4	5
Jacks of Better	1	2	3	4	5
Two Pair	2	4	6	8	10
Three of a Kind	3	6	9	12	15
Straight	4	8	12	16	20
Flush	5	10	15	20	25
Full House	8	16	24	32	40
Four of a Kind	25	50	75	100	125
Straight Flush	50	100	150	200	250
Royal Flush	250	500	750	1000	4000

Progressives

Besides the straight machines discussed above, there are progressive machines, as in slots. All payoffs, like the straight machines, are fixed except in the case of a royal flush, where this grand-daddy pays the accumulated total posted above the machine on the electronic board.

This total slowly but constantly rises, and on a quarter machine in Las Vegas can rise into the thousands of dollars. Then the game gets more interesting!

WINNING HANDS IN VIDEO POKER

Jacks or Better - *Two cards of equal value. Jacks or better refers to a pairing of Jacks, Queens, Kings or Aces.*

Two Pair - *Two sets of paired cards, such as 3-3 and 10-10.*

Three of a Kind - *Three cards of equal value, such as 9-9-9.*

Straight - *Five cards in numerical sequence, such as 3-4-5-6-7 or 10-J-Q-K-A.*

Flush - *Any five cards of the same suit, such as five hearts.*

Full House - *Three of a kind and a pair, such as 2-2-2-J-J.*

Four of a kind - *Four cards of equal value, such as K-K-K-K.*

Straight Flush - *A straight all in the same suit, such as 7-8-9-10-J, all in spades.*

Royal Flush - *10-J-Q-K-A, all in the same suit.*

Winning Strategy

The big payoff in video poker on the jacks or better machines is the royal flush - a whopping 4,000 coins are paid for this score when five coins are played.

On progressive machines, if five coins are played, the total could be a great deal higher, possibly as high as $3,000 (12,000 coins) on a quarter machine.

Of course, the royal doesn't come often. With correct strategy, you'll hit one every 30,000+ hands on the average. This doesn't mean, however, that you won't hit one in your very first hour of play!

Meanwhile, you'll be collecting other winners such as straights, full houses and the like. With proper play, all in all, you can beat the video poker machines.

To collect the full payoff for a royal flush, proper play dictates that you always play the full five coins for each game. Of course, those that want to play less seriously can play any amount of coins from 1 to 5.

On the next page you'll find the correct strategies for the **9-6 Flattops**.

JACKS OR BETTER: 9-6 FLATTOP STRATEGY

1. Whenever you hold <u>four cards to a royal flush</u>, discard the fifth card, even if that card gives you a flush or pair.

2. Keep a <u>jacks or better pair</u> and any higher hand such as a three of a kind or straight over three to the royal. Play the <u>three to a royal</u> over any lesser hand such as a low pair or four flush.

3. With <u>two cards to a royal</u>, keep four straights, four flushes, and high pairs or better instead. Otherwise, go for the royal.

4. Never break up a <u>straight or flush</u>, unless a one card draw gives you a chance for the royal.

5. Keep <u>jacks or better</u> over a four straight or four flush.

6. Never break up a <u>four of a kind</u>, <u>full house</u>, <u>three of a kind</u> or <u>two pair</u> hands. The rags, worthless cards for the latter two hands, should be dropped on the draw.

7. The <u>jacks or better pair</u> is always kept, except when you have four cards that could result in a straight or royal flush.

8. Keep <u>low pairs</u> over the four straight, but discard them in favor of the four flushes and three or four to a royal flush.

9. When dealt <u>unmade hands</u>, pre-draw hands with no payable combination of cards, save in order; four to a royal flush and straight flush, three to a royal flush, four flushes, four straights, three to a straight flush, two cards to the royal, two cards jack or higher and one card jack or higher.

10. Lacking any of the above, with no card jack or higher, discard all the cards and draw five fresh ones.

(These strategies are not applicable to the 8-5 Progressives).

12. SEEING THE SIGHTS

Okay, now that we've gotten you here, picked out a place to stay, filled your stomach and taught you how to play, it's time to get down to business. Namely, what do you do during the day when you're not gambling? The biggest attractions are, of course, the major hotels, but that doesn't adequately prepare you for what's inside them (or sometimes outside). But that's not all there is to see and do, as you'll soon find out. Please note that all hotel attractions are free of charge unless otherwise noted.

For hotels, casinos, and various sights on or near The Strip, see the map on pages 62-63.

THE STRIP

Las Vegas Boulevard South is the official designation for **The Strip** – one of the most famous thoroughfares in the world and the single most important street in Las Vegas. Covering a distance of approximately 4-1/2 miles from Russell Road to the Stratosphere Hotel, which is a little north of Sahara Avenue, it certainly ranks as one of the most unusual streets in the world. It is filled with magnificent and sometimes wacky hotel-casinos but it may be even more unusual for what it doesn't have. Where else but in Las Vegas could you encounter the main street of a city on which no one lives, that doesn't have a supermarket or an office building, a post office or many other types of structures that one usually associates with "Main Street"? But that's what makes Las Vegas what it is.

The Strip is the only road in America that has been designated as a "nighttime scenic byway" and a slow drive along this brightly lit avenue is a must for the first time visitor. Not that it's bad by day, either, but it is after dark when the special quality of The Strip really takes hold.

However, the best way to explore The Strip, day or night, is by foot. Take care when crossing Las Vegas Boulevard. The bustle and lights as well as the general crazy atmosphere can distract both pedestrians and drivers. At Tropicana Avenue four pedestrian bridges provide a safe means of crossing. In fact, at this location concrete barriers prevent you from crossing at street level. The Flamingo Road intersection has two bridges in place. Completion of the other two has been delayed by haggling between the county and casino owners. Although you will be able to cross at street level until the other bridges are completed, do use the existing two bridges whenever possible. At all other intersections exercise caution and hold on to your children.

HOTEL/CASINO ATTRACTIONS

The hotels are listed in alphabetic order. However, to avoid a lot of unnecessary running around (especially since almost all of the hotels are huge and require a considerable amount of walking), it's best to attack them in a planned manner. Concentrate on one major Strip section at a time if you're going to be doing most of the hotels. For example, many are clustered around the intersection of Flamingo Road (referred to as the Old Four Corners) and Tropicana Avenue (the New Four Corners). All of the following are located on The Strip. To make it easier for you to find we've included the major cross streets or other landmark.

BALLY'S LAS VEGAS, *southeast corner of Flamingo Road. Tel. 702/739-4111.*

Bally's is the former MGM Grand Hotel (not to be confused with the present MGM a mile to the south). It has been extensively remodeled since the time of owner Kirk Kekorian and the damaging 1980 fire. Currently owned by Park Place Entertainment, Bally's casino has more than a thousand slot machines and is among the city's biggest. While it lacks a theme (thereby showing it's age), it is still a lovely place and is on the elegant side. This is especially true of its high stakes salon. Bally's shopping arcade is most attractive.

There are two towers arranged in an L-shape along The Strip. Everyone thought it was great when first built, but with so many architectural superstars these days, it looks rather like a modern office or apartment building. The most attractive feature of the exterior are the gardens and topiary that surround the moving walkway that leads from Las Vegas Boulevard to the main entrance that is set far back from the street. Surrounded by glass tubes and towers that are kind of bland during the day, the entire walkway takes on a special appearance at night when the walkway lights constantly go through a changing kaleidoscope of colors.

BELLAGIO, *southwest corner of Flamingo Road. Tel. 702/693-7111.*

Steve Wynn's triumphant vision of elegance brings a degree of class to The Strip that even it's usual worst critics can't find much to complain about. You won't find glitz here (even the slot machines are subdued – framed in a fancy marble looking encasement and few bright lights flashing above them); only a well thought out environment that reminds one of a stately European palace. Actually, Bellagio is meant to be the recreation of a tiny Italian lake district town of that name. We wouldn't be surprised if the hotel is larger than the town. While the exterior fits that bill quite well, the interior is much more elaborate.

The main entryway to the 119 acre Bellagio is via a long winding drive or sidewalk (although pedestrians are more likely to come in via the moving walkway through the marquee, a Las Vegas first, or through the shopping arcade that begins at the Flamingo Road bridges – but more about that later). The massive property is fronted by an artificial lake that covers almost nine acres. It makes for a dramatic and beautiful sight but especially when the fantastic **Fountains of Bellagio** begin their musical act. Spread out along an 1,100-foot long row, the fountains are capable of shooting bursts of water up to a height of 240 feet! A new technology uses very little energy – compressed air forces the water out with a burst that sounds like the popping of a champagne cork.

But the fountains are far more than high jets of water. To the accompaniment of one of nine different musical themes ranging from Aaron Copeland to Frank Sinatra and from a Strauss waltz to Luciano Pavarotti, the mesmerizing waters sway back and forth in a beautiful and gracefully choreographed ballet. While diners watch from the row of upscale restaurants in the hotel that front on the lake, the throngs on The Strip have ample room to spread out and enjoy the show from numerous vantage points. *The fountains play every hour from 5:00pm to midnight except on Saturday when they begin at 2:00pm. We suggest that you wait until after dark to see them for maximum effect.* During the evening when the lights on the trees that front the lake are on, the Bellagio property becomes an enchanting sea of tranquility along a thoroughfare that is better known for glitz and eye-catching wild attractions. Although we like the glitz, too, one has to admit that the change of pace is simply refreshing.

Step inside the main lobby and you're immediately confronted by a scene not often found in Las Vegas casino hotels – you don't see the casino and there are plenty of comfortable sofas to sit down and relax after a long walk. Marble is in abundance. Throughout the hotel there is a dramatic interplay of rich, colorful carpeting interspersed with tile. The effect is outstanding. The lobby, however, is dominated by the *Fiori di Como*, a unique chandelier that covers 2,000 square feet and consists of 2,200 individual pieces of hand blown colored glass (each weighing between 30 and 50 pounds) that are supposed to be flowers but appear more like parasols to some viewers. The chandelier alone cost $10 million, which gives you an idea of how Mirage Resorts spent $1.6 billion on the joint.

Behind the lobby is the fabulous **Conservatory**, a glass roofed paradise of exploding color and beauty. The flowers are contained in

1,200 bins each measuring 20 x 40 inches. The result is that the floral display is so tightly packed that you can't even see a slither of ground between them. The Conservatory's floral arrangement changes six to eight times a year, according to the season. We haven't seen them all, but based on the Thanksgiving, Christmas, and Spring/Easter displays, all should be delightful. The hotel has even constructed its own greenhouse to grow the flowers for the Conservatory and to serve as a staging area for the next display. The rear of the Conservatory is where you'll find the entrance to the **Bellagio Gallery of Fine Arts**, a unique feature of any Las Vegas hotel. The outstanding collection of 19th and 20th century masters includes works by Degas, Monet, Picasso, Renior and van Gogh. Even Andy Warhol is represented. The collection, compared to most museums, stresses quality rather than quantity and cost $285 million to acquire. While the works are technically for sale if the offering price is right, it isn't expected that the pieces on display will change that much, at least in the short term. *The Gallery is open daily from 9 am until midnight. The admission is $10 ($14 with the audio tour). You can reach the gallery without going through the casino if you have children and would prefer them not to enter a gaming area.*

Another gorgeous sight at Bellagio is the expansive pool area that covers five acres and, architecturally speaking, encompasses aspects of several styles of Mediterranean gardens. There are six separate pools, some with fountains, trellis lined walkways, statues and plenty of trees. While non-guests cannot enter the pool area itself it can be viewed in all its glory from the Pool Promenade or the Monet Patio. The former is along a small shopping arcade while the latter is in the convention center area.

We've already alluded to the richness rather than the glitziness of the casino itself. Everything about it exudes a European style and luxury, from the gaming tables and change booths to the rich textured cloth wall coverings. Especially pleasing are the colorful canopies throughout the casino. Each and every one of the several bars in the casino are works of art in themselves. Do go into the **Fontana Bar** (entertainment during the evening), a round room that adjoins the lake. Outside on the patio is a dramatic view not only of Bellagio's lake but of the Paris Hotel across the street. Because the patio is reached through the bar, no one under 21 years of age, unfortunately, will be able to get the view from this vantage point.

Last, and certainly not least, is the **Via Bellagio**, a magnificent glass domed shopping street that leads from the casino out to The Strip. It is reminiscent of the early enclosed European shopping centers, especially like one in Milan, only it is more dramatic. Lined by exclusive shops and restaurants (see the shopping chapter for more details), the Via is filled with potted plants and other dramatic artistic enhancements. In fact, no matter which way you enter the Bellagio from, you'll be amazed from the moment you set foot inside.

Strollers and persons under age 18 are not permitted at Bellagio unless you are a registered hotel guest.

CAESARS PALACE, *northwest corner of Flamingo Road. Tel. 702/731-7110.*

Caesars Palace (no apostrophe, please) is now over 30 years old but renovations and expansions have kept it looking spanking new. It was truly the first of Las Vegas' mega-hotel/resorts and set the standards by which all that followed have had to live up to. Despite the fact that Bellagio now sits across the street from it, Caesars can still compete with any other facility for the most amazing place in town. Caesars is everything you ever imagined Vegas was or should be. It's a huge place, with the interior done-up in neo-Roman luxury, but it has a kind of decadent feel that is in tune with what this town is all about. The theme is carried through in great detail to every part of Caesars wonderful empire.

You know it's a special place from the moment you approach it – fabulous fountains and statues grace the main entrance while equally impressive statues line the long north entrance driveway. Among the more famous recreations are the winged "Victory at Samothrace" and "Venus de Medici." Perhaps the most beautiful of all the statues is the new grouping of three statues (two equestrian) right out in front of the main entrance pool and fountain. The gleaming white life-size sculpture is truly a work of art. Also on the outside, near the central Strip entrance way, is an authentic replica of a Thai Buddhist shrine. It supposedly brings good luck. A gift from a wealthy Thai newspaper tycoon, the 14-foot high statue weighs more than four tons.

Three different "people-movers" bring guests from The Strip into the casino (some people refer to them as human vacuum cleaners). One starts at a beautiful circular marble building and passes a holographic display of ancient Rome. (Look quickly otherwise you can easily miss it.) The street entrance to the Forum Shops is highlighted by the magnificent golden **Quadriga Statue** – a charioteer urging on his team of four horses, followed by a moving walkway passing under a series of triumphal arches. The statue is lit up at night by gas-lit flames.

The inside is no less spectacular. The original **Forum Casino** is home to high rollers so you may not want to play there. More casual bettors can be found in the unbelievable **Olympic Casino** where statues, frescoes, and a painted ceiling make for one of the most impressive gaming rooms in Las Vegas. You might even see Caesar himself along with Cleopatra and a burley Centurion occasionally walking through the casino and chatting with guests. **Cleopatra's Barge** is a floating cocktail lounge (open evenings only) that's worth a look even if you don't patronize it. The street level of the new tower is a large and magnificent area with so much marble that you would think that they had to raid every quarry in the world to get enough. At the rear of the tower is the entrance to the **Garden of the Gods Swimming Pools**. Featuring three large pools and several spas, all with inlaid marble, it is among the top two or three pool areas in the city for beauty. The main pool is round and in the center is a small island with a temple-like structure in the middle. Surrounding the pools are lovely gardens and dozens of classically inspired statues and columns. Even the lifeguard chairs are something unique – they look like Caesars' throne!

There are also several small Roman style edifices that house, among other things, a snack bar. Non-hotel guests can only visit the pool area during the winter months. At other times, however, you can still get a decent view of it by going up to the third floor of the convention center and looking out of any of the huge windows along the main concourse. (Even the convention area is striking to look at.)

The new and older sections of the hotel are connected by the **Appian Way** that house a small number of very exclusive shops and galleries. A full size replica of Michaelangelo's *David* is located here. The hotel's main lobby was recently refurbished and is now a showplace of gleaming white marble and gold statues. The **Palace Tower** houses guest rooms as well as the hotel's convention facilities, but the marble luxury of the street level is something that should be seen if you have the time. Among the sights worth seeing here are the beautiful open lounge area of the garden-styled Terrazza restaurant, located underneath a magnificent rotunda. While the exterior of the older Caesars Palace towers were anything but Roman in appearance, the Palace Tower, distinctive for its graceful fluted columns and Corinthian capitals, is a lavish looking classical work topped by a Greco-Roman facade on the three pediments. The center bears a gold-leafed profile of Caesar himself. If ancient Rome had built near-skyscrapers, this is definitely what it would have looked like!

Caesars Magical Empire is a dinner theater and magic show that is described in the *Nightlife and Entertainment* chapter; however, during the day they try to drum up business for dinner by presenting a free show called the **Luminaria**. You're taken through the catacomb like chambers of the Magical Empire into a central rotunda that is 70 feet high. Here, a wizard conjures up some legendary mighty forces that created Rome. Plenty of special effects are used during the show and flames (which are very popular at Caesars), burst forth from the fountain and warm the room in response to the wizard's incantations. Good fun for all ages. *Performances are given Friday through Tuesday, approximately every half hour, between 11 am and 3:30 pm. They last about 10 minutes.*

Another entertainment option at Caesars is the **Omnimax Theater**, visible from the outside of the hotel as a dark globe shaped building. At night geometric patterns light up the globe. Theater presentations change periodically and cover a wide variety of topics. *Tel. 702/731-7900. Call for exact time schedule. Admission is $7 for adults and $5 for children.*

Despite all of the wonderful things that we've already mentioned about Caesars there is no doubt that the highlight of a visit to the empire is the incomparable **Forum Shops** – the "shopping wonder of the world." However, let us state right up front that even if you have no intention of buying a single thing, it would be a great mistake not to come to the Forum Shops. There's that much to see and do. So let's begin. The shopping aspects of the Forum Shops will be detailed in *Chapter 15*, although we have to at least mention at this point **FAO Schwarz** with its imaginative two-story Trojan Horse (you can go inside) whose wooden head moves and eyes shine. The store also has the most delightful mechanical teddy bear display we've ever seen. Of course, the theme is ancient Rome. The mall (which lacks only department stores) resembles an ancient Roman street scene. The ceiling is one of the most realistic sky paintings you'll likely to see anywhere. And it gradually changes over a period of about twenty minutes from day to night and then back again. A magnificent **Neptune's Fountain** graces the center court and has to be one of the most photographed sights in town. The **Festival Fountain** contains a large statue of a seated Bacchus, god of wine and merriment, surrounded by smaller statues of Apollo, Venus and others. These seemingly stone monuments come "alive" as part of a laser light show projected on the domed ceiling. Bacchus welcomes guests to his party and tells you a bit about other goings-on in the Forum Shops. Get there early to be sure of a good viewing spot. *Free ten minute shows daily on the hour beginning at 10 am.*

At the far end of the Forum Shops is the beautiful **Great Hall**, closely modeled after the famous Pantheon in Rome. There's a huge 50,000 gallon semi-circular aquarium with colorful fish to look at, but the main attraction is the **Sinking of Atlantis**. The legend involves the aging Atlas who wishes to turn Atlantis over to either his son or daughter, both of whom are evil and fighting for control. Well, to make a long story short, other gods intervene and destroy Atlantis. It's not the story that counts but the effects. The life-likeness of the mechanical participants is fantastic, it surpasses anything we've seen at Disneyworld as you can even see the folds of their "skin" as they move. (The bad daughter is kind of cute, by the way.) Accompanying the dialogue of the regal family are bursts of fire and water and imaginative videos on huge screens high up on the walls of the rotunda like Great Hall. *Free shows lasting about ten minutes are given every hour on the hour beginning at 10 am.*

There are also several motion simulators in the Forum Shops. The **Cinema Ride** are for the inexperienced simulator rider and are located on the lower level. *Tel. 702/369-4008. Open daily from 11 am to midnight. Prices vary depending upon the* ride. The **Race for Atlantis**, located off of the Great Hall, combines three dimensional IMAX film technology with one of the wildest simulators to be found anywhere. Your "mission" is to save the lost city of Atlantis and it's a lot of fun if you like these types of rides. On the other hand, if they're not for you, we understand fully. But you should at least go into the ride's entry area where a mammoth statue depicts a mythological hero slaying an evil dragon. The art work is something that can be appreciated by all ages. *Tel. 702/733-9000. Race for Atlantis hours are daily from 10 am to 11 pm (to midnight on Friday and Saturday) and the admission is $9.50 for adults and $6.75 for children age 12 and under.*

CIRCUS CIRCUS, *north of Convention Center Drive at Circus Circus Drive. Tel. 702/734-0410.*

Bigtop Pee Wee meets Nick the Greek at Circus Circus and the result is a wild ride great for both kids and adults. It's one heck of a show with the emphasis on fun, whether it's in the casino, on the Midway or in the theme park. The exterior features a huge marquee in the form of a jolly clown and one of the glitziest canopies anywhere along The Strip. The main building is shaped like a giant circus tent. Stone gorillas, clowns and other circus characters dot the outside area along Las Vegas Boulevard. The casino is one of the biggest in the city and, after a recent refurbishment, is not quite as pink as it used to be. It tends to be one of the most crowded and noisiest of the casinos. That's annoying to some people but others enjoy it because it makes it more exciting.

Above the main casino is the **Midway**. This is like a perpetual carnival with games of skill mainly in the old low-tech style – you know, throw the baseball and hit the jar sort of thing. Those interested in more modern electronic versions can go to the arcade. Then there is the **circus** itself where trapeze artists, clowns and other performers strut their stuff as people watch from a seating area or from around the Midway's promenade. The various acts are performed at intervals of approximately 45 minutes and last about ten minutes each. There's a schedule posted but if you hang around long enough you'll likely see just about every type of circus act there is. The circus acts used to be visible from the casino floor but that was changed because it was disturbing to some of the gamblers. *The Midway is open every day from 11 am to midnight. Circus acts also begin at 11 am. Admission is free but there is a charge for each Midway game played. Prices begin at 50 cents but most cost at least a buck.*

The theme park that used to be known as Grand Slam Canyon is now called the **Adventuredome**. It's housed underneath a huge dome (it is the largest indoor theme park in the United States, covering about five acres) with pink glass that gives everything inside a rather unusual color. It has a big roller coaster, log flume and many other rides and attractions along with restaurants, snack bars and live entertainment. The laser tag facility is kind of unusual for a theme park. The Adventuredome is designed to reflect the canyon country of the American southwest and the artificial mountains and other landscaping are kind of attractive, making this an interesting place to just walk around for a while even if you don't want to go on the rides. *Tel. 702/794-3939. Theme park open daily from 10 am until 6 pm (until midnight on Friday and Saturday). Admission is free but there is a fee for rides. You can purchase individual ride tickets ($2-5 each) or passes good for unlimited rides on a single day. These cost $12-16 depending upon height.*

The other main point of interest in Circus Circus is the attractive shopping promenade located outside of the theme park entrance above the hotel's main lobby. There are some unusual shops and a couple of good places to eat. Circus Circus is a huge property and you can save some walking between the Strip side and the theme park side by taking their small monorail.

DESERT INN, *between Sands Avenue and Convention Center Drive. Tel. 702/733-4444.*

You won't see too many tourists oohing and aaahing at the Desert Inn (or DI as it's known to the locals) because it doesn't have anything crazy or glitzy about it. This is where the rich people used to stay before the arrival of some of the other classy hotels. What you will see at the Desert Inn are lovely grounds that are more reminiscent of a Floridian or Hawaiian resort than Las Vegas. The atrium lobby of the new wing is also beautiful.

EXCALIBUR HOTEL & CASINO, *southwest corner of Tropicana Avenue. Tel. 702/597-7777.*

The medieval Camelot theme is done up in great style at this big and fun-filled hotel that appeals almost as much to grown-ups as it does to kids. Two L-shaped towers flank a multi-turreted castle of King Arthur. The white turrets are topped in gold, red or blue and make a most colorful sight. It's one of the prettiest hotel exteriors by day but at night is simply fabulous – a sight that is still capable of mesmerizing the visitor despite the addition of ever more exotic looking hotels. To get the best view (one that isn't blocked by the new tram station) stand on one of the pedestrian bridges that span Las Vegas Boulevard and Tropicana Avenue near to the MGM Grand. You approach the main entrance in front via a moving walkway that crosses the moat (a castle has to have a moat, after all). The back entrance has a similar view. The main difference is that there is no moat. However, a floral display and two topiary knights make an attractive picture.

Returning to the front, at night you can watch Merlin the Magician do battle with a ferocious fire breathing dragon. Kids will simply adore it but then again, so do we! The huge dragon moves along the water of the moat on tracks that you can't see; it's head moves and eyes light up. *The free shows last about eight minutes and are staged nightly on the hour beginning after dark with the last show at 11 pm. They are subject to cancellation during bad weather.*

Inside, the 100,000 square foot casino is among the biggest in Las Vegas. The medieval theme is continued here with stuffed mounted knights, heavy wrought-iron chandeliers and more. Above and below the casino level is where all of the non-gaming action takes place. Beneath the casino is the **Fantasy Faire** where kids can play one of many arcade or carnival type games of skill. Also here are the **Magic Motion Machines**, one of the best motion simulator attractions in town. *Simulators operate daily from 9 am to midnight (from 10 am on Sunday and to 1 am on Saturday). The cost is $3 per ride.* Refer to the entertainment section for information on **Tournament of Kings**.

Upstairs is the **Medieval Village** with many interesting shops and several restaurants. Free entertainment is held from time to time on the **Court Jester's Stage** according to a posted schedule. On this level you'll also find the moving walkway that leads to the adjacent Luxor Hotel. The Excalibur side of the walkway has several shops that form a continuation of the Medieval Village.

Excalibur is a classic example of Vegas recreation of suspended reality, replete with knights in shining armor and damsels in distress (those losing at the tables, anyway) who sometimes parade around the casino and other areas of the hotel. Don't expect to find a lot of glitz and glamour at Excalibur. It's all designed for good fun.

FLAMINGO HILTON, *just north of the northeast corner of Flamingo Road. Tel. 702/733-3111.*

Way back when, the Flamingo was the first of the modern glitzy casino hotels. It was opened in December 1946 by the infamous Bugsy Siegel. Nothing, however, remains of the building that Bugsy built. Acquired by the Hilton chain, the Flamingo underwent a series of enlargements and enhancements that has put it among the biggest and most beautiful of all Strip hotels. The exterior of the L-shaped glass and concrete tower features the unmistakable floral Flamingo Hilton logo as well as a glass facade of pink flamingos. The interior boasts a large and elegant casino as well as a small but attractive shopping arcade.

However, the real star attraction is the magnificent grounds, which we rate as among the two or three best of any Las Vegas hotel. All of the grounds are in the rear as the hotel itself sits right on The Strip and does not have any fronting property. The large tropical garden is filled with palm trees and other vegetation that cover 15 acres and are threaded by winding paved paths. They lead first pass the animal habitat that contains a dozen Chilean flamingos and a pond that houses a colony of African penguins. They're small (only 18 inches high) and cute to watch. Twice daily feedings (*at 8:30 am and 3:00 pm*) are popular, especially with kids. Beyond the habitat is a large waterfall, artificial lake and a fountain surrounded by four pink stone flamingos spraying water into the fountain. The pool area sits behind all of this and is an elaborate maze of interconnected pools, water slides and lagoons. A bridge crosses this marvelous landscape and is a great spot for pictures. The grounds also house the Flamingo's pretty wedding chapel which fronts the upper level pool area. Opposite the wedding chapel entrance is a short trellis lined walkway which ends at a stone cairn that holds a monument which pays tribute to the role played by Bugsy Siegel in developing this resort city. Only in Las Vegas!

HARRAH'S LAS VEGAS, *between Flamingo Road and Sands Avenue. Tel. 702/369-5000.*

It wasn't that long ago that Harrah's used to be recognized by its familiar showboat facade. That's all gone now as this older property made extensive additions and changes to make it more competitive with the mega-resorts that surround it. The new carnival theme is colorful and quite attractive. Harrah's combines style with a fun atmosphere in a pleasant way. The exterior is highlighted by a huge facade consisting of hundreds of large brightly colored lights surrounding a fantastic mural that depicts traditional Las Vegas entertainment. Also decorating the outside are big blue Harrah's logo globes, life size gold court jesters and the new **Carnival Court**. What looks like an old style carousel from a distance is actually a covered stage where you can watch live entertainment, mostly in the form of bands. A schedule will be posted to let you know when the action begins to heat up. The Carnival Court is surrounded by several interesting shops.

The interior of the Harrah's casino is large and equally colorful. We especially like the ceilings in some areas of the casino that feature thousands of tiny bulbs that create a dazzling atmosphere. Also be sure to see the life-size statue in the casino called *Virtue Wins*. The statues' gambling themes change peridocially as they are rotated to other areas of Harrah's locations. But they're always whimsical. To the rear of the hotel near the attractive check-in area are several more interesting shops.

IMPERIAL PALACE, *north of Flamingo Road, adjacent to Harrah's. Tel. 702/731-3311.*

This palace doesn't measure up to the standards of most of its neighbors when it comes to eye appeal. The Oriental theme inside and out is alright but isn't done with any particular style or grace. What it does have, however, is one of the best automotive museums in the world. The **Imperial Palace Auto Collection**, on the fifth floor of the main garage, has one of the biggest collections of antique and customized cars in existence. More than 200 are on display at any one time (some are always on view while others rotate). Many of the vehicles were owned by celebrities or world leaders. Included in the latter are Hitler's custom built Mercedes and Mussolini's Alfa Romeo. Several cars used by American presidents are also on display as well as Model T's, a 1947 Tucker (only 51 were made) and several 1930's Caddies. A separate room houses the largest collection of Duisenbergs in the world. *Open daily from 9:30 am to 11:30 pm. There is no admission. (Previously, there was a $7 charge that most people never paid because of the availability of free coupons. If a fee is reimposed, you'll likely still be able to get coupons entitling you to free entry in many visitor magazines or frequently from hotel employees outside on The Strip.)*

LUXOR, *southwest corner of Reno Avenue (one block south of Tropicana Ave.). Tel. 702/262-4000.*

Originally built in 1993 at a cost of $375 million, an additional $240 million was pumped into a recent expansion and renovation that turned what was previously an unfulfilled great idea into one of the most spectacular properties on The Strip. In a city of unique hotels, the Luxor may well be the most unusual of them all, despite competition from places like New York, New York and the Venetian.

Set behind a tall, slim obelisk and a man-made lake with temple "ruins," the Luxor is a 350-foot high glass pyramid, actually the fourth largest pyramid in the world. In front of the pyramid, which is the main building, is a ten-story high Sphinx that doubles as the hotel's *porte cochere* and main entrance. The pyramid is placed far enough back from The Strip so that you can approach it on foot by walkways lined with dozens of lion statues. To the north are the new twin stepped pyramid towers. All over both the exterior and interior are authentic Egyptian hieroglyphics and beautiful art works. It is important that during your visit to Luxor that you shouldn't move along too fast – take some time to really appreciate the detail that has been incorporated into the design. Almost everything is a true copy of something that existed in ancient Egypt. The pyramid is topped with what is said to be the brightest light in the world. Attention is focused on it by blinking lights that run up and down the four corners of the pyramid. It's a good thing they have those lights, too, because with its dark glass exterior, you would have trouble seeing the Luxor at night.

Stepping into the fabulous lobby is an eye-popping experience. The beauty is awesome and lovers of ancient Egyptian architecture will go insane. Huge Pharaoh figures standing five stories high sit in front of subtly lit pools flanked by heroic lions. Off to the right is the equally dramatic registration lobby that contains more monumental statues as well as gorgeous and life-like paintings of ancient Egypt. Generous use of marble and tile adds to the luxurious surroundings. The beautiful 100,000 square foot casino is round and also features an Egyptian motif.

Some of the things you should look for around the casino perimeter are the gold statue of Queen Nefertitti outside the lounge that bears her name; the reclining figure of a topless Cleopatra in the middle of the **Nile Bar**, and the fabulously ornate entrance to the **Ra Nightclub**. (More about the latter for nightclub patrons in *Chapter 13*.) Also, take a peek on the lower level at the entrance to the buffet area even if you aren't going to be eating there. It's a highly imaginative recreation of an Egyptian archaeological site complete with unearthed mummies. And for visitors who aren't going to be seeing the show at Luxor we'll mention that the theater is absolutely the most lavish and beautiful in Las Vegas. So try taking a peek if you can (although if you're chased out we'll adamantly deny sending you on this secret mission).

The Luxor's shopping area is known as the **Giza Galleria** and features several interesting shops with Egyptian art works, most notably the **Cairo Bazaar**. Outside the entrance to the shopping area are two talking camels who'll be glad to tell you a bit about the hotel. Again, further details on the individual stores will be in the chapter on shopping but, just as an attraction, some of the stores are well worth seeing for their beautiful wares and the same can be said about the tomb-like surroundings of the Galleria itself with its statues and deliberate ruined look. The Giza Galleria is off to the side of the hotel where the moving walkway to the Excalibur begins. Again, the decor in this section is mind boggling. A larger shopping mall more on the scale of those at Caesars or the Venetian will soon be added between the Luxor and Mandalay Bay.

Upstairs via escalators to the left of the main lobby as you come into the hotel is the so-called **Attractions Level**. This level offers the best views of the massive interior of the pyramid, an atrium covering 29 million cubic feet and which is capable of housing nine Boeing 747 aircraft! Of course, they might have a little difficulty getting them through the front doors! You can also get a good look at the lobby areas from up here. The Attractions Level houses several shops, a restaurant, food court and the hotel's big arcade area in addition to its main visitor attractions.

The first is **In Search of the Obelisk**, a wild motion simulator ride housed inside a structure designed to resemble the exterior of an ancient temple. The second is the **Luxor Imax Theater** where different high-tech motion pictures are shown. The theater is a black glass structure that is decidedly futuristic looking for this Egyptian themed hotel except for the two large Pharaoh statues that stand guard at its entrance. Finally, **King Tut's Tomb and Museum** is a highly imaginative walk-through journey of an exact replica of the famous young king's tomb as it was found in 1922 by Harold Carter. High quality recreations of many of the artifacts found in the tomb are on display. *Attractions hours are daily from 9 am to 11 pm (except for the IMAX which runs from 10 am to 10 pm).. Admission is $6 for the* *simulator ride and $5 for King Tut's Tomb. Prices for the Imax vary depending upon the movie being shown but usually range between $8-10. Call Tel. 702/262-4555 for exact Imax show schedule and information on all attractions.*

That about concludes the inside of Luxor but you're not quite finished with your tour as yet. The pool area is also quite a sight with cascading waters and plenty of other big statues to remind you what hotel you're in.

MANDALAY BAY, *north of Russell Road, adjacent to Luxor. Tel. 702/632-7777.*

Although this is an upscale hotel, it doesn't mean that this isn't a fun place to visit. A lot of that has to do with their entertainment program and some of the wild restaurants that were previously described. But it's a whole lot more than just that. Going one better on the tropical theme in evidence at several Las Vegas hotels, Mandalay Bay goes beyond tropical to exotic. It could easily have been called Shangri-La and have been well named, for it even takes exotic to new, mysterious levels. The 950-million dollar mega-resort covers more than 40 acres at the southern end of The Strip and debuted on March 2, 1999.

Exploring its sights isn't that easy. Not only is it huge, like so many of its neighbors, but the layout can be a bit confusing. You should pick up a map at the reception area to help you get around. For now, we'll do our best to be your guide, starting with the Strip pedestrian entrance at the hotel's north end. Two huge winged gargoyles (frequently found throughout Mandalay Bay) stand guard at a colonnaded entrance way. The walkway winds through an enchanting area of waterfalls surrounded by round pagoda-like mythical temples. One of the larger temples has a dozen elephants on its facade. Large barrel like fixtures have flames soaring out of them at night. The 40-plus story golden glass Y tower stands proudly behind the almost jungle-like landscape and the whole scene is imposing by either day or night.

Eventually you reach the lower (or Beach Level) entrance. Escalators will take you up to the main level, but since you're already down here, lets continue on. Going past the entrance to the elaborate spa, you'll soon go outside and reach the **Lagoon Entry Pavilion**. This 11-acre area contains Mandalay Bay's wedding chapels, several pools (including one with a swim-up shark tank), a sand beach, lazy river ride, eating places and more. Unfortunately, only hotel guests are admitted to the Lagoon area. However, you can get a glimpse of it from the hotel's registration area (which we'll get to soon) or take a walk around its perimeter on a paved path. It makes for a pleasant stroll.

The casino level carries out the exotic theme quite well. Within the casino, tiered ceilings and statues make for an attractive place to play. The centrally located **Island Lounge** is a great spot to sit, have a drink and watch the action. The pretty **Coral Reef Lounge** feaures even nicer statuary and colorful aquariums. Rattan furniture helps to get you in the right mood. Just off of the *porte cochere* on the casino level is the hotel's registration area. Lush tropical foliage and small waterfalls line the wall behind the registration desk. The lobby itself is luxurious and has cages containing colorful exotic birds as well as a beautiful aquarium that looks like a pagoda. At the far end of the lobby is a large glass wall that looks out on the Mandalay Bay lagoon. From this vantage point there is a fabulous view of a magnificent fountain flanked by six large lizard-like creatures paying homage to a central winged gargoyle. Waterfalls are an integral part of the fountain.

The restaurant area in the rear of the hotel has a partial tropical theme. You'll also find more birds here. Sometimes there is a free live show where the birds are put through their paces along with exotically clad dancers. It pays to walk around in the restaurant area regardless of where you plan to eat. Among the things you'll see are the big statue of Lenin outside of *Red Square*. His head is missing, although the top is "delicately" covered with faux pigeon poop. (The statue did have a head when the hotel first opened but, after less than a month, it was removed because too many people thought that having Lenin around was a bit offensive. We thought it was great – the personification of communism in the most capitalist city in the world!) In the evening you'll see people standing outside the *Aureole* restaurant craning their necks to see through the window as wine stewards are hoisted up like rock climbers in order to retrieve a bottle from their 40-foot high wine cellar tower!

Back off the casino area is the **House of Blues**, an unusual looking restaurant and entertainment complex that looks more Arabian than the far-eastern atmosphere the rest of Mandalay Bay seems to be attempting to create. (See the *Where to Eat* and *Nightlife & Entertainment* chapters for further information.) Even if you don't eat here or go for a show, it's worth taking a walk through. The Mandalay Bay also has a 12,000 seat multi-function arena (the largest hotel facility of it's type after the MGM's Grand Garden Arena).

The **Treasures of Mandalay Bay** is an exhibit of more than $40 million worth of rare gold and silver coins, paper money, gold bars and other valuables. The collection includes permanent items as well as some that are on temporary loan and will change from time to time. It's mildly interesting but somehow doesn't seem to fit in all that well with the theme. *Open daily from 9:00am until midnight and costs $6 for those age 12 and up.*

The hotel is connected to the other company-owned hotels on the Miracle Mile by a tramway. Unlike most of the other hotel trams and monorails, which leave you a good walk from the middle of things, this one is conveniently located on The Strip side of each property rather than being tucked away somewhere in the back. There is also an enclosed walkway to the Luxor that will eventually be lined on both sides with fashionable shops. They're under construction right now.

MGM GRAND, *northeast corner of Tropicana Avenue. Tel. 702/891-1111.*

The MGM has now completed a major overhaul that lasted about two years. They've transformed the place from the World of Oz to what is now billed as "The City of Entertainment," an appropriate name for the world's largest hotel (more than 5,000 rooms). Walking from one end to the other it does, indeed, seem city-sized. It covers 114 acres. If you saw this place when it first opened, you'll hardly recognize it today. Even the main entrance has completely changed. You used to enter through the mouth of a gigantic lion that sat on the corner of The Strip and Tropicana Avenue. People complained that it looked like a paper-mache lion and was childish. So they've replaced it with a smaller gold lion (which we still think looks kind of cheap – like gold aluminum foil). On a more positive note, however, the lion is surrounded by fountains and impressive statues holding lighting fixtures that look something like Atlas holding up the world. Huge electronic message screens flank either bridge entrance and the whole thing is rather impressive, especially at night, despite the chintzy lion.

The other complaint in the past was that the entirely green building, because of its size, was ugly. They've softened the green with touches of beige and by putting big yellow lettering and more lion symbols along the top. It has made an improvement even though it still is far from being the most striking edifice on The Strip. The size, however, is definitely notable. On The Strip side behind a row of stores at the north end of the property is a striking new structure with a large glass canopy. This houses the new Mansion suites. You won't be able to see them but the building is a plus to the MGM's look, even though it's partially blocked by a row of cheap souvenir shops that line Las Vegas Boulevard.

Walk inside and you'll find that what used to be the Emerald City has been replaced by another casino addition. But what a place it is – the round area is exquisitely adorned with fabulous statues and show business themed murals in an attractive art deco style. The rotunda like ceiling makes it seem even bigger than it already is and various MGM movies and other features constantly play on a huge overhead screen. A recent addition is four daily live shows on the stage in front of the view screens. The entire area, which is called the Pleasure Dome, is best viewed from one of two balconies that can be accessed via escalator from the main level or directly from the two pedestrian bridges that lead into the MGM from New York, New York or the Tropicana. Adjacent to one of the entrances is the Las Vegas home of the wacky **Rainforest Cafe**. Even if you don't eat here it's definitely an interesting place to look at. While there are similar places in other cities, we believe that this is the most elaborate of any Rainforest Cafe. From outside the restaurant on either the first or second level of the lobby you can look in and see the extravagant jungle-like setting, watch the "animals" (or people) and just rejoice in the remarkable color and detail of the scene. Their gift shop is equally wild and something you shouldn't miss. Be careful, though, because the shop contains big snakes and an alligator, among other creatures.

The 172,000 square foot casino is one of the more attractive gaming establishments in town. Covering the equivalent of four football fields, you have to take a stroll around it to get a real feel for how big it is. The high stakes area is particular beautiful and is reminiscent of a lavish European casino for the jet set.

Also of interest on the inside is the huge registration lobby with tons of white marble, another gold lion (this one is real nice), elaborate draperies of plaster that look like the real thing, and a massive multi-screen area behind the desk that advertises the hotel's shows amongst other things. Two places to shop in the MGM are **Star Lane** on the lower level and the beautiful **Studio Walk** which connects the casino to the theme park and convention center. The Studio Walk has many unusual shops and also houses a good number of the hotel's fabulous restaurants.

At the far end of the hotel is the **MGM Grand Adventures Theme Park** with a multitude of rides, shows and attractions. Those who claim that Las Vegas isn't for children can point to the fact that this theme park hasn't been an outstanding financial success. It seems that the moguls don't know what they want to do with it. It's changed focus several times and has recently been shrunk to make way for convention and recreational facilities. There are an assortment of thrill rides including a log flume, river ride and various types of roller coasters and simulators. We like to stand and watch the screaming people as they fly through the air on the *Sky Screamer*, kind of a hybrid between bungee jumping and sky diving.

There are also many live shows throughout the day in various parts of the park. One of the best is **Dueling Pirates**, a comical and entertaining romp in an outdoor amphitheater where the noble pirate captain saves a lovely princess from his crew. *The theme park is closed during the winter. Call for exact operating hours and fees.* Even if you don't love rides, it's fun to just stroll around for an hour or two and maybe grab a bite to eat or do some shopping while you're there.

Continuing with the great outdoors, the beautiful pool area is worth taking a look at. Although it's only open to guests, visitors can get a good view from the end of the promenade that leads to the theme park entrance or from the walkway leading to the art-deco style convention center. The path to the latter is lined with pictures of famous celebrities who have graced the MGM's many entertainment venues. But back to the pools. This seven acre facility consists of a series of five interconnected pools, a flowing river, several bridges, fountains and waterfalls.

What else can you say about a hotel that even has its own 13,000 seat arena? For one thing, it seems like they're never going to finish it. For instance, scheduled to open just as we went to press is the **Lion Habitat** located off The Strip entrance lobby. Based on what the hotel has done with lions in the past though, you can expect to see one or more full grown lions, maybe with a trainer, and cute lion cubs that will pose with you for pictures in an elaborate setting.

THE MIRAGE, *west side of The Strip between Flamingo Road (Caesars Palace) and Spring Mountain Road (Treasure Island). Tel. 702/791-7111.*

If Caesars Palace was the birth of the Las Vegas mega-resort, then the Mirage represents its coming of age. It is a tropical paradise that can rival any resort in the world. The building is a beautiful white and gold structure that brilliantly captures the strong desert sun in a multitude of ways depending upon the time of the day. It is set back quite far from The Strip via an arc-shaped driveway. Between the drive and Las Vegas Boulevard is an immense landscaped area with beautiful palm trees, waterfalls, statues and much more.

It is these waterfalls, gorgeous by day, that turn into the famous smoke and fire belching volcano attraction each evening. You'll first hear the rumbling of the volcano and see it begin to smoke before it explodes in a fiery eruption that looks an awful lot like the real thing. Even if you're standing far away you'll be able to feel the heat of the gas-generated flames that set the waters of the lake ablaze. The show can be seen from just about any vantage point along The Strip that fronts the Mirage's. You can also watch from in front of the main drive-up entrance although there's far less room there. Although it attracts big crowds you usually won't have a problem finding a good spot because there is so much room to watch. *Free "eruptions" take place approximately every 15 minutes beginning after dark until midnight. The spectacle lasts about five minutes. It will be cancelled during periods of heavy rain or high winds.*

One other thing to see outside on The Strip side of the Mirage is the larger than life sized heads of Siegfried and Roy with one of their famous white tigers. It's nice during the day but is even better at night when it's illuminated.

The interior of the Mirage has its own share of wonderful sights. Upon going through the main entrance, turn right into the hotel check in area. Behind the desk is a 53-foot long, 20,000 gallon aquarium filled with colorful and often unusual species of fish as well as sand sharks. Then turn around and head into the 90-foot high glass dome that houses a lush tropical paradise. You'll think you're in the South Seas, a theme that is carried out in many areas of the hotel's beautiful interior, including the large and elaborate casino. Be sure to visit the tiger habitat on the south side of the casino. There is almost always at least one of the rare big cats on hand behind a sturdy glass wall. Tourists pack the area to get a glimpse. If you're lucky the animals will be in an active mood and not just lying around.

If you really want to see animals, however, you'll have to fork over some money to visit **The Secret Garden of Siegfried and Roy**. This tropical setting sits behind the hotel adjacent to the Mirage's very attractive pool area. Besides white tigers there are many other types of animals roaming around a beautiful natural setting. There's also an extensive dolphin habitat. Proceeds from admission tickets are used to fund educational and conservation programs (at least that's what Steve Wynn says). *The Secret Garden is open daily except Wednesday from 11 am to 5:30 pm. Admission is $10 for everyone over age 10. You can visit the dolphin habitat alone on Wednesday for $5. Strollers are not allowed in the Mirage unless they are registered guests. This is not quite as strictly enforced as at Bellagio.*

MONTE CARLO, *between Tropicana and Harmon Avenues. Tel. 702/ 730-7777.*

The French Victorian styled hotel is modeled after the famous Place du Casino in Monte Carlo, Monaco. While it doesn't have anything wild or crazy like most of the other newer hotels, it does have a degree of class and elegance about it. That includes the beautiful 90,000 square foot casino with its magnificent chandeliers and immense potted plants. The exterior entrances at both the north and south ends are graced by a central fountain that is flanked by large statues in niches that are brilliantly illuminated at night. The "main" entrance, in between the two access points just described, is hardly ever used because of its location. However, it's worth taking a look at if you like beautiful architecture.

Of interest, if you can get in, is the lovely pool area that includes various wave pools, mini-waves crashing against artificial rocks, and the opportunity to ride an inner tube along the long and winding "Easy River." The **Street of Dreams** shopping arcade is a pleasant place for a stroll and it ends at the tram station for those desiring to go next to the Bellagio. The view of the pool from the station is good.

NEW YORK, NEW YORK, *northwest corner of Tropicana Avenue. Tel. 702/740-6969.*

Since it opened in January 1997, New York, New York has been wowing visitors and has become one of the big must-sees in Las Vegas.

This is likely to continue regardless of what else is built on the increasingly unbelievable Strip. The exterior recreates the skyline of Manhattan Island with replicas of some of its most famous structures. Each one is approximately a one-third scale of the real thing.

The tallest point of this "skyline" is the 48 story high Empire State Building. Other buildings include the AT&T, CBS, Chrysler and Seagram's towers. The casino low-rise building is also composed of replicas. Some of these are the Soldiers and Sailors Monument, the immigration station on Ellis Island, and Grand Central Terminal. However, the absolute highlight is right on the corner of The Strip and Tropicana Avenue. Dramatically angled in front of the whole structure is the 150-foot high Statue of Liberty replica. It's even on its own "island," flanked by two New York City fire boats that spray water into the air. Visitors can enter the casino through one of the pedestrian bridges or through entrances located alongside the 300-foot long Brooklyn Bridge.

If that wasn't enough, the whole thing is surrounded by the **Manhattan Express** roller coaster. It rises to a maximum height of more than 200 feet, goes 65 mph and has a 144-foot drop at one point in addition to a gravity defying loop! Only thrill seekers need apply. *Operating hours are daily from 10 am to 10 pm (until 11 pm on Friday and Saturday) and the cost of a ride is $7.* All in all New York, New York probably possesses the most architecturally diverse landscape on the entire Strip, both modern and eclectic – but mostly beautiful! It's advertised as the "greatest city in Las Vegas."

Unfortunately, we aren't so enthralled by the interior of New York, New York as we are by the outside, although it does have some good points. The biggest negatives are the overall crowded atmosphere (maybe that's appropriate because New York is that way, too) and the drab and dark ceiling. The best features begin with the recreation of a part of Grand Central Terminal. From the second floor balcony you get a great overview of the inside of the casino. Other parts of the interior recreate a portion of Central Park, Rockefeller Center and the New York Stock Exchange. Another area is designed to look like Greenwich Village, complete with subway station entrances, graffiti and garbage cans. However, there's no foul smell and no one has reported being mugged (except by a slot machine). A cute thing to take notice of are the casino change carts which are made to look like New York City yellow cabs.

PARIS, *just south of the southeast corner of Flamingo Road, adjacent to Bally's. Tel. 702/739-4612. Scheduled to open in September, 1999. Descriptions are based on our own observations of the exterior and information provided by hotel management.*

The newest resident on the fabulous Strip, Paris is also the latest hotel to be themed to a geographic location. Few places can compare with the romantic appeal of "Pah-ree" and it's likely that this appeal will also apply to the reincarnation of the city by the Seine in the desert. Paris was not yet open as we went to press so we can only report on what has been promised, aided by our keen observations of the exterior, which was complete at press time.

What would Paris be without the **Eiffel Tower**? Not the same, of course, so a 50-story high replica stands out front right on The Strip. You can even dine at the tower, just like the real thing – a gourmet French restaurant is located about ten stories up. Or, for a panoramic view that is simply marvelous, take a ride in a glass elevator to the observation deck atop the tower! Other famous Paris landmarks that have been recreated are the Opera House, the Louvre, the Hotel de Ville (Paris' city hall), and the Arc de Triomphe. The attractive hotel tower itself is in the Hotel de Ville style. The replica structures range in scale from about half actual size to about two-thirds. Finally, the exterior sights include a huge, colorful hot air balloon that serves as the hotel's signature marquee. In a city of unusual marquees, this may be the best yet.

The pool area sits amid a two-acre roof-top French garden complete with flower beds and sculpted hedges. This is on top of the casino section. We don't know if it will be open to the public to get a close-up look but, if it isn't, you'll still be able to clearly see it as you ascend the Eiffel Tower. On the inside you'll be able to sample a number of fashionable shops (including authentic French boutiques) as you wander down the quaint cobblestone streets and winding alleyways of Paris' Rue de la Paix district. The large and elaborate casino will feature 40-foot high painted ceilings that emulate a Parisian sky, along with cobblestone walks, ornate street signs and a replica of the Pont Alexander III, a famous picturesque bridge. At this Paris, the bridge will overlook the casino and shopping area as well as serving as the entry way to the Eiffel Tower elevators. Finally, we don't often recommend that you take a look at the meeting facilities, but an exception is in order here. The outer area of the main ballroom is designed in the style of the elaborate Hall of Mirrors at the Palace of Versailles. All in all, sounds like it's going to be a "natural" for Las Vegas.

RIVIERA HOTEL, *opposite Circus Circus at Riviera Avenue. Tel. 702/ 734-5110.*

One of the older hotels on The Strip, the Riviera is nothing to rave about but it does have two things worth looking at. The front section of the building that faces The Strip is a dark green glass wall with huge advertisements for the shows and restaurants found inside. When lit up at night it is one of the more spectacular displays of any Strip hotel. Outside the entrance is a life-size bronze sculpture of the cast of one of the Riviera's shows – *Crazy Girls*. The statue depicts seven half-naked girl dancers (with bikini-bottom) facing toward the wall and duplicates what has become one of the more famous billboard advertisements in town. No one we know finds it objectionable although a few women's groups complained about it because men were touching the girls for good luck. They would prefer to have the statue moved to a place where you can look but don't touch. Whatever your view, it's very Las Vegas!

STRATOSPHERE, *at the intersection of Main Street about two blocks north of Sahara Ave.. Tel. 702/380-7777.*

The 1,149 foot high Stratosphere Tower is not only the tallest structure in Las Vegas but is the biggest free standing tower in the United States. The locals are sharply divided as to whether it's an eyesore or a thing of beauty and grace. We tend to lean towards the latter. The location of the Stratosphere has caused some problems for the giant complex. It is only a few blocks north of where The Strip traditionally ends at Sahara Avenue, but those few blocks make a big difference. Las Vegas Boulevard at this point is not an attractive place when compared with the fabulous four miles south of it. The city is attempting to improve the area with landscaping and by razing some of the run-down buildings. All of that, of course, is a long-term project.

The Stratosphere has a large and attractive casino with all the things you would expect from a Strip operation. But many people just come to take the ride up to the top of the **Stratosphere Tower**. The views from either the indoor or outdoor observation decks or the revolving restaurant are simply spectacular. The nighttime view is absolutely unreal. If you're going up during the day we suggest you make sure it's a clear day so as to maximize what you see. Thrill seekers want much more than just a fast elevator ride and they'll find it, too. The appropriately named **High Roller** is a roller coaster that spins around the pod portion of the tower about a quarter of a mile above the street! You might think that such a setting would make it one of the more hair-raising roller coasters in and of itself but riders say it goes to slow to put it in that category. It sure scares the heck out of us!

Definitely more gut wrenching is the **Big Shot** that shoots fruitcakes – oops, we mean visitors – 160 feet into the air through a metal gantry at the top of the tower before it drops them, free-fall style, back to the launching pad. *The elevator ride to the top of the tower costs $6. The tower elevators and thrill rides operate daily from 10 am to 1 am (until 2 am on Friday and Saturday). The Big Shot costs $6 and the High Roller is $5. Combination passes which offer a discount on the total cost are available.*

More sedate activities at the Stratosphere can be pursued along the **Tower Shops** promenade that leads to the tower elevators. It's a nice shopping area that is separated into areas representing Paris, New York and Hong Kong.

TREASURE ISLAND, *southwest corner of Spring Mountain Road. Tel. 702/894-7111.*

The full name of this marvelous hotel/casino is Treasure Island at the Mirage, because it is owned by Mirage Resorts and is right next door to the hotel of that name. They're even connected by a short tram ride if you don't want to walk. But Treasure Island, themed from the Robert Louis Stevenson novel of the same name, stands well all by itself when compared to any Las Vegas mega-resort. The building itself is a gracefully curved "Y" in soft pastel colors, and boasts a splendid marquee that show's off the hotel's pirate theme.

The Strip side entrance is via a boardwalk that crosses a small artificial lake and goes into the hotel through **Buccaneer Bay Village**. Several colorful "buildings" are on the edge of the bay and look like an authentic Caribbean town of the late 17th century. The 80-foot long *Hispaniola* pirate ship is moored there, while the frigate *HMS Britannia* is docked past "Skull Point" out nearer to The Strip – which brings us to the nightly **Battle of Buccaneer Bay**, perhaps the wildest, most extravagant and popular of Las Vegas' free hotel attractions. The show packs in the crowds almost without fail so you should plan to arrive early in order to get a good spot.

Unlike their neighbor with the volcano, viewing space is somewhat limited. The ten minute show begins with the British warship sailing into Buccaneer Bay where it finds the pirates unloading their treasure. After some humorous dialogue between the staid British captain and the plucky pirate leader, the battle begins. Each side fires cannon at the other; there are explosions on both ships and in the village behind. Flames leap out and spectators can feel the heat as masts tumble. When it looks like the pirates have had it, a lucky salvo at their enemy's magazine sinks the British ship to the delight of the crowd. Stay around for a minute and you'll see its reemergence from the Bay. *Free performances are held every day (weather permitting – no shows when winds are high) beginning at 4:00 pm and then every 90 minutes through 10 pm with an extra show at 11:30 pm on Friday and Saturday nights.*

Now for the interior. Few hotels (except for those that have come about in the last couple of years) are quite so thorough in carrying out their theme as does Treasure Island and the result is truly special. The casino and surrounding areas nicely combine a healthy dose of whimsy with a touch of elegance. You'll notice chests of treasure and plenty of booty scattered all over the place but especially in niches located above the casino. Worth an extra look is the extravagant **Gold Bar** which is almost buried in treasure. **Mutiny Bay** is one of the better arcades on The Strip. Besides the fun and games for kids, adults will appreciate the detail in the Caribbean village setting. We're especially fond of the talking skeletons at the arcade entrance. To the rear of the casino is Treasure Island's small but attractive shopping promenade. Most of the stores flanking the wide concourse have a pirate themed decor as well. Huge figures of the type usually found on the bows of pirate ships jut out from over the store entrances and are colorful as well as extremely detailed.

Here, too, good humor is in abundance in the names of some of the stores – our favorite is *Damsels in Dis Dress*, apparently owned by a pirate from Brooklyn. If you're looking for a good souvenir, T.I.'s gift shops have what may be the cutest hotel mascot teddy bear around – a little pirate teddy complete with eye patch and leather vest.

TROPICANA, *southeast corner of Tropicana Avenue. Tel. 702/739-2222.*

Bring your lucky Hawaiian shirt to the Tropicana. One of the oldest joints on The Strip (its nickname for years was the "Tiffany of The Strip"), the Tropicana is now referred to as "The Island of Las Vegas." While parts of the main casino are beginning to show their age, it remains a lovely place and there are several things that should be seen.

Out in front of the main entrance is a spacious garden. Although it isn't as nice in our opinion as the old Pacific island village that they used to have, it does provide what is definitely the best view in town of New York, New York. Also in this area, near the bridge leading to the Excalibur, is a group of artificial rocks with a nice waterfall. They've recently constructed a small habitat for tigers out front, apparently trying to emulate the success of the one at the Mirage. There are occasionally free animal shows held in this general area so be on the lookout for any posted schedules.

The Tropicana casino's main pit area is still one of the most attractive in the city. We especially like the huge Tiffany glass ceiling over the main table game area but have mixed emotions about the green and red floral carpet design. In the registration lobby just off the main casino is "Cash Mountain," a pyramid constructed of ten million dollars in crisp bills! It's inside a thick glass enclosure so if you have any ideas of getting a sample, forget it. You can try your hand at winning all of it by guessing eight numbers in the proper sequence. If you figure the odds out on that one you'll soon realize that this is something you ain't gonna get your hands on!

The main attraction at the Tropicana is the grounds. They're reached via a raised enclosed walkway formerly called the Wildlife Walk because it housed exotic birds. The birds are now on display outside during daylight hours. Occasional shows are also staged. The aforementioned grounds contain five acres of pools amid lush tropical flora. There is more wildlife on the grounds including flamingos, ducks and several unusual species of birds. It's almost like taking a walk through a zoological park.

Also in this area is the hotel's wedding chapel which looks like a big Polynesian styled hut from the outside. There are good views of the grounds and the towers of adjacent hotels from this vantage point.

Another Tropicana claim to fame is that it is the only place in town where you can gamble from inside a swimming pool. The "swim-up black jack" area has special machines that will even dry out your money!

Speaking of gambling, the Tropicana's latest addition is the fascinating **Casino Legends Hall of Fame**. The collection has 15,000 objects, including casino items, clips of movies about Las Vegas, costumes of performers, photographs and more memorabilia that brings the history of Las Vegas gaming to life. There's even a section on showgirls, naturally, since this is the Tropicana, home of the Follies Bergere! The initial 30 members of the Hall of Fame are saluted. The list includes entertainers, gaming figures, movie personalities and others. (30 more people are scheduled to be inducted in September of 1999. Included in that group will be Elvis.) *Hall of Fame open daily from 8am to 9pm (until midnight on Friday and Saturday) and the cost of admission is $4 for adults. Free passes are often available.*

THE VENETIAN, *just south of Sands Avenue. Tel. 702/733-5000.*

Simply spectacular. We could leave it at that but, since you bought the book, you're entitled to find out why. Las Vegas is unreal in many ways. Paradox after paradox presents itself to the observant visitor and perhaps none is greater than the theme of the Venetian. For the famous city of water has been meticulously recreated in the parched desert. Unlike many other Vegas hotels that have scale replicas of famous buildings, statues, or whatever, the Venetian took a different approach – they went for full scale reproductions. So the **Campanile Tower**, for instance, is the same as the real 315-foot high, golden angel topped architectural masterpiece. In fact, except for the moving walkways leading from the Strip and through the Campanile, you could well think you're in the real Venice. Everywhere are graceful arches, colorful Old World facades, and huge reliefs of the heroic winged Venetian lion.

No one thing dominates the scene as you enter from the Strip, but the graceful **Rialto Bridge** comes close. While the real bridge crosses the Grand Canal, this one spans the main roadway into the hotel. The lagoon along Las Vegas Boulevard (550,000 gallons of water) fronts some of the other notable recreations. These include the fabulous colonnaded **Doge's Palace**, the **Ca D'Oro (Palace of Gold)**, **St. Marks Libary** and the **Bridge of Sighs**. The latter is so called because prisoners had to cross the bridge from the Doge's Palace to get to the New Prison. The hotel, fortunately, doesn't recreate that unpleasant portion of Renaissance Venice. Between the Palace of Gold and the Doge's Palace, an imaginative use of painted walls and indentations of the building gives the appearance of a canal leading far off into the distance from the lagoon. You should also spend a few moments taking careful note of the many statues (no two are alike) and other details that have been carefully researched and recreated with the greatest degree of authenticity possible.

As everyone knows, a replica of St. Mark's Square wouldn't be accurate if it didn't have the famous pigeons. Well, the creators of the Venetian didn't overlook that either. 500 pigeons are released five times a day and take a spin around the bell tower before returning to their coops. These are homing pigeons, not you're usually dirty street variety – which doesn't mean you can't get "dropped" on if you're standing in the wrong place. But, don't worry, that's supposed to be good luck. Sure!

Fabulous, too, are the interior features. So let's go inside. The casino is, of course, the usual dazzling room you would expect from a major Strip hotel. We also love going upstairs to the second level and stepping outside on the balcony that overlooks the lagoon. Even better are the remarkably vivid hand painted frescoes, surrounded by gold moldings, that adorn many of the ceilings in the Venetian's public areas. They are equalled only by those found in the great palaces of Europe. One would have thought that such skills were a lost art but apparently, to our good fortune, can still be done with amazing artistry. The **Gallery**, which connects the hotel's main entrance and registration area with the casino, is the best example of this kind of work. The lobby has a beautiful fountain beneath a domed ceiling, while the Gallery itself is a spacious arched room where you can just stand there and stare almost endlessly at the elegant scene.

But as wonderful as all this is, perhaps the best piece of recreation is the huge **Grand Canal Shoppes**. Highlighting the area is the 1,200 foot long Grand Canal that runs the length of the mall and has its own fleet of working gondolas (and the gondoliers will sing for you). Along either side of the canal are fashionable shops and restaurants. The ceiling recreates the Venetian sky before sunset. Also within this magnificent shopping arcade is a replica of **St. Marks Square**. Those who have been to Venice will immediately recognize it – the recreation is that good. To many onlookers, the colorful Venetian facades and painstaking detail will be enough to make a walk along the Grand Canal a delightful experience. The historian, however, will be pleased to note that several real Venetian neighborhoods are recreated. *Fee basis gondola rides are available during the operating hours of the shopping center.* (Right now, the Grand Canal Shoppes and the Canal itself are only half the size we just described – the second half will commence construction soon.).

Another point of interest in this $1.2 billion dollar mega-resort is a branch of the world famous London-based wax museum, **Madame**

COMING SOON....

One of the constants of Las Vegas is that things never stay the same. No sooner than a hotel or two or three opens up than another is announced and up before you even know it. With the recent completion of Mandalay Bay, Phase I of The Venetian, and Paris, a major Vegas construction explosion was finished. However, there is still some more on the horizon.

The old Aladdin is history but a bigger and better one is rising from the dust on the same site. The new **Aladdin** *will have an elaborate casino done up in an Arabian Nights theme complete with a colorful tent-like ceiling. The original Aladdin did little with their theme beyond the name. The Dessert Passage will be a major shopping center that surrounds the hotel and connects with another hotel. The name of it hasn't been determined yet but it will have a music theme. The Aladdin will be completed in 2000, the other hotel at a future time.*

Mandalay Resort Group intends to complete its "Miracle Mile" with another property to the south of Mandalay Bay. We'll have to wait some time for that one, however. Finally, Mirage Resorts isn't finished with their Strip contributions either. They purchased the Boardwalk Hotel, which certainly doesn't fit in with their mega-resort style. Although nothing has been announced, word is that the Boardwalk is history and that it will be replaced by another super hotel to be linked up with the Bellagio property.

Several other potential projects are currently being bantered about but it's too early to say with any certainty whether any will come to fruition. A San Francisco-themed hotel as well as one based on the Titantic are among this group. Keep watching.

Tussaud's. Approximately half the size of the one in London, the Vegas version occupies two floors of a recreation of the **St. Mark's Library Building**. The museum features approximately a hundred figures in settings appropriate to the depicted person. There is some emphasis on people who've been important to Las Vegas such as Frank Sinatra and Tom Jones, among many others. Although all of this may sound a bit corny or even childish to you, don't dismiss it out of hand. It's a high quality museum done by the best in the business and the result is an entertaining experience. *The wax msueum is open daily from 10:00am until 11:00pm and the adult admission price is a rather hefty $14.*

In a city where using the word "big" to describe the hotels is a gross understatement, the Venetian will also bring new meaning to that word. It will eventually become the world's largest hotel (the approximately 3,000 rooms that it opened with in May 1999 is going to be doubled when a second tower is completed). Each tower will have its own 116,000 square foot casino and the shopping center will be larger than the Forum Shops. How's that for BIG! Do we have any complaints? Just one little one. The hotel's fabulous pool area is located in a place where it cannot be seen by anyone who isn't a hotel guest. Oh, well. You just can't have everything.

OTHER STRIP DIVERSIONS

SHOWCASE, *north of Tropicana Avenue immediately adjacent to the MGM Grand.*

This is one of the more difficult attractions to categorize. On the mundane side are some movie theaters and an **All-Star Cafe** if you get hungry, but everything else about Showcase is unusual. Starting with the colorful facade that includes a multi-story soda bottle and humongous packages of candy, it consists of the following features:

GameWorks: A 45,000 square foot arcade on the lower level where kids (and even more adults) will be in high tech game heaven. It even has it's own restaurant and bar for grown-ups. For a change of pace you can go mountain climbing. Well, sort of. Two artificial rock towers are said to be the tallest indoor climbing mountains in the world. There's no shortage of people attempting the climb but they're outnumbered by the hordes of visitors who come to watch from the street level overlook. *Tel. 702/432-4263. Open daily from 10 am to 4 am. Admission is free but there is a separate charge for each activity.*

World of Coca-Cola: A combination museum and super gift-shop, this attraction traces the history of Coca-Cola and has all sorts of interesting memorabilia. The three story high Coca-Cola bottle that's visible from the street is actually an elevator that leads up to the entrance of the museum. *Tel. 800/720-2653. Hours are daily from 10 am until midnight and the admission is $2 (children 6 and under are admitted free) including free drinks of any Coca-Cola product. No charge for entering the gift shop area.*

M&M's World: What the World of Coca-Cola is to soda, this is to the popular candy. Again you'll find a big gift shop and plenty of colorful and cute exhibits. But the highlight is the *M&M's Academy* where you'll walk through a fantasy tour of how the little candies are made. It's not like a real factory – just a highly imaginative and oversized piece of fun that even the majority of adults will enjoy. A professor conducts you through the M&M "labs" and you'll also see a ten minute movie featuring the misadventures of Red and Yellow (two pieces of candy, of course), in a very effective 3-D mode. *Tel. 702/597-3122. Operating hours are 10 am to midnight. The M&M Academy is open Thursday through Monday from 11 am to 7 pm (until 9 pm on Friday and Saturday). There is a $4 admission charge for the Academy only.* Also on the premises of the M&M's World is an outlet for *Ethel M.*

Chocolates, which is manufactured by the same company. (Tours to their factory in Henderson leave periodically from this location; see the Henderson section for more information on that attraction).

There are a few other attractions on The Strip worth mentioning. The **Don Pablo Cigar Company**, *3205 Las Vegas Blvd. South*, is interesting if you want to see how the pros roll cigars the old fashioned way. The rollers are mostly Cuban and if you've never seen one of these babies being rolled by an expert, you're in for a treat. *Tel. 702/369-1818. Open Monday through Saturday from 9 am to 6 pm and on Sunday from 10 am to 4 pm. Admission is free.*

The **Guiness World of Records**, *2780 Las Vegas Blvd. South*, features both Vegas and real-world feats displayed through mock-ups, life-size dolls, photos, computers and TV screens. See what some people will do to get their name into the record book. *Tel. 702/792-3766. Open daily from 9 am to 6 pm. The admission is $5 for adults, $4 for seniors and $3 for children.*

Finally, the **Magic and Movie Hall of Fame**, *3555 Las Vegas Blvd. South (on the upper level of O'Shea's Casino)*, tells all about magic, the movies and ventriloquism through exhibits and memorabilia. It's mildly interesting if you like this sort of thing (magic, that is). The admission includes a magic show. *Tel. 702/737-1343. Hours of operation are Tuesday through Saturday from 10 am to 6 pm. Admission is a hefty $10 although it's more reasonable if your visit is timed to include the 4:30 pm magic show.*

OFF-STRIP

There are three hotels in the immediate off-Strip area that are worth visiting – The Rio, the Las Vegas Hilton and the Hard Rock Hotel. All have something special in their own way but the Rio is definitely one of Las Vegas' must-sees.

HARD ROCK HOTEL, *Harmon Ave. at Paradise Road, about 3/4 mile east of The Strip. Tel. 702/693-5000.*

You can't miss either the hotel or the adjacent **Hard Rock Cafe** – both can quickly be identified by their giant guitars. In the case of the hotel itself the guitar goes right through the porte cochere. The casino is one of the few in Las Vegas that is round. It's not one of the bigger casinos but it is attractive with its overhead globe (the world of rock, of course) and saxophone shaped chandeliers. Harley Davidson motorcycles and other interesting items dot the casino. Many TV screens are scattered throughout and show music videos.

But the big attraction is the veritable museum of rock and roll that completely surrounds the casino. Here you can see the original gold records, costumes and instruments of more than a dozen famous rockers from the '60's through the '80's. There's also a special Beatles display and a sports memorabilia collection. You may also be interested in knowing that Hard Rock's management donates a portion of the proceeds from slot play to help save tropical rain forests.

LAS VEGAS HILTON, *Paradise Road immediately north of the Las Vegas Convention Center. Tel. 702/732-5111.*

This used to be the largest hotel in the city before the building boom of the late 1980's began. It's still huge. In fact, it is one of the more easily recognizable structures in town as is the big gold colored marquee. The casino is big and elegant but somewhat understated, like in the style of the Desert Inn. The showroom used to play host to Elvis Presley (when the hotel was called the International) and some of his costumes and instruments are on display in a lobby showcase along with a statue paying tribute to him. Also of interest is the Race and Sports Book. Called SuperSports, it is Las Vegas' biggest such operation and looks like it could substitute for NASA Mission Control. Actually, after NASA, it has the largest display of big screen monitors in the world. Late in the evening when sports action is over for the day, those monitors are used to show music videos.

The biggest attraction at the Las Vegas Hilton is **Star Trek: The Experience**. This 40,000 square foot, $70 million dollar extravaganza has Trekkies from all over the world salivating. It's about as close to the "real" thing as you can get. (Even the advertising slogan plays on the great resemblance to the movies and TV shows as they claim "this time, it's real.") The entrance area of the Experience is quite dramatic with its large models of Starfleet ships suspended from a painted ceiling that looks like outer space. The attraction itself consists of several sections but the two main parts are the *History of the Future,* which displays Star Trek memorabilia and the *Voyage Through Space.* The voyage includes an unusually long (22-minute) motion simulator ride. Portions of the "journey" are mild and others are quite a ride. Visitors are "beamed" aboard the USS Enterprise and taken on an adventure through the 24th century. You can get dressed up as a Starfleet officer or as an alien.

Also within the Star Trek attraction area is a recreation of the promenade from *Star Trek: Deep Space Nine.* It houses, among other things, a big gift shop with all sorts of ST merchandise and *Quark's.* The latter is an interesting restaurant and even has a Ferengi wait staff. And if you have to ask what that means you probably won't enjoy your visit. *Tel. 888/462-6535. The Experience is open daily from 11 am until 11 pm. The admission is $15 per person. Senior and Nevada resident discounts are available.* Outside the Star Trek area is the **Spacequest Casino**, a real casino that gives you a possible taste of what gambling will look like in the future. For example, you can activate the slot machines by passing your hand through a light field. Just what the world needs, right?

THE RIO, *Flamingo Road about 3/4 mile west of The Strip. Tel. 702/252-7777.*

Rivaling anything you can see on The Strip, the Rio has been popular since it opened both with visitors and locals alike because it's such a fun place. It has an intangible quality to its atmosphere that is hard to describe but seems apparent to just about every visitor we've taken there. Maybe it's the little things, like Rio Rita, a Carmen Miranda type character who roams through the casino, that make the Rio special. The carnival and tropical theme is most evident in the original part of the casino. The very attractive pool area is also worth taking a stroll through.

The 51 story tower is the highest hotel structure in Las Vegas (if you don't count the Stratosphere) and is clearly visible from The Strip with its blue and red glass facade in geometric patterns. The top floor is the **Voo Doo Lounge** and it offers a panorama of The Strip that we feel is even better than from the Stratosphere because it's closer. Now, the Rio doesn't like to let it be known that you can go up there for the view and not have a drink in the lounge but if it's before 5 pm you can do so without being hassled. Of course, if you want to sip a drink out on the open observation deck, so much the better for you and the hotel. Children are not allowed on the deck at any time since it is considered to be a part of a drinking establishment. (The floor beneath the lounge is a restaurant of the same name and offers the same view from behind glass and children are welcome patrons there.)

The first two levels of the tower are the glitzy and exciting **Masquerade Village**. More than twenty stores and eateries line both sides of each level. In the middle of it all is another casino. Shopping or window-shopping is nice but the real reason to come to Masquerade Village is for the fabulous **Masquerade Village Show in the Sky**. While live entertainment in the form of ornately costumed dancers takes place on a stage in the middle of the casino, performers are circling above the two-story village on exotic "floats" suspended from the ceiling and traveling along a 900-foot track. (For a fee of $10 visitors can get dressed up and join the performers on one or more of the floats). The cast of almost 40 performers are high energy all the way. Few free shows in Vegas can compare. The shows last approximately 15 to 20 minutes including the pre and post-show goings on.

Three similar shows rotate. The themes are different – carnival in Rio, Venetian carnival, and New Orleans – but the floats are the same. Only the costumes and music change. There is also a fourth show which features a '60's rock theme and is more interactive with the spectators. At the end of each show the performers throw colorful beads to people on both levels and managing to secure one seems to be a big priority for lots of visitors. (We have quite a collection at home.) It's terrific fun and attracts big crowds so you should arrive early. The best viewing area is on the upper level on the side of the casino facing the main stage. However, if you've seen one show and are going for another (or if you like to concentrate more on the stage performers than the floats) you can watch from directly in front of the stage on the first level. *Performances are given daily except Wednesday, every two hours from 2 pm until midnight. Except for the aforementioned fourth show (which is given at 4 pm and at 4 and 10 pm on Saturday), the three carnival shows rotate. Admission is free. Children must watch the show from the upper level.*

If you're staying on The Strip and don't have a car you can still get to the Rio without having to take a taxi. Free shuttle service is provided from the corner of The Strip and Harmon Avenue.

Here's the rundown on two off-Strip non-casino/hotel attractions of interest. Most popular in this group is the **Liberace Museum,** *1775 E. Tropicana Ave., about 1-1/2 miles east of The Strip.* This museum gets excellent reviews from just about everyone, including those who weren't particularly fond of Mr. Showmanship himself. The extensive collection includes several of his pianos – one of them a rhinestone-encrusted Baldwin; about a half-dozen of his one-of-a-kind automobiles, stage jewelry and his lavish costumes and furs. Among the latter are a full-length Black Diamond Mink cape and a King Neptune costume that weighs an incredible 200 pounds. The museum also has an excellent gift shop with many musically oriented items. *Tel. 702/798-5595. Hours of operation are daily from 10 am until 5 pm (opens at 1 pm on Sunday). The admission is $7 for adults, $5 for seniors. Children under 12 are free.*

The **Marjorie Barrick Museum of Natural History,** *on the UNLV campus (enter at Harmon and Swenson),* houses a number of exhibits which change from time to time. The permanent collection emphasizes the natural history, archaeology and anthropology of the desert southwest. *Tel. 702/895-3381. Open Monday through Friday from 8 am to 4:45 pm and on Saturdays from 10 am to 2 pm. Admission is free.*

DOWNTOWN

The Downtown hotels are unlike their Strip counterparts in lots of ways, but especially when it comes to their appeal as attractions. Maybe unappeal would be more fitting because there isn't too much to see in these hotels unless you just like to look at casinos. Several, such as Binion's, have an old-time atmosphere and feel to them, which might be of interest to some. **Binion's Horseshoe** has had for many years a display of one million dollars (a hundred $10,000 bills bearing the portrait of Salmon P. Chase) arranged in a horseshoe shaped piece of glass. The 30-plus year tradition of having your picture taken for free in front of all that loot was recently discontinued, but you can still take your own picture since it isn't inside the casino. The **Golden Nugget** displays the *Hand of Faith Nugget*, the largest solid gold nugget on public display in the world. It weighs in at 62 pounds. Try putting that on your ring finger! A number of other sizable specimens are also on display. The Golden Nugget's pool area and casino are the nicest to be found downtown.

Main Street Station, a couple of blocks north of Fremont, is filled with authentic antiques and is second only to the Golden Nugget in the downtown beauty pageant – but it's more interesting. The theme is generally Victorian. The lamp posts out front are from Belgium and date from World War I. There's a lot of stained glass and fine wood paneling all around. Of interest is a small section of graffiti covered stone from the Berlin Wall. Unfortunately, it can't be seen by the ladies since it is housed over one of the urinals in the men's room off the casino. Despite that setback to equal access, both men and women should take some time to stroll around and appreciate all the little art things to be found. You can pick up a brochure which will direct you to and explain 19 different antiques, artifacts and other points of interest.

The majority of Downtown's hotels line up on either side of a four-block stretch of Fremont Street. Besides the hotels there are lots of gift shops and other assorted businesses. But it also is home to one of the most spectacular attractions in town – the **Fremont Street Experience**. The four block long pedestrian only street is covered by a curving white canopy. Each night one of the greatest sound and light shows takes place when more than two million lights are computer synchronized into a show that travels across the canopy accompanied by music from numerous speakers. It's quite a sight to see all the hotel lights of Glitter Gulch go off and leave you in momentary darkness until the Experience begins. At the end the lights come back on and Fremont Street returns to normal – everyone goes back into a hotel to gamble, eat or whatever else you want to. Shows rotate and include the imaginative *Odyssey* but we especially like the *Las Vegas Legends* and *Country Western* performances. *Tel. 702/678-5777. The shows are free of charge and begin on the hour after sunset. If you're staying on The Strip and do not have a car, you can avoid the tedious city bus trip downtown by taking the free Fremont Street Experience shuttle bus. It departs from 3734 Las Vegas Blvd. South, immediately adjacent to the north side of the Boardwalk Hotel & Casino.*

The Fremont Street Experience was downtown's answer to the glamour of The Strip. While it has been helpful, one attraction can't compete with the myriad stars along Las Vegas Boulevard. So, the next step in the downtown revitalization process is now under construction immediately to the east of the Fremont Street canopy. It's called **Neonopolis** and will be a multi-story entertainment center with movie theaters, clubs, restaurants and who knows what else. It's scheduled for completion in 2000, but we all know what "scheduled" means.

Several attractions are located a few blocks north of the Downtown casino center in the vicinity of Cashman Field. First in this group is the **Las Vegas Natural History Museum**, *900 Las Vegas Blvd. North*. This seven year old museum is finally coming into its own as a quality cultural attraction. Exhibits concentrate on the desert Southwest and Nevada. The dinosaur exhibit and live shark are probably the most popular features. *Tel. 702/384-3466. The museum is open daily from 9 am until 4 pm and there is an admission charge of $5 for adults, $4 for senior citizens and $2.50 for children ages 4 through 12.*

The **Lied Discovery Children's Museum**, *833 Las Vegas Blvd. North*, has interactive exhibits and is especially good for youngsters up to the age of 12. *Tel. 702/382-5437. Open daily except Monday from 10 am to 5 pm. The admission is $5 for adults and $4 for children ages 2 through 17.* Finally, the **Old Mormon Fort**, *908 Las Vegas Blvd. North*, contains the oldest surviving building in Nevada. It will give you an idea of what Las Vegas was like when it was first settled by Mormons from Utah in 1855. The fort has been undergoing extensive restoration in recent years and may be subject to temporary closures. *Tel. 702/486-3511 for hours and more information.*

AROUND LAS VEGAS

While there are quite a few casino/hotels around town there's only one that is worth a visit from a sight-seeing point of view. **Sam's Town**, *Boulder Highway at Nellis and Harmon, Tel. 702/456-7777*, is, as the name implies, a western or cowboy themed property that is popular with locals as well as visitors. Of most interest is the beautiful atrium known as **Mystic Falls Park**. Surrounded by the hotel tower and designed to look old, the park borders on several of the hotel's restaurants and shops. Within the park are meandering pathways that take you past small streams and automated animals of all sizes that sure look like the real thing. At night the little lights on the park's many trees give a perennial Christmas appearance.

Also in the atrium is the **Sunset Stampede**, a lively high-tech display of lasers, sound, light and water. *Performances lasting about ten minutes are given daily at 2, 6, 8 and 10 pm and are free of charge.* A last item of interest at Sam's Town occurs each weekend when the atrium area plays host to the **Festival in the Park**. This features the work of local artists and musicians. *Saturday and Sunday from 11 am through 5 pm.*

The remainder of the attractions are scattered all about the valley and your interests will dictate which ones are appropriate for your available time. For a little scenery you might want to get a close up look at **Sunrise**

Mountain on the east side. The natural area that encompasses this distinctive and colorful peak can be reached via Lake Mead Drive (Highway 147). If you continue east on that route, you'll eventually reach the Lake Mead National Recreation Area, which is described in the chapter on excursions.

Carroll Shelby Factory & Museum Tour, *6755 Speedway Blvd. (adjacent to the Las Vegas Motor Speedway.* This interesting tour takes visitors through the manufacturing facility while the museum houses a collection of Shelby's high performance race cars that span more than 35 years. *Tel. 702/643-3000. Free tours are given daily at 11:30 am. You can also arrange tours by appointment.*

Desert Demonstration Gardens, *3701 W. Alta Drive, off of Valley View.* This facility is run by the Las Vegas Valley Water District and was designed to acquaint desert residents with ways to landscape their homes using low-water techniques. Called xeriscaping, you don't have to live in the desert to find this interesting. The displays of desert flora are attractive, too. *Tel. 702/258-3205. Gardens open daily (except holidays) from 8 am until 5 pm and there is no admission fee.*

Gilcrease Bird Sanctuary, *8101 Racel Road.* The sanctuary is home to a large number of game and exotic birds as well as birds of prey. They are all here through the efforts of the Wild Wing Project and are being rehabilitated from injury. *Tel. 702/645-4224. Open 11 am to 3 pm, weather permitting, from Wednesday through Sunday. The admission fee is $3 for adults and $1 for children.*

Jurassic Chinasaur/Chinatown Plaza, *4255 Spring Mountain Road,* The fossil remains of nine dinosaurs are on display. *Tel. 702/221-8448. There is a $5 admission charge for adults, $4 for seniors and $3 for children ages 4 to 12.* Chinatown Plaza houses a number of shops and restaurants where you can experience the Orient. The architecture is Chinese and includes a ceremonial gate.

Las Vegas Art Museum, *9600 W. Sahara Ave.* Yes, there is art in Las Vegas besides what you can find in the Bellagio. This isn't one of the great art museums of the world but it does have a number of interesting works in its permanent collection, including some by Salvador Dali. *Tel. 702/360-8000. Hours of operation are Tuesday through Saturday from 10 am to 5 pm and Sunday from 1 to 5 pm. Admission is $3 for adults, $2 for seniors and a $1 for children.*

Las Vegas Mormon Temple, *827 Temple View Drive (off of the east end of Bonanza Ave.).* Visiting religious shrines may not come to mind to many people planning a trip to Las Vegas, but like all Mormon temples, this one is an architectural work of art surrounded by nicely landscaped grounds. The temple itself is closed to non-Mormons. Excellent views of The Strip and mountain background can be had from this high vantage point in the eastern foothills.

Nevada State Museum, *700 Twin Lakes Drive, in Lorenzi Park*, This museum has exhibits on both the natural and human history of Nevada, with special emphasis on the Las Vegas area. Of special interest is the exhibit which shows what Las Vegas was like in the 1940's – quite a contrast from today! Another exhibit on how animals adapt to the brutal conditions of life in the desert is highly educational. *Tel. 702/486-5205. Open daily from 9 am to 5 pm. There is a $2 admission charge for those over 18 years of age.*

Southern Nevada Zoological Park, *1775 N. Rancho Drive*. While not terribly large, Nevada's only zoo (if you don't count some of the animal collections in some Strip hotels) is a nice place to get some fresh air and see some wildlife. The zoo features a mix of animals from all over the world, with emphasis on the southwest. A petting zoo for children is a good place to take the little ones. *Tel. 702/647-4685. Open daily from 9 am to 5 pm and the admission is $6 for adults and $4 for children ages 2 through 12.*

HENDERSON

The city of Henderson occupies the southern portion of the Las Vegas Valley. More than half of it is surrounded by colorful mountains. The Lake Mead National Recreation Area forms a part of its eastern boundary. Henderson covers a big area (larger than the city of Las Vegas) and stretches for more than 15 miles from east to west.

Getting to Henderson from The Strip is easy. You can take either Flamingo Road or Tropicana Avenue east to I-515 and then go south to Henderson. (From Downtown just hop I-515 south all the way.) From the southern end of The Strip you can drive east on Sunset Road right into Henderson. Alternatively, take I-15 south to I-215. That road is part of the not yet completed Las Vegas Beltway.

Most of the casinos in Henderson are rather small and geared towards locals. However, there are two casino/hotels that you should take a look at if you're in the area. **Sunset Station**, *Sunset Road at Stephanie Street, two blocks west of the intersection of I-515, Tel. 702/547-7777*, is the most elegant of Station Casino's four area properties and would fit well on The Strip. It is designed in Spanish Mediterranean style and features painted ceilings and other attractive features. The focal point is the main table gaming area and its central **Gaudi Bar**. The noted designer has fashioned a multi-colored glass ceiling that looks like waves and has no straight lines in it.

The Reserve, *Lake Mead Drive at I-515, Tel. 702/558-7000*, is the only African safari themed hotel in the Las Vegas Valley. The outside is a rather drab dark brown but is highlighted by colorful murals of wildlife and large

AMERICA'S FASTEST GROWING CITY

What is now **Henderson** *began as a small town called Basic back during World War II. It was built to provide housing for the titanium plant that made the light-weight and durable metal for aircraft. The plant is still there (in a larger industrial park that is actually on a plot of land that isn't part of Henderson but is surrounded by it), but there are few other remnants of the old Basic. A walk down Water Street in the old "downtown" is like a stroll through an earlier period except for the modern City Hall and other public buildings that cover a portion of upper Water Street.*

Henderson had only 6,000 residents back in 1950 and a mere 50,000 as recently as 1988. However, recent growth has been phenomenal. The 1999 population is estimated to be in excess of 160,000 people, surpassing Reno and making Henderson the second largest city in Nevada! There is little sign of any significant slowdown as building continues at a torrid pace. They don't build new houses in Henderson, they build whole neighborhoods at a single time.

In addition to the old Basic area, Henderson has sizable new residential areas on the east side. However, the best known and heaviest populated areas are in the west where the established communities of Green Valley and Whitney Ranch have recently been joined by award-winning master-planned communities like Green Valley Ranch, McDonald Ranch, Seven Hills, Anthem and others.

monkeys up on the towers. Inside is much more colorful, with tusk-framed change booths (the outside marquee is also designed to look like two giant tusks), a brilliant elephant mural behind the registration desk and a bunch of naughty simians who inhabit the appropriately named *Funky Monkey Bar*. Also be sure to see "Congo Jack's" plane wreck. Sometimes Congo Jack himself along with Monsoon Mary can be seen strolling through the casino.

When it comes to non-hotel attractions the best known places in town are collectively referred to as the **Henderson Factory Four**. In close proximity to one another they can be seen in quick succession and make for an interesting little trip. The four are Ethel M. (fine chocolates), Ocean Spray (cranberry juice products), Favorite Brands & Co. (marshmallows) and Ron Lee (porcelain clown fixtures). All can be thoroughly enjoyed by children. If we had to pick ones that are suitable for adults unescorted by little ones we would choose Ethel M. first. The others, except for the marshmallows are, however, all capable of being enjoyed by grown-ups. Admission to all four facilities is free and the three food manufacturers provide free samples. All have gift shops which feature company logo items and more. Ethel M, especially, has a nice selection of gift items.

Ethel M., *2 Cactus Drive (off of the intersection of Sunset Road and Mountain Vista)*. A subsidiary of the folks at M&M's, Ethel M manufacturers more expensive boxed chocolates. The self-guided factory tour leads you past all of the stages in the making of their delicious morsels. Signs and videos explain the process in more detail. There is a nice gift shop that sells all sorts of southwestern items plus a factory store where you can purchase any Ethel M product. Free samples are available. Outside the factory is a beautiful cactus garden with winding paths that lead you past a variety of desert flora. During the Christmas season is an especially good time to visit as the gardens are illuminated with thousands of tiny white lights. *Tel. 702/433-2500. Hours are 8:30 am through 7 pm.*

Ocean Spray's **Cranberry World West**, *1301 American Pacific Way*, features a video on the history of cranberry production as well as on Ocean Spray's worldwide operations. Afterwards you can see a portion of the factory through glass windows. The tour exits through the large gift shop where you can sample a variety of the company's juice products as well as food made with their juices. *Tel. 702/566-7160. Hours are daily except Sunday from 9 am to 5 pm..* **Favorite Brands International**, *1180 Marshmallow Lane, off of American Pacific and Gallagher Way*, follows the same process. You view production from behind glass windows and proceed to the gift shop for more free samples. As you can imagine, kids

DEVELOPMENTS AT LAKE LAS VEGAS

In the northeast corner of Henderson near the Lake Mead National Recreation Area is one of the largest private development projects in the state. **Lake Las Vegas** *is an upscale residential community (lots and new homes are still available) that surrounds an artificial lake that is two miles long and almost a mile across. Mountains surround the community, making it one of the most attractive settings in the Las Vegas Valley. The community will have five separate golf courses, all designed by the famous Jack Nicklaus.*

While the more than 4,000 homes that are ultimately to comprise Lake Las Vegas may not be of particular interest to you, the hotels and the accompanying golf and lake recreation may be. Hyatt is building a world-class resort on the lake's north shore that will be open in December 1999. Grand Bay is another upscale hotel slated for the early new millenium while the project as a whole may eventually have six hotels. There will be gaming but the casinos will be on the small side – nothing like on The Strip. First class shopping will also be included.

and others who love sweets will thoroughly enjoy the initial trio of the Henderson Factory Four. *Tel. 702/564-5400. Hours are daily from 9 am to 5 pm.*

For a change of pace **Ron Lee's World of Clowns**, *330 Carousel Parkway (off of Warm Springs Road west of Gibson),* isn't a food maker. Rather, Ron Lee produces hand made pewter, porcelain, and other fixtures, all with a clown theme. Their workmanship is beautiful and will delight adults as much as children. In addition to the self guiding factory tour that takes you through each phase of the production process, the lobby has on display Mr. Lee's own personal collection of figurines. Many are elaborate works of art. The gift shop, too, has fine specimens that you can look at to your heart's content. They're available for purchase but, be forewarned, the prices are quite high. It's best to visit during the week if you can because the most interesting part of the factory tour is to see the employees painstakingingly at work. There is an old time carousel on the premises that your children will just have to take a ride on. *Tel. 702/434-3920. The operating hours are Monday through Friday from 8 am to 5 pm and Saturday from 9 am to 5 pm. There is a nominal charge for the merry-go-round.*

The **Clark County Heritage Museum**, *1830 Boulder Highway,* is conveniently on the way to Hoover Dam. This museum has exhibits on the Native American inhabitants of the area and then moves on down through the ages to the first settlers. The mining era is then traced before you reach a number of exhibits on Las Vegas since the legalization of casino gambling. Of even greater interest are the outdoor exhibits that have actual houses along "Heritage Street" from portions of Southern Nevada. There's also a recreated ghost town, railroad terminal (complete with 1905 Union Pacific steam engine) and mining equipment. *Tel. 702/455-7955. Hours are daily from 9 am to 4:30pm. The admission charge is $1.50 for adults and $1 for children.*

The **Henderson Bird Preserve**, *3400 Moser Street (off of E. Sunset Rd. & Boulder Highway).* This 147-ace migratory bird stop encompasses an area of wetlands and ponds. Handicapped accessible boardwalks and easy trails cross the entire preserve and there are blinds for viewing the birds. The fall migratory season (October) is the best time to visit. During the summer you should come early to avoid the hottest part of the day. *Tel. 702/565-2063. Hours are daily from 6 am to 3 pm and there is no admission charge.*

Finally, the Green Valley section of Henderson has commissioned many life-size sculptures such as people waiting for a bus, children playing, and so on, that are scattered throughout the area. They're especially concentrated in the area around Sunset Road and Green Valley Parkway. For a listing of all the sculptures and their locations, ask for a brochure available in many Green Valley retail shops.

When you're ready to work your way back to Las Vegas you might consider taking a different route from whence you came. **Horizon Ridge Road** is our suggestion. It curves along near the mountain foothills, providing a good view of both the mountains and some of the many attractive planned communities in Henderson. The road begins at the intersection of Horizon Road and the I-515 highway exit of that name. As you swing around the first turn there is, on clear days, a stunning panorama of the distant Strip and the entire Las Vegas Valley. As the road dips and rises the mountain and city views will keep disappearing and reappearing. Take Horizon Ridge to Eastern and then go north to I-215 which will bring you back to The Strip.

CASINO-ONLY ESTABLISHMENTS

It's almost inevitable that sometime during your trip to Las Vegas when you're walking down The Strip or other part of town, you may get an urge to gamble. If so, you don't have to go into one of the big hotel casinos to part ways with your money. There are lot's of casino-only establishments where you can play. There are more of these casinos than you can throw a pair of dice at, but here are some good casino-only joints:

- *Barley's Casino & Brewing Company, 4500 E. Sunset Road, Henderson*
- *Ellis Island Casino, 4178 Koval Lane (off-Strip)*
- *Eureka Casino, 595 E. Sahara Avenue (off-Strip)*
- *Jerry's Nugget, 1821 Las Vegas Blvd. North, North Las Vegas*
- *Joker's Wild, 920 N. Boulder Highway, Henderson*
- *O'Sheas Casino, 3555 Las Vegas Blvd. South*
- *Sassy Sally's, 32 Fremont Street (Downtown)*
- *Silver City, 3001 Las Vegas Blvd. South*
- *Slots-A-Fun, 2880 Las Vegas Blvd. South*

13. NIGHTLIFE & ENTERTAINMENT

Las Vegas rightfully claims its place as the "capital" of many things, but perhaps nowhere is their leading status more evident than in entertainment. There is so much nightlife on or near The Strip that your biggest problem will be trying to see and do everything you want in the time available. There's surely something for every taste. Glitzy revues with gorgeous showgirls, high-tech production shows, magic and the biggest celebrities in show biz are only the start. There are also sophisticated nightclubs, western dance halls and wild strip joints. Throw in comedy improv clubs and countless hotel lounges for good measure and you get the idea.

Show-going is a big part of a trip to Las Vegas for millions of visitors so it should come as no surprise that getting into the show of your choice isn't always an easy thing to do. If possible, try and purchase your tickets for the most popular shows before your arrival. Unfortunaely, this isn't always possible to do because some shows only sell tickets three days to a week in advance. On the other hand, many shows have advance sales of six months or even more. Be prepared to pay dearly for some of the better known acts. Prices typically start at around $35 but do go up to $100. Big name celebrities will often garner even higher prices. Alas, entertainment isn't as cheap as it used to be in Las Vegas but comparable shows elsewhere would still likely cost you a whole lot more.

The last several years have seen several trends in showroom policies that are better for the visitor. First of all, almost all showrooms have pre-assigned seating. Not only do you know where you're going to sit before you enter the room, but you no longer have to give a bribe – er, excuse us – a tip to an unfriendly maitre'd in order to be assured a good seat. There are almost no dinner shows left anymore and that's good because the small tables and so-so food weren't a great dining experience. Even cocktail service has changed quite a bit. While table service is still available in a number of showrooms, the trend is to have a self-service bar just outside the theater. One of the reasons for this is due to another trend: the replacement of nightclub style table seating with theater style seats. The result is that you're less crowded in, don't have to cram your neck to see the stage and generally have a more comfortable place to watch the show.

In addition to the "dark" night or nights that most shows have, we want to reiterate that many of the larger shows close up shop during traditionally slow periods. The two biggest entertainment "gaps" are during the November Comdex convention and from early December to just before the holiday season gets in full swing. If shows are an important part of your Las Vegas plans, you may want to think twice before arranging your trip during one of those periods.

Read each show description carefully to determine exactly what's included in the price. Also, shows can change quite suddenly. A show that was supposed to be "indefinite" can often have a definite departure if patronage falls below expected levels.

PRODUCTION SHOWS

Twenty years ago if you asked for the definition of a production show it would simply have been the traditional Las Vegas revue – showgirls, feathers, brilliant costumes, colorful sets and lavish entertainment. That still exists but this high-tech world has spawned shows that are minus (or mostly minus) the showgirls and related specialty acts. Big magic shows and shows heavy with acrobatic performances are also included in this major category.

AMERICAN SUPERSTARS (Stratosphere). While *Legends in Concert* is considered to be "the" celebrity impersonator show, American Super-stars has become a worthy rival. It started as a lounge show and has been considerably upgraded in the past few years The talented and energetic performers do rock, country and pop performers with incredible realism. The dances are also quite good. This may well be one of the better entertainment values on The Strip. *$23 for adults, $17 for children ages 5 through 12 plus tax. Nightly except Thursday at 7 and 10 pm. No one under age 5 admitted. Tel. 702/380-7711.*

AN EVENING AT LA CAGE (Riviera). This show has been around for more than ten years so it must be good. Well, it is, if you like female impersonators. The star of the show is Frank Marino, who is excellent. He does a Joan Rivers that's better than the real thing. The supporting cast is also good. We do want to emphasize that despite the nature of the performers, the audience is definitely mainstream, so you don't have to feel embarrassed about showing up. *$22 and up plus tax and tip. Nightly* *except Tuesday at 7:30 and 9:30 pm. Additional 11:15 pm show on Wednesday and Saturday. No one under age 18 admitted. Tel. 702/794-9433.*

THE BEST OF THE FOLIES BERGERE...SEXIER THAN EVER (Tropicana). A long name for a show so just call it the *Folies Bergere* like everyone else does. This show opened in 1959 and has the distinction of being the oldest show on The Strip (or anywhere in Las Vegas for that matter). This version takes the most popular acts from over the years, including the famous "Can-Can" number, and combines them in a fast paced tempo that improves on more recent editions. The costumes and sets are excellent (lots of feathers) but not as elaborate as in "Jubilee," and the action isn't as exciting (save for the aforementioned Can-Can) as, say, "Enter the Night." It lacks the technical wizzardry of other shows and the Tiffany Showroom is revealing its age. Despite all of these shortcomings, it is the most traditional of all Vegas revues, and that alone makes it worthwhile. So do the gorgeous showgirls! *$50-60 including tax. Nightly except Thursday at 8 and 10:30 pm. No one under age 21 admitted. Tel. 702/739-2411.*

NIGHT MADNESS (San Remo). This is a small and intimate theater – quite a contrast with the big showrooms. The advantage is that you're up close and personal with the performers. A new show, it features a talented cast and continues the San Remo's tradition of adult-oriented musical entertainment. None have been that successful. However, for the budget-minded individual who doesn't have unrealistic expectations, it's fine. *$25 including two drinks plus tax and tip. Nightly except Sunday at 7:30 and 9:30 pm. No one under age 18 admitted. Tel. 702/597-6028.*

CHICAGO (Manadaly Bay). A revival of the award winning Broadway show by Bob Fosse, a talented cast of 17 singers and dancers (including Chita Rivera and Ben Vereen) brings great energy to the production and, if you like Broadway style entertainment, makes for a good choice. It's certainly not your ordinary Strip production show. On the other hand, Broadway style entertainment has not been a rousing success when transferred to Las Vegas hotels. Then again, Steve Wynn says that shows like this are going to become a regular feature of the Las Vegas entertainment scene. Time will tell, but the dark and subdued mood of *Chicago* might not be in keeping with the upbeat style that seems to be favored by visitors to Las Vegas . While most Vegas shows run about 90 minutes, so you can make tracks back to the gaming tables, Chicago runs 2-1/4 hours including an intermission. So, the price is certainly right – a whole lot cheaper then seeing it on Broadway.

The show debuted with the March 1999 opening of Mandalay Bay and as, we went to press, it was too early to tell if it's going to be a success that starts a new trend in Vegas showrooms, or a big flop. How long a run it will have is anyone's guess (even hotel management doesn't believe it will be a permanent fixture). However, it is Mandalay Bay's intention to replace it when the appropriate time comes with another Broadway play. The 1,800 seat theater is attractive and comfortable. *$55-75. Shows at 7:30pm on Tuesday, Thursday, Friday and Sunday; and at 7:00 and 10:30pm on Wednesday and Saturday. Tel. 702/632-7580.*

CRAZY GIRLS (Riviera). The Strip's most topless revue. It's a good tease for the guys although we think most women will be kind of bored. The dancers aren't as talented as those in the main shows but, then again, most of the male audience doesn't seem to care. If you compare this show to a traditional Las Vegas revue, it definitely doesn't match up. If, on the other hand, you take it for what it is – a good natured jiggle show – then you can have an entertaining evening for little cost. *$19 and up including two drinks plus tax and tip. Nightly except Monday at 8:30 and 10:30 pm and additional midnight show on Saturday. No one under age 18 admitted. Tel. 702/794-9433.*

EFX (MGM Grand). The biggest and most technically oriented of the new style Las Vegas production shows, EFX dazzles the audience with its sets and costumes, but especially the wonderful special effects. The cast of 72 fills a tremendous stage in this huge 1,600 seat theater with an array of dance numbers. It's entertainment that is well suited to all ages. The demanding nature of the starring role has taken its effect – first Michael Crawford, then David Cassidy. The show now stars the long-legged Tommy Tune of Broadway fame. He's definitely a talented performer, but EFX continues to prove to us that the production is bigger than whoever the leading man is. The H.G. Wells "Time Machine" sequence is the show's highlight and compares favorably with any show in town. The rest of the show is good but doesn't quite live up to the hotel's promotional claim that to miss EFX is to "miss Las Vegas." *$52-72; $37 for children ages 5-12. All prices include tax. Tuesday through Saturday evenings at 7:30 and 10:30 pm. No one under age 5 admitted. Tel. 702/891-7777.*

ENTER THE NIGHT (Stardust) This show plays in a relatively small, old style showroom with tables and chairs. Although we definitely like regular theater seats better in general, there is something nice about the old arrangement for Enter the Night. That's probably because of the extensive use of runways that go through the audience and bring everyone close to the action. A combination of the old time Las Vegas revue with a generous sprinkling of modernism and even some surrealism, this show is a lively and colorful production that is highly entertaining at a much lower cost than many other Strip productions. The late show has quite a bit of topless acts with great looking dancers and showgirls. Excellent is the word to describe some of the specialty acts – particularly the ice skaters and the wacky Argentinian gauchos. The latter have been entertaining Vegas audiences for many years. *$30 including two drinks plus tax and tip.*

Sunday and Monday at 8 pm; Tuesday through Thursday and Saturday at 7:30 and 10:30 pm. All 7:30 performances are family shows (age 6 and up); all others no one under 21 admitted. Tel. 702/732-6325.

GREAT RADIO CITY SPECTACULAR (Flamingo Hilton). It's been rumored time and again that this show is on the way out. Perhaps it should be since the biggest audience for it seems to be Asian tour groups. We think the problem is basically this – the Rockettes are good, but they do pale in comparison to the more acrobatic achievements of other Las Vegas dancers. This show rotates a celebrity star such as Susan Anton, Paige O'Hara and others. They usually don't help much. *$52.50 for 7:45 pm dinner show and $42.50 for 10:30 pm cocktail show. Both include tax and tip. Nightly except Friday. No one under age 5 admitted. Tel. 702/733-3333.*

IMAGINE, A THEATRICAL ODYSSEY (Luxor). One of a new breed of spectacular Las Vegas production shows that's quite hard to describe. It has a loose theme that ties together numerous acts that showcase excellent dancing, acrobats and even some magic. In that sense it does take some features of other shows such as *Mystere, EFX* and maybe even a little from Siegfried and Roy. That's a negative to some people because they claim it isn't original. Maybe not, but unless you plan to see all of the same type shows in a single trip, that shouldn't present any problem. The performers are all excellent and this is a most enjoyable theatrical experience. In addition, the Luxor Theater is second to none in Las Vegas or anywhere else for that matter. It carries Luxor's ancient Egyptian theme to new and spectacular heights. This may sound ridiculous to some, but the theater itself is almost worth the price of the show. *$40 including tax. Nightly except Thursday at 7:30 and 10 pm. Tel. 702/262-4400.*

JUBILEE! (Bally's). The city's biggest traditional revue, *Jubilee!* features the largest cast, the most elaborate costumes, and greatest sets of any show. A couple of acts stand out in particular for their overwhelming beauty and artistry. These are the destruction of Delilah's temple by a revengeful Samson and the sinking of the Titanic. Just for the record, this show has been putting the famous liner into a watery grave each night long before the current Titanic craze. For feathers and costumes, beautiful long-legged showgirls, and top notch dancers, *Jubilee!* has never had an equal and probably never will. *$50-66 including tax. Nightly except Friday at 8 pm; also at 11 pm on Thursday and Saturday. No one under 18 admitted. Tel. 702/967-4567.*

LANCE BURTON: MASTER MAGICIAN (Monte Carlo). Wholesome family entertainment is the best way to characterize this show. Mr. Burton is definitely one of the most accomplished magicians in the world, so anyone who likes magic is sure to thoroughly enjoy this show. If you're not a real enthusiast of this kind of art, you should still leave the theater with a smile on your face. That's because Burton is an entertainer who is very at home interacting with the audience. A supporting cast of six female dancers are pleasing to the eye and helps keeps things moving along at a nice pace. The star gets a break to allow some time for a comic juggler who is also quite good. *$35-40 including tax. Tuesday through Saturday evenings at 7:30 and 10:30 pm. Tel. 702/730-7000.*

LEGENDS IN CONCERT (Imperial Palace). This was the original celebrity impersonator show. When it opened it was supposed to run for six weeks. Instead, it has been around for more than ten years, has spawned offspring in other cities as well as numerous imitators. It is, however, still the best of its genre. In most cases you'll be hard-pressed to tell the impersonator from the real thing. The band is one of the best in town and special kudos also go to their dance team which definitely enlivens the proceedings. Recently, the costumes have gotten a whole lot better as well. The celebrity line-up changes from night to night but a typical evening could well be a cast of Gloria Estefan, Rod Stewart, Diana Ross, Garth Brooks, the Four Tops and, of course, Elvis. *$35 including tax, tip and two drinks; $20 for children under age 12. Nightly at 7:30 and 10:30 pm. Tel. 702/794-3261.*

MICHAEL FLATLEY'S LORD OF THE DANCE (New York, New York). Replacing the awful *Madhattan* that flopped in the same show-room, this *Lord of the Dance* doesn't star Michael Flatly. It just uses his name. The cast of 40 dancers accompanied by several musicians is talented and energetic, but unless you are stimulated by the thought of ninety minutes of Celtic dancing, it can become rather tedious after the first third. *$50, except $60 on weekends, both including tax. Shows 7:30 and 10:30 pm on Tuesday, Wednesday and Saturday; 9 pm only on Thursday and Friday. Tel. 702/740-6815.*

MYSTERE (Treasure Island). The first and still best of the "new-age" surreal production shows, *Mystere* is a delightful time for audiences of all ages. The effects and costumes are all wonderful and some of the acrobatic performances border on the unbelievable. To make things even better, *Mystere* has something that most shows of its type lack – a true sense of humor and comic relief. Staged in an excellent theater that was specially designed for this show, it is something that you will always remember, even if you have a difficult time in describing what you saw. We can best summarize it by saying that it is one part circus, one part Las Vegas production show, and one part sheer imagination. The sum of it all is possibly the best evening of theater entertainment you'll ever likely to experience. This is a hot show and tickets are sometimes difficult to get. *$64 plus tax. Wednesday through Sunday evenings at 7:30 and 10:30 pm. Tel. 702/894-7722.*

"O" (Bellagio). A short name for a big show. And an unusal name as well. "O" is the pronunciation of the French word *eau*, which means water. And water is at the heart of this $92 million dollar production extravaganza created by the always imaginative folks at Cirque du Soleil. The stage is often covered by a movable platform but is essentially a lake that reaches a depth of up to 25 feet and contains 1.5 million gallons of water. Designed to be a sort of tribute to the theater, "O" is more than a waterborne version of Cirque's fabulous *Mystere* that was just described above, although it does have the surreal atmosphere, acrobats and other things common to their shows. This is a fast paced ten act show with a talented and active cast of 74 in colorful costumes that is sure to please viewers of all ages. The magnificent three-tiered theater holds 1,800 people and, with it's brilliant oval shaped domed ceiling, is only one of a small number of casino/hotel showrooms that can compete on looks with the theater at the Luxor. It has some of the feel of a gracious European opera house. *$90-100 including tax. Friday through Tuesday evenings at 7:30 and 11 pm. Tel. 702/693-7722.*

SIEGFRIED & ROY (The Mirage). The masters of the disappearing white tiger have been doing their thing at the Theater Mirage since 1990. Long considered by many as the "best" show in town and as the one "must see," we don't think it quite meets those standards. An excellent show to be sure, Siegfried & Roy, doesn't quite justify it's place as the second most expensive show (after "O") in town. There are several others that are better. The magical gifts of the German dynamic duo are not in question, nor is their ability to communicate well with the audience. They are indeed master showmen who have earned an almost legendary place in the annals of Las Vegas showdom. It is far more than a magic show as all of their work is either accompanied by or sandwiched in between rather lavish production numbers featuring a large supporting cast. You may be a little disappointed that the famous white tigers play such a small role in the show. A few new major acts have recently been introduced, so if you saw this show in the past, you might consider an encore visit. *$90 including tax, tip and two drinks. Friday through Tuesday evenings at 7:30 and 11 pm. No one under age 5 admitted. Tel. 702/792-7777.*

SPELLBOUND (Harrah's). This is first rate magic for those who like that sort of thing and it isn't cluttered by production show ornamentation. That is, depending upon you opinion of magic, either very good or very bad. . *$35 plus tax. Nightly except Sunday at 7:30 and 10 pm. No one under age 5 admitted. Tel. 702/369-5222.*

SPLASH (Riviera). This show has consistently been quite popular among visitors to Las Vegas. Locals (and especially the critics) tend to pan it as the worst thing to hit The Strip. The truth lies somewhere in the middle. It's a revue set largely to water and features a 20,000 gallon tank for several of its numbers. Those who claim it's outdated should think twice when they praise the watery aspects of "O" – after all, Splash, in a way, did it first. The male dancers are handsome, the female dancers beautiful and well endowed, and the costumes are good – all necessary ingredients for a successful revue. On the other hand, there's nothing to fill you with awe and you may well leave with the mixed emotions we have. *$40-50 plus tax. Nightly at 7:30 and 10:30 pm. The early performance is the family show; no one under 18 for the late show. Tel. 702/597-5970.*

TOURNAMENT OF KINGS (Excalibur). Up until February of 1999 this show was known as King Arthur's Tournament. It was renamed and revamped because, although quite successful, the theory in Las Vegas is that if you keep things the same for too long, you die. The basic concept is the same as it has been for years. Guests sit around a medieval style arena and cheer on their own knight in shining armor in this elaborately staged feast of chivalry and jousting. It's a natural for children but we've seen plenty of adults get really caught up in the fun and action. The latest version encourages even more audience participation and has been further enhanced by completely new (and more elaborate) castle set and colorful costumes. The finale depicts a corronation in a cathedral set and is definitely a great conclusion to the evening's festivities. Oh, yes, the food isn't anything special but you get to eat it medieval style – no utensils. It brings new meaning to "finger lickin' good." *$34.95 for a dinner show plus tax. Nightly at 6 and 8:30 pm. Tel. 702/597-7600.*

LOUNGE ACTS & OTHER SHOWS

The "lounge" show is a Las Vegas fixture that goes back to the town's earliest days as a casino mecca. Almost all of the major hotels have a lounge show in addition to their main showroom. Lounges are much smaller than the showrooms, often only containing less than a hundred seats, although some can fit in several hundred. There is generally no admission charge to a lounge show but there is a cover charge, usually in the form of a two-drink minimum, so this can be a cheap way to take in some entertainment.

Lounges are located in or off the casino and in almost all cases you can see the goings on in the casino from them – a reminder to come out and gamble. Some lounge acts stay around indefinitely while others are only booked for a short time. Because of that, it is always best to check current magazine or newspaper listings to see who is appearing (although, more often than not, it isn't likely that you will have heard of the performer). In a lounge act you'll usually see a singer (or singing group) backed by live musicians although other forms of entertainment can also be featured. You'll also find that quite a few hotels have, in addition to one or more lounges with entertainment, a piano bar.

The following shows aren't easy to fit in any particular category so we'll put them in with the lounge shows for lack of a better place.

CAESARS MAGICAL EMPIRE (Caesars Palace). Guests are escorted into one of two small and beautiful dining chambers for a complete meal along with their own personal "wizard" who performs feats of magic close up. Other aspects of an eving at the Magical Empire include more magic in a larger theater (combining diners from both rooms and others waiting their turn to eat; and a get together in the beautiful rotunda where more weird happenings take place amid special effects with fire (as in the free "luminaria" show described in the *Seeing the Sights* chapter). It's an enjoyable evening that hasn't met with a great deal of positive public response. Perhaps it's the price – you could see Lance Burton and have a decent dinner for quite a bit less money. *$75; discounts available for off-peak dining. Open Friday through Tuesday evenings beginning at 4:30 pm. Tel. 702/731-7333.*

CLINT HOLMES (Golden Nugget). While the late show at this hotel is geared for the grown-up set (see "Hot Stuff" below), this is a family style show. It's a pleasant enough evening and Mr. Holmes has considerable talent but it just doesn't do much for us. *$40 plus tax. Show at 8:00pm Monday, Tuesday, Thursday and Friday; and 7:30 and 10:00pm on Saturday and Sunday. Tel. 702/386-8100.*

THE DREAM KING (Holiday In Boardwalk). Las Vegas has more Elvis impersonators than any other place in the world. Sometimes you'll think you are walking around Graceland rather than down The Strip. Be that as it may, Trent Carlini does a credible job as the "Dream King" and if you like Elvis then you most certainly will enjoy this little no frills show. *$20 plus tax. Nightly except Monday at 8:30 pm. Tel. 702/730-3194.*

FOREVER PLAID (Flamingo Hilton). This has become a big hit at Bugsy's Celebrity Theater. Both critics and show goers seem to really like it. We mention this only because we aren't able to share the same enthusiasm of this tale of four 1950's nerds called "The Plaids" trying to make it big in the music world. It's a schmaltzy story with equally schmaltzy music but we have to admit the talented cast does pull off a fairly enjoyable evening, especially for the price. *$20 plus tax. Nightly except Monday at 7:30 and 10 pm. No one under age 5 admitted. Tel. 702/733-3333.*

HOT STUFF (Golden Nugget). This hotel just can't seem to find a show that has staying power. After the ill-fated *History of Sex*, they're trying another "adult" variety show. The adult aspect is, to say the least, on the milder side but some women may find it a little too much like a strip club. In fact, the intention is to make this show a throwback to the 1960's when some of the Strip hotels had this sort of entertainment. So, if you like the entertainment found in a "gentlemen's club" (although the quality of the dancing, as well as other acts, is better here), but don't wish to be seen in those sort of places, this is a respectable way to see a respectably good show. *$30 plus tax. Showtime is 11:00pm on Monday, Tuesday, Thursday and Friday; and midnight on Saturday. No one under age 21 admitted. Tel. 702/386-8100.*

HURRAY AMERICA (Westward Ho). A pleasant if short (about 60 minutes) musical-comedy revue with a cast that trys real hard; maybe a bit too hard. Our biggest objection (especially considering the bargain prices) is the showroom. It's actually a converted meeting hall and so the table arrangement isn't conducive to watching the stage, especially if you're not right up front. Two-for ones, discounts, and even free tickets are often available so this is a good bet for the bargain entertainment seeker. This show has been running for a long time but there are rumors that it is soon to be on the way out. *$13 plus tax. Nightly except Wednesday and Saturday at 7 pm. No one under 21 admitted. Tel. 702/731-2900.*

KENNY KERR'S BOYLESQUE (Jackie Gaughan's Plaza). Relocated from the Debbie Reynolds Hotel when that property started having an identity crisis prior to its eventual sale. Kenny Kerr is an old hand at the Las Vegas female impersonator trade. He's funny and talented and backed by a good supporting cast. Like most of the other shows in this genre, if you don't have an objection to it on some grounds, it can be a relatively inexpensive way to see an enjoyable show. *$24 plus tax, includes one drink. Tuesday through Saturday evenings at 8 and 10 pm. No one under 21 admitted. Tel. 702/386-2444.*

Lounge Acts "Plus"

In addition to the above "miscellaneous" shows, there are a couple of new miscellaneous facilities – sort of a cross between the lounge show and the bigger ones. The first is the **RioBamba Cabaret** in the Rio Hotel. This place only opened its doors at the end of 1998 so we don't have a big track record of the types of entertainment you'll see. The first act was a crooner in the Frank Sinatra mold. It appears that the policy will be two shows nightly and will run you about $20 bucks including tax, tip and two drinks. The **Luxor Live Theater** used to be a part of their ancient Egyptian "trilogy" attraction, but the part housed in this nice theater was never very popular. They've now installed various evening shows and, like the RioBamba, it's still to new to definitely characterize. Ticket prices will run around $25. The initial show starred a good singing impersonator.

Finally, **Hawaiian Hot! Luau & Polynesian Revue** in the Imperial Palace Hotel is an entertaining dinner and show that is conducted poolside (weather permitting) from spring through early fall. The "Drums of the Islands" show may not be as good as the better ones in Hawaii, but if you've never been to the islands, this is a good second place. Island lei greetings, hula lessons, sing-alongs, and a generally good time for one and all. It's quite popular, so get there early for a good seat. *$28 including buffet dinner. Tuesday and Thursday evenings. Doors open around 6 pm but inquire as to exact time when making reservations. Tel. 702/794-3261.*

CELEBRITY ENTERTAINMENT

You have to scan the newspapers or events magazines (as well as hotel marquees) to find out who is in town when you're there. If you like to plan your trip around celebrity entertainers then contact the Convention and Visitors Bureau for a schedule. Most name entertainment is scheduled several months in advance. You can also call the major hotels that feature celebrities to find out who is going to be in town when you are coming to visit.

Caesars Palace, the **Desert Inn, Mandalay Bay** (in the arena and House of Blues), **MGM Grand** (Hollywood Theater and Grand Garden Arena), **Sahara**, and **The Venetian** are the important Strip hotels that regularly schedule name entertainment. We didn't forget Bally's – they have closed their celebrity showroom to make way for a passage to the new Paris hotel next door. However, they do have celebrities on some nights when their production show is dark. Quite a few hotels with long-standing production shows, such as **The Mirage**, also schedule name entertainment when their resident show is off on vacation. Off-Strip hotels also often have celebrity entertainment. Among the places you can count on seeing some stars in this category are the **Orleans** and **Arizona Charlies.** *The Joint*, at the **Hard Rock Hotel** is a major venue for rock performers.

Of all the venues just mentioned, the **House of Blues** is the most unusual. Featuring decor that can only be described as outrageous, the facility is a mixture of theater and nightclub and is ideally suited to all types of audiences. The more sedate concert-goer can sit in the upper level in comfortable theater style seating. Those who never bother to sit during a performance can choose downstairs where there aren't any seats to get in the way – the pit-like floor fronts the stage and has plenty of room to move about to the beat of the music. Railings provide some support and help to keep the crowd organized.

DANNY GANS (Rio). Mr. Gans has become a celebrity through his Las Vegas career, several times having been named Entertainer of the Year. Danny-boy is extremely talented but, in our opinion, the show is good but not worthy of any special honors. Although he can project an incredible number of voices, he attempts to try to cover too many different people and the show loses some focus.

We strongly believe that, considering the lack of big production values, it's quite overpriced. Not that this is any fault of Mr. Gans. In fact, he has consistently complained to the Rio about the constant price increases and has refused to take a salary increase. Because of this dispute it is almost a sure thing that he will leave the Rio upon the expiration of his contract at the end of 1999. Talk about town is that several Strip hotels will be glad to provide employment for him, so you can expect to see Danny carrying on somewhere in Las Vegas whenever you get here. *$99 including tax and two drinks. Wednesday through Sunday evenings at 7:30 pm. No one under age 6 admitted. Tel. 702/252-7776.*

AFTERNOON DELIGHTS

While Las Vegas' reputaion as a night town is nowhere more in evidence than in entertainment, there are a few shows that have found a home during the daylight. These are low cost, low-tech shows with small casts and not a lot of staging. But, then again, if you don't have enough money in your budget for the big shows, a matinee performance may be the way to go. If your expectations are reasonable, there's no reason why you shouldn't enjoy them. Daytime shows seem to come and go even quicker than some of their sister night acts, but here are a few that are likely to be around:

The Illusionary Magic of Rick Thomas (Tropicana): A low-tech and low-keyed Siegfried & Roy genre show, complete with white tiger. Need we say more? $16-21. Daily except Friday at 2 and 4 pm. Tel. 702/739-2411.

Viva Las Vegas (Stratosphere): This show traces its origins all the way back to the now imploded Sands and is the longest running daytime show in town. Don't expect Jubilee!, but on the other hand it's good fun for the price and the hard working cast is quite good. $10 plus tax (discount tickets readily available). Daily except Sunday at 2 and 4 pm. No one under 5 admitted. Tel. 702/380-7777.

Comedy Magic (Maxim): Simply a daytime version of the evening comedy clubs. $8-12 plus tax and tip. Daily except Sunday at 1 and 3 pm. Tel. 702/731-4300.

NIGHTCLUBS & DANCE HALLS

THE BEACH, *365 Convention Center Drive, Tel. 702/731-1925. Nightly.*
Dancing all the time; semi-name live entertainment. Also known as a big pick-up place with a tougher reputation than in the hotels.

CLEOPATRA'S BARGE (Caesars Palace), *Tel. 702/731-7110. Nightly.*
Live music and dancing. This place specializes in keeping people entertained during the wee hours. Classy setting on a modern day version of the Nile queen's pleasure barge. It actually floats!

CLUB RIO (The Rio Hotel), *Tel. 702/252-7977. Wednesday through Saturday.*

This 900 person capacity room led to numerous other dance clubs being established in some of the big hotels. This is, however, still among the best. It certainly is popular. DJ, boogie nights, some top 40 acts and almost anything else you can think of.

DYLAN'S DANCE HALL, *4660 Bouldler Highway, Tel. 702/451-4006. Thursday through Saturday.*

A combo western and rock place. Good fun. Lots of locals.

NAUGHTY LADIES SALOON (Arizona Charlies), *Tel. 702/258-5200. Nightly.*

Live entertainment and dancing.

THE NIGHTCLUB (Las Vegas Hilton), *Tel. 702/732-5422.*

One of the more elaborate major hotel clubs, this one often has some fairly big names performing. Full choreographed shows.

RA (Luxor), *Tel. 702/730-5900. Wednesday through Saturday.*

Along with Studio 54 (see below), truly one of the exquisite "in places" for the "beautiful people." Trendy with semi-big to big name rock entertainment. The decor is the wildest ancient Egyptian you could imagine. It starts at the main entrance where you're greeted by two golden (and topless) statues of trident-wielding wild ancient Egyptian women. However, the high boots and platform heels adds a definite touch of modernity. The blue lit entryway is flanked by eight statues of Egyptian gods complete with human bodies and animal heads. Upon entry you're overwhelmed by a huge winged statue of Ra, the Egyptian sun god. The 900-person capacity club is covered with silver walls and features, high tech lighting, dramatic sound, laser lights and other special effects, and even several caged dancers. This is most definitely much more than simply a place to go dancing. Dress code.

ROCKABILLY'S, *3785 Boulder Highway, Tel. 702/641-5800. Nightly except Sunday.*

Country western dancin' and bronco bustin'. Bring your chewing tobacco.

STUDIO 54 (MGM Grand), *Tel. 702/891-7254.*

A '90s reincarnation of the famous late 70's pop culture club in New York that started it all. It's just as picky about what you wear and who'll they'll let in. If you're the type that wants to "be seen," then this is the place. Some big name entertainment appears here. The place definitely rocks. The three story club features state-of-the-art sound and lighting, four separate dance floors, four bars, private clubs, and a gallery of celebrity photographs taken at the original Studio 54.

UNDERGROUND NIGHTCLUB (Hard Rock Hotel), *Tel. 702/693-5066.* This new (May 1999) 8,000 square foot high-tech facility is designed to compete with Studio 54 and Ra. We're sure, given Hard Rock's popularity with the in-crowd, that is will be among the most popular night spots in town.

UTOPIA, *3765 Las Vegas Blvd. South. Tel. 702/740-4646.* Wednesday through Sunday. One of the real hot spots on The Strip. More casual than Ra or Studio 54 but still sophisticated. Great rock music.

VOODOO CAFE & LOUNGE (The Rio Hotel), *Tel. 252-7777.* Nightly. Good bands and good fun in addition to an unforgettable nighttime view of The Strip. Definitely stays with the tradition of the Rio as a place to go to have a good time.

WESTERN DANCE HALL (Sam's Town), *702/456-7777.* Nightly. One of the most popular dance places in town with the local cowboys and cowgirls. DJ on most nights but live entertainment from Thursday through Saturday. During the early evening hours the joint offers free dancing lessons (uh, oh guys – there goes your excuse not to go dancing).

Several "local" casino/hotels also have nightclubs that aren't as well known as the ones just listed. Palace Station **(Trax)** and Boulder Station **(Railhead Junction)** are in that category.

In addition to the above venues, microbreweries are a popular place to pass some time during the evening when in Las Vegas. The Monte Carlo Hotel was the first of The Strip resorts to have one. While that hasn't set a big trend, there are plenty of other of these pubs around. These include the **Holy Cow!**, *2423 Las Vegas Blvd. South, Tel. 702/732-2697;* **Gordon Biersch Brewery**, *3987 Paradise Road, Tel. 702/312-5247;* and **Triple 7 Brewpub**, *located downtown in the Main Street Station Hotel & Casino, Tel. 702/387-1896;* and **Sunset Brewing Company**, *in Sunset Station Hotel, Henderson, Tel. 702/547-7777.*

COMEDY ACTS

We have mixed feelings about all of the comedy shows. Sometimes they can be hilarious and at other times, well, real duds. It all depends on how good the line-up is on a particular evening and you never really know for sure. We're acquainted with people who regularly seek out the comedy shows while others have had their fill of them after one or two attempts. You'll have to be your own judge as to whether this type of entertainment is for you. There are usually age restrictions as most of the acts feature adult oriented humor.

The main comedy shows are:

CATCH A RISING STAR (MGM Grand). *$18 including tax. Nightly at 7:30 and 10 pm. Tel. 702/891-7777.*

COMEDY MAX (Maxim). *$16-20 including drink (or buffet for the higher rate) including tax and tip. Nightly at 7 and 9 pm. Tel. 702/731-4300.*

COMEDY STOP (Tropicana). *$15 all inclusive. Nightly at 8 and 10:30 pm. Tel. 702/739-2714.*

THE IMPROV AT HARRAH'S. *$17 plus tax. Nightly except Monday at 8 and 10:30 pm. Tel. 702/369-5223*

RIVIERA COMEDY CLUB. *$15 plus tax and tip. Dinner options available. Nightly at 8 and 10 pm with an additional show at 11:45 pm on Friday and Saturday. Tel. 702/794-9433.*

GENTLEMEN'S CLUBS

There's no doubt that quite a few men come to Las Vegas with their buddies for a raunchy good time. And Las Vegas obliges as there is no shortage of "gentlemen's clubs" – a nice euphamism for topless go-go bar, nudie club, or whatever other term you wish to apply.

Clubs are of two basic types: the first is the **topless** joint, indicated by **(T)** in the listings; the other are those where the dancers are totally **nude (N)**. All offer lap dancing. In general, the topless clubs serve all alcoholic beverages while the nude clubs aren't allowed that privilege.

Some of these clubs advertise that they welcome couples. While we're sure they do, you won't find many women guests and we certainly don't recommend that in general. There are a couple of clubs that are "higher class" and do, indeed, see couples in attendance. These are **Club Paradise** (T), *4416 Paradise Road, Tel. 702/734-5848* and the **Olympic Gardens** (T), *1531 Las Vegas Blvd. South, Tel. 702/385-8987*. Both of these establishments offer, in addition to the usual things found at these clubs, cabaret style entertainment that isn't too bad, talent wise.

Among some of the other popular men's clubs near The Strip and downtown are:

• **Cheetah's** (T), *2112 Western Avenue, Tel. 702/384-0074*
• **Crazy Horse Too** (T), *2476 Industrial Road, Tel. 702/382-8003*
• **Girls of Glitter Gulch** (T), *20 E. Fremont Street, Tel. 702/385-4774*
• **Little Darlings** (N), *1514 Western Avenue, Tel. 702/366-0959*
• **Palomino Club** (N), *1848 Las Vegas Blvd. North, Tel. 702/642-8587*
• **Showgirls** (N), *3247 Industrial Road, Tel. 702/893-3409*
• **Spearment Rhino** (N), *3344 S. Highland Drive, Tel. 702/796-3600*
• **Talk of the Town** (N), *1238 Las Vegas Blvd. South, Tel. 702/385-1800*
• **Tally-Ho** (N), *2580 S. Highland Drive, Tel. 702/792-9330*

We always believed that what's good for the goose is also good for the gander. So, with fair play in mind we would be happy to present the flip side of gentelemen's clubs and offer some suggestions for the bachlorettes on the prowl for a fun time. Unfortunately, there aren't any permanent clubs of that genre to choose from. It is suggested that ladies seeking out entertainment by scantily clad men scan the local entertainment publications and newspapers upon their arrival. Oftentimes there is such entertainment available, at least temporarily.

CULTURAL OFFERINGS

While some of The Strip shows (as opposed to strip shows) are truly artistic presentations, the high-brow visitor may still consider them a tad beneath their demeanor. For those unfortunate souls, here's a quick rundown on some other entertainment possibilities.
- **Charleston Heights Arts Center** (theater), *Tel. 702/229-6383*
- **Las Vegas Civic Ballet**, *Tel. 702/229-6211*
- **Nevada Dance Theater** (ballet), *Tel. 702/895-3827*
- **Nevada Symphony Orchestra**, *Tel. 702/792-4337*
- **University Dance Theaer**, *Tel. 702/895-3827*

Two venues for various performances are the **Artemus W. Ham Concert Hall**, on the University of Nevada-Las Vegas campus, *4505 S. Maryland Parkway, Tel. 702/895-3801* and the **Nicholas J. Horn Theater** at the Community College of Southern Nevada, *3200 E. Cheyenne Ave., Tel. 702/651-5483*. Major hotels sometimes present Broadway style productions as do other venues throughout the city. Scan the entertainment pages of the newspapers for current happenings.

ODDS & ENDS

There are theaters on The Strip and nearby that show first run movies (**Showcase**, for example) but we can't possibly imagine why anyone would waste their time going to see a movie in Las Vegas when they can easily do it at home. On the other hand, there are some special motion pictures that may well be of interest to a lot of visitors, such as the IMAX films at Caesars Palace or the Luxor and which were described in the preceding chapter under those hotels.

14. SHOPPING

As recently as five or six years ago there was nothing too special in the way of shopping in Las Vegas. Besides the hotel gift shops and plenty of souvenir joints (most of them offering cheap, tacky merchandise), there wasn't much else to choose from. Oh, sure, you could go to one of a few local malls, but they had the same stores you could find anywhere. In short, Las Vegas was definitely not a shopper's paradise. Boy, has that changed!

Beginning with a few upscale shops called the Appian Way in Caesars Palace and Bally's Avenue Shops arcade, the hotel owners realized they had a good idea on their hands. There has literally been an explosion in the growth of hotel shopping on The Strip as well as concurrent growth in malls, outlets and other types of specialty shopping throughout the Valley. Las Vegas has become a true shopping destination that rivals any city in the world. Yes, the world because you have everything from flea markets like Istanbul's bazaar to the most sophisticated stores usually found only on New York's Fifth Avenue, Rodeo Drive in Beverly Hills or in Paris. The best is on The Strip but the avid shopper will also find much else that is of interest in many other locations throughout Las Vegas. And if you still want that cheap trinket to bring back to the folks at the office, you can still find that with ease.

First we'll take a look at the major shopping arcades, malls and so forth by our usual geographic breakdown. Then we'll move on to some specific store suggestions for the most popular categories of goods that Vegas visitors usually look for.

THE STRIP

Hotel Shops

The Forum Shops at Caesars Palace, is The Strip's and Las Vegas' premier shopping destination. Beyond the spectacular street scene, the talking statues and the impressive fountains, there are more than 90 stores and restaurants covering just about anything you could imagine. By all accounts the Forum Shops, measured on a sales per square foot basis, is the most successful shopping center in the world. The only thing it's missing are department stores but, then again, with the incredible choices available, who needs them? The unusual is just as easy to find here as is the ordinary. Among the most notable and recognizable stores are **Gucci**, **Victoria's Secret**, **FAO Schwarz**, **Gap/Gap Kids**, **The Museum Company**, **Polo Store/Ralph Lauren** and **Ann Taylor**. Numerous fine arts stores are located throughout the Forum Shops. You'll find prices reaching to $25,000 or even higher! There are also many restaurants in the Forum Shops, ranging from **Planet Hollywood** to European style "outdoor" cafes. There's also a deli and ice cream shop.

One of the most unusual stores in town is **Antiquities**, a natural for the Forum Shops. It features photographs, old time gadgets, movie posters and the like. Much of the merchandise is limited editions signed by famous celebrities (e.g., a negligee worn by Madonna). If this wasn't enough, a Phase III expansion of the Forum Shops will soon be under way and should be complete sometime in 2001. The fabulous Forum Shops isn't the only shopping place within Caesars' empire – the **Appian Way** houses a small number of exclusive fashion shops, jewelry stores and art galleries.

Now vying for equal billing with the Forum Shops are the **Grand Canal Shoppes** at the Venetian. As was just the case with the Forum Shops, we won't bother to repeat from the Seeing the Sights section what the place has to offer from a non-shopping standpoint. If you can drag yourself away from looking at the Venetian street scenes and riding the gondolas along the Grand Canal, you'll notice almost a hundred different places to shop for all sorts of things. Of course, like all good Strip shopping centers, the stores are mostly of an upscale nature, so be prepared to spend. Located above the Venetian's casino, some of the major retailers here include **Movado**, **Cesare Paciotti** (Italian designer fashions), **Donna Karan Couture**, **In Celebration of Golf**, **Gallerie San Marco** (art gallery), **Marshall Rousso**, **Toys International**, **Ann Taylor**, **Banana Republic** and **Kids Karnivale**. Many of the stores are first-timers on the Las Vegas scene and are unknown to shoppers who haven't been to Europe. In addition to the Grand Canal Shoppes, the Venetian also boasts the unique **Sephora**, a leading perfume and cosmetic store from France. Among the treasures here that will certainly interest women shoppers are the *Lipstick Rainbow* collection that offers 365 different shades – one for each day of the year.

Bally's **Avenue Shops**, with about 40 stores, is a lot smaller than the malls at Caesars or the Venetian, but you'll find a slower paced environment to shop for high quality goods. There are also several fast-food eateries. Across the street is the beautiful sky-lit shopping street of the

Bellagio called the **Via Bellagio**. Built on the style of the first enclosed pedestrian shopping malls in Italy, the upscale shops here include **Tiffany**, **Georgio Armani**, **Chanel**, and **Hermes**.

Luxor's **Giza Galleria** concentrates mostly on Egyptian themed gift items. While a couple of places here have prices in outer space, a more reasonable range can be found at the colorful **Cairo Bazaar**. Additional shopping is available immediately after the end of the moving walkway from the Luxor to the Excalibur. Here you'll find a smaller selection of interesting shops, covering a wide range of prices. Some are geared to the medieval Excalibur theme while others are more general. A major retailing center on the Luxor/Mandalay Bay site has been announced. Construction had begun at press time but management has been hush-hush on details except that it will be anchored by **Nordstrom's**.

Star Lane at the MGM Grand contains about a dozen shops on the promenade leading to the monorail and can be reached via escalator off of the hotel's main lobby. Additional shopping at the MGM is located along the pricier **Studio Walk**. This promenade has clothing and gift shops, art stores and assorted other retailers along with many of the hotel's better restaurants and a food court.

The **Tower Shops** at the Stratosphere were designed by the same people who brought you the Forum Shops. While it isn't nearly as elaborate or beautiful, the street scene design that includes Paris, New York, and Hong Kong is attractive and contains more than 50 stores ranging from the ordinary to the unusual. Most of the stores are recognizable national chains.

While the above constitute the biggest and the best of the hotel shopping centers they aren't the only ones by any means. Attractive shopping facilities can be found in just about all of the major hotels. The hotels with the next tier of good shopping include Circus Circus (on the promenade outside of the theme park entrance), Flamingo Hilton, Mirage, Monte Carlo, New York, New York, and Treasure Island.

Non-hotel Shopping

The hotels definitely offer the most interesting shopping on The Strip. The remainder generally consists of cheap gift shops and the like. However, one exception to this is the **Fashion Show Mall**, *3200 Las Vegas Blvd. South, across the street from Treasure Island (Tel. 702/369-8382)*. Here you'll find mostly upscale shopping in more than 130 stores including small boutiques and large department stores like **Saks**, **Nieman-Marcus**, **Macy's** and **Dillards**. The Strip entrance to the mall has a few visual novelties including an Italian restaurant with a huge painting of the Mona Lisa. On the opposite side is the **Dive!** restaurant, which is shaped like the front of a submarine and periodically makes diving sounds.

The **Showcase** isn't exactly shopping in the usual sense of the word, but refresh your memory by referring back to the Seeing the Sights chapter for what's inside.

OFF-STRIP

Other than some typical local strip malls there isn't too much in the vicinity of The Strip to offer shoppers. The notable exception are the 22 stores in the Rio's exciting **Masquerade Village**. The stores are on two levels surrounding a part of the casino and the venue for the Sky Parade. So, if you're not too busy watching the show or gambling, you might want to check out some of the nice (and mostly very expensive) shops. There's also a small food court as well as some better restaurants.

The **Las Vegas Hilton** has a nice selection of stores that include several for children's items such as clothing and toys. And most of them aren't *Star Trek* linked.

DOWNTOWN

Fremont Street Experience is home to, besides hotels, plenty of small stores that specialize in gifts and souvenirs. Not far from Downtown lies Vegas' antique row, although most stores are scattered over a fairly broad area. Many are located along **East Charleston Boulevard** and they sell all manner of collectibles from all over the world, not just from Las Vegas' short but glorious past.

AROUND LAS VEGAS

Two major regional shopping malls are located not far from The Strip or Downtown. The first is **The Boulevard Mall**, *3528 Maryland Parkway, Tel. 702/735-8268*. The stores are mostly the usual national chains but they are generally less expensive than shopping at Strip hotels. The department stores are **Dillards**, **Macy's**, **Sears** and **JC Penny**. The mall has a huge food court if you get hungry. The **Meadows Mall**, *4300 Meadows Lane, Tel. 702/878-4849*, has 150 stores on two levels, including four department stores and a food court. For the most part the stores at the Meadows are a little more down-scale from those at The Boulevard but, again, most are nationwide chains.

If you're looking for outlet stores then try the **Belz Factory Outlet World**, a little south of The Strip at *Las Vegas Boulevard South and Warm Springs Road, Tel. 702/896-5599*. With about 160 stores, this is one of the biggest outlet malls in the country. A lot of people seem to think that you can always find great buys at these type of places – we're not so sure, but if you just like to shop then it's worth taking the short ride to Belz. It's especially good for apparel shopping. **Saks Fifth Avenue** is among the stores having an outlet here. The 60 stores of **Vegas Point Plaza** are located at *9155 Las Vegas Blvd. South*. It used to be called the Factory Stores of America but the name was changed to give it a new image and, hopefully, more traffic. One of the problems is that it isn't enclosed so that summer shopping can be on the toasty side.

We also have to mention the **Fantastic Indoor Swap Meet,** *1717 S. Decatur Blvd. at Oakey, Tel. 702/877-0087.* Open only on weekends (extended days during the Christmas shopping season), this gigantic flea market houses hundreds of booths. You can find clothing as well as gift items, and a plethora of unusual things. It makes a great place to browse even if you aren't planning on buying anything. Locals shop here in droves because you can often get some really good buys.

HENDERSON

The Henderson building boom has certainly included plenty of new shopping areas. For the most part the opportunities are the major national retailers that you see just about everywhere although many are located in spanking new facilities. The major shopping areas are located along **Sunset Road** from Green Valley east to I-515. **Stephanie Street** south of the intersection of Sunset also has lots of stores.

The **Galleria at Sunset Mall**, *Tel. 702/434-0202*, is also located at this intersection. The two level mall has about 130 stores in a brighly sky-lit facility that is the most attractive of the regular malls in the Valley. The decor is colorful with a hint of southwestern. They also have a 600-seat food court with pretty topiary and other plantings.

I'M LOOKING FOR....

Besides the usual souvenirs that travelers are always hunting for (which we'll make some suggestions on in the section that follows), visitors to Las Vegas seem most interested in apparel, works of art, jewelry, Native American and southwestern items, and western wear. We won't bother mentioning any apparel stores beyond the one's previously mentioned simply because there are so many. They include all of the national names plus scores of local places. However, unless you're looking to make an expensive fashion statement, you're better off shopping for clothing away from stores in Strip hotels.

Art

The Forum Shops are home to some of the finest art galleries in Las Vegas. These include the **Galleria di Sorrento** and the **Galerie Lassen.** Caesars Palace also has the **Gallerie Michelangelo**, located near the entrance to the Palace Tower. Another excellent place to purchase fine art is the **Passman Gallery**, located in the Masquerade Village of the Rio Hotel. Getting away from hotel shopping, you can choose from a wide selection at **Debora Spanover Fine Art**, *1775 E. Tropicana Ave.*; the **Art Encounter**, *3979 Spring Mountain Road*; and **Carrara Galleries**, *1236 S. Rainbow Blvd.* If you're specifically looking for Egyptian artwork then there are several places in the Luxor as well as at **Egyptian Art Imports**, *3661 Maryland Parkway*. The **Crystal Galleria** in the Forum Shops has a wonderful selection of beautiful items if you're looking for quality glass and crystal.

Jewelry

Every hotel shopping arcade seems to have one or more jewelers, as do all of the local malls. However, several good choices are **Jewels of the Nile** in the Luxor and **Tiffany & Company** and **Fred Leighton**, both in the Bellagio. The Forum Shops has **Hyde Park Jewelers**. Two respected chain-store jewelers in Vegas are **M.J. Christensen** with locations in the Forum Shops, the Meadows and Galleria Malls; and the **Tower of Jewels**, *953 E. Sahara Ave.* as well as the Meadows and Galleria Malls. You can also find a good selection at reasonable prices at **Tiffin's** in the Boulevard Mall.

Native American Goods/Southwestern Crafts

We said that shopping for this category is popular for Las Vegas visitors. That doesn't mean that the selection is great, though. This is the southwest but it isn't Arizona or New Mexico. A few places that come to mind are **Amanda's**, *9155 Las Vegas Blvd. South (Pointe Plaza)*; **Viva Southwest**, *1226 S. Rainbow Blvd.*; **Nava Hopi Gallery**, *Galleria Mall*; and **West of Santa Fe** in the Forum Shops. You can also find several merchants selling these genres of goods in the **Fantastic Indoor Swap Meet**. Finally, **El Portal Gifts**, downtown on the *Fremont Street Experience*, has an excellent selection.

Western Wear

The biggest and best place is the **Western Emporium** in Sam's Town Hotel. Two places with boots in their name sell a lot more than footwear. These are **Cowtown Boots**, *2989 Paradise Road* and the **Boot Barn**, *7265 Las Vegas Blvd. South*. Three well known places with the local western wearers are **Sheplers**, *3025 E. Tropicana Ave.*; **Adam's Western Store**, *1415 Western Ave.*; and **Miller Stockman**. The last retailer has locations in the Fashion Show, Meadows and Galleria Malls. **West of Santa Fe** (Forum Shops), has a decent selection of western wear in addition to southwestern and Native American goods.

HOW ABOUT THOSE SOUVENIRS?

It's only natural to want to bring home a souvenir of Las Vegas for your friends and family or to put on display in your own home. The choices are endless. Every hotel has a gift shop which has their logo on everything from t-shirts to glasses to you name it. Prices do vary quite a bit and, surprisingly, things aren't always the highest in the more expensive hotels. Shop around and look for your favorites before you buy.

You can get "generic" Las Vegas stuff in scores of gift shops that are scattered on The Strip but especially downtown on Fremont Street. Although some of the merchandise is qualty, things are generally chintzier in these stores than in the hotel shops. A store that bills itself as the world's largest gift shop is **Bonanza**, *2400 Las Vegas Blvd. South at the intersection of Sahara Ave.* We don't know if it actually is the largest but the size of the selection is impressive.

GAMBLING PARAPHERNALIA

If you're looking for something different to bring home, how about a slot machine (either mini or full sized)? Or a poker table. Maybe just some authentic Las Vegas chips. They're all available for sale in several places that sell to the pros as well as to the casual visitor. When buying gaming equipment please be aware of restrictions that may be imposed by the state in which you live, even if it's for private use. Store personnel can assist you with this.

*The biggest gaming equipment emporiums are the **Gambler's General Store**, 800 South Main, Tel. 702/382-9903; the **Bud Jones Company**, 3460 S. Valley View Blvd., Tel. 702/876-2782 and **Paul-Son Gaming Supplies**, 2121 Industrial Road, Tel. 702/384-2425. All of these places can sell you slot machines, chips, dice, gaming furniture, books and much more. Speaking of books, if you want literature on gaming or Las Vegas, then check out the **Gambler's Book Club**, 630 S. 11th Street, Tel. 702/382-7555. Serving gamblers since 1964, it has the best and most extensive selection of gaming books in the country. The staff is friendly and knowledgable and can direct you to exactly what you're looking for.*

*Finally, if you're looking for old time slot machines then you should visit the **House of Antique Slots**, 1243 Las Vegas Blvd. South, Tel. 702/382-1520. Casino clothing is available from the **Dealers Room Casino Clothiers**, 3507 S. Maryland Parkway, Tel. 702/732-3932. This is a great place for those of you who have fantasies of dressing like a real-live dealer or croupier on Bingo Night or poker night with the folks back home.*

15. SPORTS & RECREATION

For fun in the sun there are few other major cities in America that can offer the variety of sports and recreational activities that Las Vegas does. There are even some professional and college spectator sports. (Gambling is not allowed on college games involving teams from the state of Nevada.) Whichever sport you like to play, or whatever sport you like to watch, you should have no trouble finding something fun to suit your needs.

And to make things even more enticing to the recreational enthusiast, Las Vegas is a place where you can partake in outdoor activity at any time of the year. It's possible to go skiing down the snowy slopes in Kyle Canyon in the morning and to waterski that same afternoon on Lake Mead. Such are the pleasures of Las Vegas. The winters are mild enough to get out on the golf course and even the summer, with its dry heat, doesn't deter too many people from physical activity. We should, however, caution those who aren't accustomed to the heat to take it slowly and try whenever possible to restrict strenuous activity to the morning hours (or after dark where available).

Here's a sport-by-sport rundown on the action.

BICYCLING

We don't suggest taking a casual bike ride up The Strip. But, if you do like to ride your bike, the Las Vegas area does have some great places. Red Rock Canyon is a fabulous place to pedal as are many of the less crowded portions of the Lake Mead National Recreation Area. Many of the Valley's residential communities have bike paths. These can be found in Summerlin and to an even greater extent in Henderson which has miles of trails already in use and many more under construction or in planning.

For information on the latter, contact the Henderson Department of Parks and Recreation, *Tel. 702/565-2063*.

BOATING

Boating choices in the greater Las Vegas area are pretty simple: if you want it close by then go to **Lake Mead**. There are six marinas to choose from within the National Recreation Area. The **Lake Mead Lodge**, *322 Lakeshore Road, Boulder City; Tel. 702/293-3484*, is very accessible and has a good selection of watercraft.

If you're willing to drive a little further, boating is also available either on Lake Mohave or on the Colorado River, both accessible from Laughlin, about a 90-minute drive from Vegas. Call or visit the **Laughlin Visitor Center**, *1555 S. Casino Drive, Tel. 702/298-3321 or 800/1-LAUGLIN.*

BOWLING

Although the Las Vegas area has more than a dozen bowling alleys spread out all over town, the most convenient ones for visitors are those that are located right in some of the major hotels. All of them are open 24 hours a day, just in case you get the urge to throw a few strikes at three in the morning:

- **Gold Coast**, *4000 W. Flamingo Road. Tel. 702/367-4700.* 72 lanes.
- **The Orleans**, *4500 W. Tropicana Avenue. Tel. 702/365-7400.* 70 lanes.
- **Sam's Town**, *5111 Boulder Highway. Tel. 702/454-8023.* 56 lanes.
- **Santa Fe**, *4949 N. Rancho Drive. Tel. 702-658-4995.* 60 lanes. This one is a little bit further from The Strip than the others but it isn't far if you're staying Downtown.
- **Showboat**, *2800 Fremont Street. Tel. 702/385-9153.* 106 lanes. Sight of some major tournaments.

BUNGEE JUMPING

Las Vegas isn't New Zealand when it comes to bungee jumping but you can try out **A.J. Hackett Bungee**, *810 Circus Circus Drive (adjacent to the Circus Circus Hotel), Tel. 702/385-4321.* They have a 201 foot high tower with a double bungee deck. An elevator takes you up to the jump-off point. Jumping is available day and night. The price is $49 for the first jump and $25 for each additional jump. A.J. always also throws in a gift for the jumpers. It could be a tee shirt, a bottle of beer or who knows what else.

GOLF

The Vegas area has some of the finest golfing in the Southwest. There are almost 30 major golf clubs, private and public. The surrounding areas also have some good venues including one in Mesquite, about 77 miles northeast near the Utah border.

The list below contains all of the major courses that are open to the general public, at least on a limited basis. Call for more exact information. If you are staying at a hotel that doesn't have its own golf course you should inquire with the concierge or guest service office about golfing opportunities since almost all the major hotels can arrange for you to play somewhere.

Another way to ensure getting a spot on the links is to contact **Las Vegas Preferred Tee-Times**, *Tel. 702/893-9008 or 888/Four-Tee*. They will arrange, at no extra cost to you, guaranteed tee times at the best courses in Las Vegas, including access to some private clubs you may not otherwise be able to get into that aren't included on the list that follows. Transportation is provided.

- **Angel Park Golf Club**, *100 S. Rampart Blvd. Tel. 702/254-4653*. Public. 36 holes.
- **Black Mountain Golf & Country Club**, *501 Country Club Drive, Henderson. Tel. 702/565-7933*. Semi-private. 18 holes.
- **Boulder City Municipal Golf Course**, *1 Clubhouse Drive, Boulder City. Tel. 702/293-9236*. Public. 18 holes.
- **Callawlay Golf Center**, *Las Vegas Blvd. South at Sunset Road, Tel. 702/896-4100*. Public. 9 holes, but extremely convenient to Strip hotels. Lighted for night play.
- **Craig Ranch Golf Course**, *628 W. Craig Road. Tel. 702/642-9700*. Public. 18 holes.
- **Desert Inn Country Club**, *3145 Las Vegas Blvd. South, at the Desert Inn Hotel. Tel. 702/733-4299*. Open to public but reservations of six months in advance are suggested. 18 holes.
- **Desert Pines Golf Club**, *3415 East Bonanza Road. Tel. 702/388-4400*. Private. 18 holes.
- **Desert Rose Golf Course**, *5843 Club House Drive. Tel. 702/431-4653*. Public. 18 holes.
- **Las Vegas Golf Club**, *4300 W. Washington Ave. Tel. 702/646-3003*. Public. 18 holes.
- **Legacy Golf Club**, *130 Par Excellence Drive, Henderson. Tel. 702/897-2187*. Public. 18 holes.
- **Los Prados Golf and Country Club**, *5150 Los Prados circle. Tel. 702/645-5696*. Semi-public. 18 holes.
- **North Las Vegas Golf Course**, *324 E. Brooks Avenue, N. Las Vegas. Tel. 702/649-7171*. Public. 9 holes.
- **Painted Desert Country Club**, *5555 Painted Mirage Drive. Tel. 702/645-24569*. Public. 18 holes
- **Rhodes Ranch Golf Club**, *920 Rhodes Ranch Parkway. Tel. 702/740-1414*. Public. 18 holes.

- **Stallion Mountain Country Club**, *5500 E. Flamingo Road. Tel. 702/436-7000.* Private. 18 holes.
- **Wild Horse Golf Club**, *2100 W. Warm Springs Road, Henderson. Tel. 702/434-9000 or 800/884-1818.* Public. 18 holes.
- **Sahara Country Club**, *1911 E. Desert Inn Road. Tel. 702/734-1796.* Semi-public.
- **Sun City Summerlin Golf Club**, *9201 Del Webb Blvd. Tel. 702/363-4373.* Semi-private.
- **Sunrise Vista Golf Course at Nellis**, *Nellis Air Force Base. Tel. 702/652-2602.* Open to public on stand-by basis only. Holders of Military ID get first preference.

HIKING

Some of the best hiking in the area is in the **Red Rock Canyon National Conservation Area**. Rock climbing is also a popular activity here. The **Lake Mead National Recreation Area** also has some good hiking possibiliies but many of them are quite difficult. Get information at the Alan Bible Visitor Center on US 93 south of Boulder City. Again, due to the extreme summer heat be sure to carry plenty of drinking water, protect yourself from the sun as much as possible and try to do the most strenuous hiking in the morning. A better idea altogether is to hike during the cooler months.

HORSEBACK RIDING

Red Rock Canyon is the venue of choice in the greater Las Vegas area for those who want to stay close to town and like to ride. Horses can be rented there from **Cowboy Trail Rides**, *Tel. 702/387-2457* or at nearby **Bonnie Springs Ranch**, *Tel. 702/875-4191.* If you want to travel a little further, then visit the **Mount Charleston Riding Stables**, *Tel. 702/872-7009.* The weather is a lot cooler at the latter location.

HOT AIR BALLOONS

The **Great Balloon Experience** isn't really a true balloon adventure because it is always tethered to the ground (making it good for everyone who has an aversion to floating around in the air). On the other hand, you'll spend ten minutes 400 feet above the Strip beneath a colorful, 118-foot high stars and striped themed balloon which provides some fabulous views. You also experience some of the "freedom" feeling that you can get in a real balloon trip but not on some observation deck in a tall building. The big gondola can hold up to 30 people. The balloon does not operate when the wind gets to around 30 mph. *Located at the south end of the New Frontier Hotel on Las Vegas Boulevard South. Tel. 702/791-2552. The fare is*

$10. Operates daily from 10:00am to midnight and until 2:00am Thursday through Saturday. Balloon trips not available when it is being used for special events such as weddings.

RAFTING

Due south of Hoover Dam you can take the **Black Canyon River Raft Tour**, 3-1/2 hours of floating fun on the lower Colorado River and Lake Mohave. The trip begins at the base of mighty Hoover Dam and winds past stunning canyon lands. It's a great way to see the magnificent landscapes of this portion of the southwest. You might catch a glimpse of bighorn sheep as well as seeing natural hot springs. This is not a whitewater experience, so it is suitable even for the previously uninitated rafter. The "expedition depot" is located at *1297 Nevada Highway (US 93) in Boulder City. Tel. 702/293-3776. Reservations are suggested. The price is $65 per person including lunch. They'll pick you up at your hotel for an extra $15.*

SKIING & ICE SKATING

Even though the majority of people don't think of Las Vegas when it comes to winter sports, if you're here in the winter months you can take advantage of some great cross-country and alpine skiing. Both can be found in the Mount Charleston area in the Toiyabe National Forest. The **Lee Canyon Ski Area**, *State Highway 156; Tel. 702/872-5462 or 702/646-0008*, is located just under 50 miles from The Strip. They have double chair lifts on each of Lee Canyon's three slopes. The runs are named Highroller, Blackjact, Keno and Slot Alley! What else would you expect – this is still Vegas. Base elevation is 8,500 feet.

Ice skating has become quite popular among the locals so visitors will have no difficulty in finding a place to lace up and take to the ice. Here's a rundown on the rinks.

- **Crystal Palace Skating Centers**, *4680 Boulder Highway. Tel. 702/458-7107; 3901 Rancho Drive. Tel. 702/645-4892; 1110 E. Lake Mead Drive, Henderson. Tel. 702/564-2790; and 9295 W. Flamingo Road. Tel. 702/235-9832.*
- **Las Vegas Ice Gardens**, *3896 Swenson Street. Tel. 702/731-1208.*
- **Sahara Ice Palace**, *953 E. Sahara Avenue. Tel. 702/862-4262.*
- **Santa Fe Ice Arena**, *Rancho at US 95 North (in the Santa Fe Hotel). Tel. 702/658-4993.*

The **Sunset Station Hotel & Casino** in Henderson is building an ice rink which was not yet done at the time this book went to press; however, it's slated for completion in 1999.

SKY DIVING

While this certainly isn't a "mainstream" recreational activity, it's been around in Vegas for quite a few years and seems to do okay. A **Skydive Las Vegas** provides a 20 minute lesson before taking you up in a jet to 13,000 feet where you jump out and go into a 45 second freefall before opening your chute and taking the six minute ride back to earth. *Tel. 702/293-1860* for information on prices and transportation as well as reservations. A little closer to earth is **Flyaway Indoor Skydiving**, *200 Convention Center Drive.* You can experience body flight in a wind tunnel after receiving instruction. *Tel. 702/731-4768 for times. The price is $35 per person.*

SPECTATOR SPORTS

Professional Sports

Auto Racing: The **Las Vegas International Motor Speedway**, *7000 Las Vegas Blvd. N, Tel. 800/644-4444*, is located in the northern part of the Valley via I-15 to Exit 54. The 1,500 acre complex opened in 1996 and has been successful in attracting a number of prestigious auto racing events, including the famous Winston Cup Series. Among the facilities are a campground and RV park and even a wedding chapel for those who want to marry and ride.

Baseball: The **Las Vegas Stars** of the Pacific Coast League (the highest level of minor league play) take to the diamond just a few blocks north of the Downtown Casino Center at *Cashman Field, 850 Las Vegas Blvd. North; Tel. 702/386-7200.* The season runs from April to September and you can watch the game close-up from any seat in this attractive little stadium. If you've never been to a minor league game, check it out. Everyone has fun regardless of who wins.

Boxing: No city in the United States is a hotbed for boxing more than Las Vegas is. Of course, a big part of that popularity comes from people with full pockets who pay huge sums to get into the fights and then wager even bigger sums on the outcome. Some of the sports' most important matches are held in Las Vegas. Popular venues are the MGM Grand Garden Arena and the Thomas & Mack Center.

Ice Hockey: Las Vegas had a minor league team but it folded at the end of the 1998-1999 season. A new team is expected to begin play in the Fall of 2000.

Rodeo: The early part of December brings the **National Finals Rodeo** to town. The main events take place at the Thomas & Mack Center but other venues are used as well. This is a popular event so reservations for hotels as well as the rodeo should be made as far in advance as possible.

COLLEGE SPORTS

The **University of Nevada-Las Vegas**, commonly known by all as **UNLV**, conducts a full schedule of men's and women's intercollegiate sports. The most popular from a spectator's point of view are men's basketball and football. The **Runnin' Rebels** play their basketball at the aforementioned *Thomas & Mack Center,* a short trip from The Strip. The team has had its share of success, including an NCAA Championship. They aren't quite that good now but are very competive.

Unfortunately, the same can't be said for the woeful football team. They try to play at **Sam Boyd Stadium**, *7000 E. Russell Road just off of Boulder Highway,* but don't seem to have a clue the last few years. Wins are few and far between but if you just want to see some college gridion, who cares? Tickets are reasonable and you can almost always get good seats. Basketball tickets are much harder to come by. For information and tickets for all UNLV sporting events, contact the Thomas & Mack box office, *Tel. 702/895-3900.*

MORE ABOUT UNLV

*Known to many people for its winning basketball teams and its former flamboyant towel-chewing coach, Jerry Tarkanian, **UNLV** actually has a good academic program as well. The campus, spread out over 335 acres, has more than 18,000 students enrolled. In addition to the many sporting events at the Thomas & Mack, the university has a full program of cultural events, some of which you can read about in the Nightlife & Entertainment chapter. The university is one of the few to offer a School of Hotel Administration, many of whose graduates help run the hotels and casinos in Las Vegas and other gambling destinations throughout the country.*

SWIMMING

Although there are quite a few municipal swimming pools for residents, it doesn't pay to even mention them because there's scarcely a hotel or motel that doesn't have a pool for its guests. Those who like a real beach can take a drive out to the Lake Mead National Recreation Area where **Boulder Beach** can fill the bill. It's open all year but the water and air can be kind of chilly during the winter. Somet hotels don't keep their pools open during the short winter season. You can count on all of them being available from April through October. Indoor swimming pools are quite rare in Las Vegas hotels.

TENNIS

There are no fewer than 300 tennis courts in and around the city. Many of the hotels offer tennis courts, particularly on The Strip, but priority is almost always given to guests. If tennis is an important part of your vacation plans you should consider staying at a hotel that has its own courts.

Hotel Tennis Courts

- **Alexis Park**, 375 E. Hzrmon Ave., Tel. 702/796-3300. Two lighted outdoor courts.
- **Bally's**, 3645 Las Vegas Blvd. S., Tel. 702/739-4111. Ten outdoor courts, five lighted.
- **Caesars Palace**, 3570 Las Vegas Blvd. S., Tel. 702/731-7786. Three lighted outdoor courts.
- **Desert Inn**, 3145 Las Vegas Blvd. S., Tel. 702/733-4444. Ten outdoor courts, five lighted.
- **Flamingo Hilton**, 3555 Las Vegas Blvd. S., Tel. 702/733-3111. Four outdoor lighted courts.
- **Frontier**, 3120 Las Vegas Blvd. S., Tel. 702/794-8200. Two lighted outdoor courts.
- **Jackie Gaughan's Plaza Hotel**, 1 Main Street, Tel. 702/386-2110. Four lighted outdoor courts.
- **Las Vegas Hilton**, 3000 Paradise Rd., Tel. 702/732-5111. Six outdoor courts, four lighted.
- **Monte Carlo**, 3770 Las Vegas Blvd. S., Tel. 702/730-7777. Three lighted outdoor courts.
- **Riviera**, 2901 Las Vegas Blvd. S., Tel. 702/734-5110. Two lighted outdoor courts.
- **Tropicana**, 3801 Las Vegas Blvd. S., Tel. 702/739-2645. Four lighted outdoor courts.

Public & Private Tennis Courts

- **Las Vegas Racquet Club**, 3333 W. Raven. Tel. 702/3621-2202
- **Pro Tennis**, 3000 Joe W. Brown Drive, Tel. 702/732-1861
- **Quail Ridge Estates Tennis Club**, 1 Goldfinch Avenue, Henderson, Tel. 702/456-0300
- **Sports Club**, 2100 Olympic Avenue, Henderson, Tel. 702/454-6000
- **Sunset Park**, Sunset Road & Eastern Avenue, Henderson, Tel. 702/260-9803
- **Twin Lakes Racquet Club**, 3075 W. Washington Blvd., Tel. 702/647-3434
- **UNLV**, 4505 S. Maryland Parkway, Tel. 702/895-3240

MISCELLANEOUS

The **All-American SportsPark**, *121 E. Sunset Road (corner of Las Vegas Blvd. South)*, is a very unusual sports participation facility with somethng for just about everyone. Two especially popular features are Slugger's Stadium, where you can play baseball like a major leaguer in front of an authentic looking scoreboard; and the NASCAR Speedpark, a "racing" facility.

In addition to those activities there are pool tables and a rock climbing wall. *Tel. 702/798-7777. Open daily from 11 am to 11 pm (till midnight on Friday and Saturday, 10 pm on Sunday). Prices vary according to activity.*

16. EXCURSIONS & DAY TRIPS

If you've come all this way to Las Vegas and never leave The Strip, or the city for that matter, you'll be missing out on a beautiful part of the country. You don't have to travel all the way to the Grand Canyon to see some breathtaking sights – they're all around you, most within an hours' drive or less. The purple hues of Mt. Charleston in twilight, the incredible workmanship of Hoover Dam, the stillness of early morning in the Valley of Fire – these and more are all scenes that are not what leap to mind when your friend or loved one says to you: "Let's go to Vegas."

But the majesty of the southwest's mountains and canyons is also part of Vegas, perhaps not as much as the neon and glitz of Casinoland, but almost. The area attractions are as exciting and interesting as you'll find anywhere. Our strong recommendation is to take a spin out to some of the sights and soak up a day or two of the great outdoors.

Depending on your travel style, you can either rent a car and see the sights yourself, or go on one of the many tours that depart Las Vegas for area excursions. A number of the tours can be done in well under a day, while some are two days or more. We'll show you all the possibilities in this chapter. If you do decide on the guided tour route than check back in *Chapter 8* for a listing of some tour operators.

Or, just dance on down to the lobby of just about any hotel in town. There'll likely either be a tour desk that can make all the arrangements for you or plenty of brochures on tour companies that you can contact yourself.

TRAVEL DISTANCES TO AREA EXCURSIONS

Bonnie Springs Ranch	*19 miles*
Death Valley (Furnace Creek)	*129 miles*
Grand Canyon-North Rim	*307 miles*
Grand Canyon-South Rim	*290 miles*
Hoover Dam	*30 miles*
Lake Mead Marina	*38 miles*
Laughlin	*90 miles*
Mt. Charleston	*34 miles*
Primm	*40 miles*
Red Rock Canyon	*16 miles*
Spring Mountain State Park	*20 miles*
Valley of Fire State Park	*52 miles*
Zion National Park	*175 miles*

HOOVER DAM

This is the most popular out-of-town destination for visitors to Las Vegas and, by itself, can be done in about four hours. **Hoover Dam**, about 45 minutes away by car, is one of the great architectural triumphs of the early twentieth century. The dam, known for its first twelve years as Boulder Dam, provides about five billion kiilowatt-hours of electricity a year to three states: Nevada, Arizona and California. Located in Bouler City, a visit to Hoover Dam is a must-see for visitors who want to see more than three kings and a pair of tens (well, that would be a pretty nice sight too).

The dam is 726 feet high with a base 660 feet thick. It's made of seven million tons of concrete and 18 million tons of reinforced steel. Thousands of workers labored five yeas and 94 construction workers died before the Dam was finished in 1935. In 1955, the American Society of Civil Engineers officially declared it one of the seven engineering wonders of the world.

The mighty **Colorado River**, responsible for the shape of Grand Canyon, is diverted here and the dammed-up result is **Lake Mead** (see below).

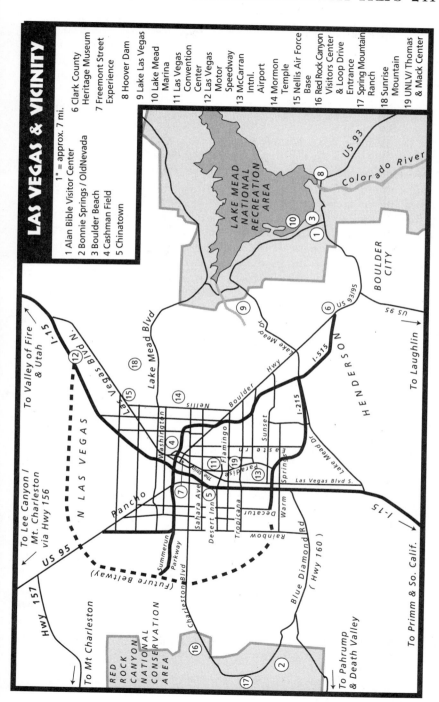

LAS VEGAS & VICINITY

1" = approx. 7 mi.

1 Alan Bible Visitor Center
2 Bonnie Springs / OldNevada
3 Boulder Beach
4 Cashman Field
5 Chinatown
6 Clark County Heritage Museum
7 Freemont Street Experience
8 Hoover Dam
9 Lake Las Vegas
10 Lake Mead Marina
11 Las Vegas Convention Center
12 Las Vegas Motor Speedway
13 McCarran Intnl. Airport
14 Mormon Temple
15 Nellis Air Force Base
16 Red Rock Canyon Visitors Center & Loop Drive Entrance
17 Spring Mountain Ranch
18 Sunrise Mountain
19 UNLV/ Thomas & Mack Center

Guided tours of the dam (highly recommended) are offered. These tours take you down to the base and through tunnels to the impressive power house where the force of the water rotates the huge turbines that generate the electric power. Tours last about 45 minutes and begin with a brief introductory film. A "hard-hat" tour takes visitors further behind the scenes for those who are more interested in the workings of the dam. You can sometimes expect to encounter big crowds and a fairly long wait for the tours, so it is advisable to get there early in the day.

In addition to the tours you can visit the sleek new gold glass colored visitor center (no charge) where you can view interesting exhibits on the construction of the dam. It's also an unforgettablae experience to walk along the top crest of the dam to view the lake on one side and the deep gorge into which the Colorado River flows on the other side. The dam itself is located within a forbidding canyon. You get some good views of it on the way down to the dam via a series of switchbacks, but even better views are available if you drive across the crest to the Arizona side of the border. There are several small parking areas with overlooks that provide spectacular views. *Tel. 702/293-8321. The visitor center is open daily (except Christmas) from 8:30 am to 5:30 pm. Tours are offered at frequent intervals and cost $6 for adults, $5 for seniors, and $2 for children ages 2 through 12. "Hard hat" tours cost $25. Call for schedule.*

Directions: Take either Flamingo or Tropicana east from The Strip to I-515 (also known as US 93/US 95) and head south. The freeway ends in the southern part of Henderson at the Railroad Pass and the old Boulder Highway loses its I-515 designation. Boulder Highway changes name to Nevada Highway, but just stay on US 93 and you'll have no trouble reaching it.

If you have time you can make a stop in Boulder City itself at the **Boulder City/Hoover Dam Museum**, *1228 Arizona Street*. It has a good collection of historical exhibits from the Dam's early history and also shows a movie about the Dam's construction. *Tel. 702/294-1988. The museum is open daily from 10 am to 5 pm and the admission charge is $1 (50 cents for kids).*

LAKE MEAD NATIONAL RECREATION AREA

The **Lake Mead National Recreation Area** is the byproduct of the Hoover Dam project and a darn nice byproduct at that. In addition to providing aquatic relief from hot summers, Lake Mead, the largest man-made lake in the Western Hemisphere, supples water to 25 million people throughout Nevada and the rest of the southwest. Las Vegas gets most of its water from Lake Mead by way of the **Southern Nevada Water Project.**

Lake Mead begins about 25 miles from Las Vegas and snakes its way to more than a hundred miles away. The lake has 550 miles of shoreline for you to enjoy fishing, boating (there are six marinas), rafting, swimming, other water sports and camping. If you're going to fish, you'll need a license. Fishermen will be pleased to learn of the variety of fish in the lake: largemouth bass, striped bass, catfish, crappie, trout, and bluegill.

If cruising along the lake in a large paddle-wheeler strikes your fancy, **Lake Mead Cruises** offers very pleasant scenic rides on *The Desert Princess*. The boats depart from a pier about a half mile north of the **Lake Mead Marina**. The 300-passenger vessel will take you out on the deep blue waters of Lake Mead, surrounded by the red sandstone cliffs. It's hard to believe that the glitter of Las Vegas is so nearby when you gaze out on the splendor that surrounds you on all sides. The boat turns around as it gets near to the rear of Hoover Dam. In addition to scenic rides, Lake Mead Cruises also offers trips with a breakfast buffet, dinner, or dinner with dancing. The scenic cruises offer interesting commentary on the natural and human history of the area. *Tel. 702/293-6180. Excursion cruises leave at 10 am, noon, 2 and 4 pm (no late trip from November through March). The fare is $21 for adults and $10 for children. Contact Lake Mead Cruises if you want information on one of the meal cruises. Reservations are recommended.*

For the do-it-yourself boater, rental boats are also available at the Lake Mead Marina. An unusual sight at the marina are the hundreds of large-mouthed bass that congregate near the shore waiting for handouts from visitors. The water is often so thick with the fish that you can hardly see the lake! Adjacent to the marina is **Boulder Beach**, a popular spot for swimming and diving. Rafting on the Colorado River is another option if you have the time. See the *Sports & Recreation* chapter for information on **Black Canyon Raft Tours**.

For the land lover we suggest an auto tour through the recreation area. There's plenty of land to see. In fact, despite the large size of Lake Mead and smaller Lake Mojave, land comprises about 87% of the national recreation area. The short tour involves taking Lakeshore Drive (State Highway 166) to Lake Mead Drive (Highway 146) and then returning west to I-515. A longer tour via Northshore Road leads about 42 miles up Lake Mead and the Overton Arm to near the town of Overton at State Highway 169. This latter route is a good idea if you are going to see the Valley of Fire (see below). Regardless of whether you do either of these routes, be sure to stop on your way to or from Hoover Dam at the beautiful **Lake Mead Overlook**. It's located about a quarter mile off of US 93.

The Lake Mead National Recreation Area is open at all times and there is no charge for admission. The Alan Bible Visitor Center has information, a desert botanical garden, and lake views. It's located on US 93 at the intersection of

Lakeshore Drive. Tel. 702/293-8907. Hours are daily from 8:30 am to 4:30 pm except for New Year's Dy, Thanksgiving and Christmas.

Directions: Same as to Hoover Dam. You reach the recreation area about five miles before getting to the dam. Use Lakeshore Drive, off of US 93, for access to other points in the recreation area including the marinas, beach and Northshore Drive.

Many visitors who want to spend a complete day away from The Strip combine Hoover Dam, Lake Mead and the attractions in Henderson. It can be done in one full day (not including Colorado River raft tour and north shore excursion) and makes a nice change of pace from the usual Vegas activities.

RED ROCK CANYON

Less than a half-hour drive west of town you'll find beautiful red sandstone and gray limestone formations and cliff outcroppings that have been carved by water and wind erosion. You'll think you're in the wilds of the great southwest rather than minutes from the hustle of The Strip. Part of the Spring Mountains, Red Rock Canyon was formerly home to the Paiute Indians. The sunlight at different times of the day changes the hues, so that the Canyon area is always a little different each time you come here.

The unique beauty and fragile environment of the area has been designated as the **Red Rock Canyon National Conservation Area**. Begin your trip with a stop at the **Red Rock Visitors Center**, *1000 Scenic Drive* to get trail guides and maps, view the exhibits on the local plants and wildlife, and get information on this Bureau of Land Management (BLM) administered facility that's as popular with the residents of Las Vegas as it is with visitors. The sandstone and the limestone come together at the **Keystone Thrust**, a fault or fracture where the ancient rocks collided with (and are now superimposed on top of) one another. The escarpment runs for 15 miles and is about 3,000 feet high. It is believed to be about 65 million years old.

In late afternoon, as the sun sets and just before darkness stretches over the land, you'll witness the muted colors of the desert, the subtle hues and tones of the scrub brush, the earthly pale reds of the ore embedded in the hills – all silhouetted against the many Joshua Trees and yucca bushes.

Red Rock Canyon has many nature and hiking trails, short and long, easy and strenuous. It is best to inquire at the visitor center about their difficulty if you have any questions. The easy way to see the conservation area is via the simple to drive 13-mile one-way scenic loop road. There are several good viewpoints of the red rock formations, especially in the beginning of the drive. The rocks are a favorite with rock climbers and you'll see dozens of people scampering over them at just about any time. If you're visiting with children take them along the short **Children's Discovery Trail**, where they'll learn about different varieties of plants and trees and see where Indians used to live beneath the natural rock overhangs.

Tel. 702/363-1921. The Conservation Area is open during daylight hours. The visitor center is open from 8:30 am to 4:30 pm. Admission is $5.00 per vehicle but National Park Service passports are honored. If visiting in the hotter months it is best to do hiking in the morning hours. Tours are available from Las Vegas for those who don't have their own wheels. Always carry water if you're going to be out on the trails.

Directions: Head west on W. Charleston Boulevard (located between the north end of The Strip and Downtown) for about 16 miles and follow sign to Red Rock Canyon.

SPRING MOUNTAINS ATTRACTIONS

There are two interesting attractions that lie within the Spring Mountains in the general vicinity of Red Rock Canyon. They can be done separately, or together with the Canyon to make for a most pleasant day long trip. The **Spring Mountain Ranch State Park** and **Bonnie Springs/ Old Nevada** both lie on the continuation of State Highway 159 just south of the exit from the Red Rock Canyon Scenic Loop Road.

Spring Mountain Ranch covers 500 acres and was built in 1869. It was expanded over the years and was once owned by Howard Hughes. The name comes from the several natural springs in the area that were once a source of water for the Paiute Indians. Of interest, aside from the excellent views of the mountains and portions of Red Rock Canyon, are the main ranch house which lies beneath the reddish Wilson Cliff Range and the wildlife that can often be seen by Lake Harriet. The state sponsors many events including the **Theater Under the Stars** program. *Tel. 702/ 875-4141. There is a $5 park entrance fee.*

The Bonnie Springs Ranch predates Spring Mountain Ranch by about 25 years. It was a wagon-train stop along the Old Spanish Trail to California. On the premises are a petting and feeding zoo as well as opportunities for horseback riding. Adjacent to the ranch is the Old Nevada Village, a restoration of an Old West frontier town with wooden sidewalks and saloons, ice cream parlors, a blacksmith shop, museums and souvenir shops. There's also a miniature train ride, gunfights and even hangings on the main square. The first two will delight children for sure although we're not so positive about the hangings. Adults will find a real saloon decorated with dollar bills. *Tel. 702/875-4191. Call for hours and prices.* Travelers on SR 159 will frequently encounter wild burros. Drive carefully, as there have been numerous accidents. You cannot stop on the main road. Pull completely off of the road in order to observe them from a safe distance. Do not attempt to feed or even approach the burros as they are unpredictable.

Directions: If coming from Red Rock Canyon simply turn right at the end of the loop road and you'll reach the two attractions in a few moments. If you're coming directly from Las Vegas proceed via Charleston Boulevard (as described in the directions for Red Rock Canyon and continue to Spring Mountain Ranch and Bonnie Springs.

MT. CHARLESTON

The **Spring Mountains National Recreation Area**, which is administered by the **Toiyabe National Forest**, is situated to the north and west of the Red Rock Canyon Conservation Area. This huge tract of land is a good place to go for great hiking, camping, backpacking, wagon rides, horseback riding, and in the winter, skiing and sleigh-riding. There is abundant wildlife (including coyotes, bighorn sheep, cougar and deer) and several dozen species of plant life, so much so that you'll wonder whether you're really still just a hop, skip, and a jump away from all that blazing neon.

The mountains reach over 10,000 feet in the Spring Mountain Range, which of course affects the weather: be forewarned that it often gets chilly at night, although the summertime daytime highs are a much more comfortable 20 degrees cooler than in the Valley. There is also considerably more precipitation in the higher elevations than in Las Vegas – the rain (or snow) comes in from the west and falls on the mountains but often doesn't make it over them. Imposing **Mt. Charleston** rises to a height of 11,918 feet. You can reach the area in about an hour from Las Vegas. Whether you're gazing at the area's tallest peak or looking out below and beyond from up on top, the view is spectacular.

Campers can drive to a campsite and do their thing from May 1 through September 30 only, although you can winter camp if you walk in. There are some beautiful trails here, several of which originate behind the **Mt. Charleston Lodge**, which is a great place to eat if you're coming up this way.

Directions: Take US 95 north until you reach Lee Canyon Road, which is State Highway 156. Turn left and proceed up the Canyon and in about 15 minutes you'll reach the Mt. Charleston ski area. We suggest an interesting scenic return route rather than just reversing the above directions. About six miles from the ski area turn right off Route 156 onto Route 158. This road winds its way along high ground for nine miles and offers excellent vistas. It ends at Route 157. A left turn here and a drive of 17 miles down Kyle Canyon will return you to US 95. (This route is actually three miles shorter than the way into Mt. Charleston but takes a little longer due to the slow going on Route 158.

VALLEY OF FIRE STATE PARK

If you like to hike or camp, hunt for old rocks, or just enjoy contemplating the nature of the Earth's geological history and the beauty it has created, this is just the place to do it. Red sandstone juts out in all directions, creating a picture-perfect desert landscape of rock formations with names like **Mouse's Tank**, **Seven Sisters** and **Elephant Rock**. Look for the bighorn sheep, burros, desert tortoise, wild horses and other Southwestern animals roaming about. Within it's more than 20 square miles are formations that have been dated back about 150 million years. The name comes from the vivid colors that are in abundance when reflected by the sun's light. In addition to the natural wonders, visitors can see some excellent examples of prehistoric petroglyphs. They were believed to have been carved by the Basketmaker people who predated the Ancestral Puebloans of the southwest. The best petroglyphs are reached by a strenuous metal staircase that ascends **Atlatl Rock**.

Most of the important formations in the Valley of Fire are alongside the road or reached by relatively short and easy trails. However, for the more adventurous, the park offers a good selection of longer and more difficult trails. The roads are good and consist of two routes. One is the state highway that runs east-to-west through the park. The other ascends a narrow gorge beginning at the visitor center and leads to some trailheads as well as overlooks that provide sweeping vistas of the surrounding desert and mountains. The visitor center has exhibits and you can get more detailed information on trails. Camping is available. Mid-day visits in the heart of summer should be avoided.

Tel. 702/397-2088. The park is open for day visits between dawn and dusk. The visitor center is open daily (except Christmas and New Year's) from 8:30 am to 4:30 pm. There is a $4 vehicle entry charge.

A nearby attraction in the town of Overton is the **Lost City Museum**. This fine facility specializes in the Ancestral Puebloan Indian culture (until recently more commonly known as the Anasazi) that predates the days of the Spanish explorers. *Tel. 702/397-2193. Open daily except Thanksgiving, Christmas and New Year's from 8:30 am to 4:30 pm. The admission charge is $2 for everyone 18 years of age and up.*

Directions: Take I-15 north about one hour (roughly 45 miles) to Exit 75 and then follow State Highway 169 east for 19 miles into the park. You have three options for the return trip, the first being to simply reverse the route you came by. A second choice is to exit the park on the east side and take Route 169 north through Overton to I-15 south. This allows you to visit the Lost City Museum in Overton. Finally, you can continue from the east exit for a mile to Route 167 and turn right. This will return you to the Las Vegas area via the Lake Mead National Recreation Area's North Shore Drive, a slower but pleasant trip. Route 167 ends at Route 147 which will take you back to I-515 and access to all parts of Las Vegas.

THE DESERT TORTOISE

Most people are surprised to hear that the deserts of southern Nevada are home to a tortoise, believing that these creatures like a watery environment. But such is not the case with this arid-loving cute little fella. It has become an endangered species as civilization encroaches upon its natural habitat. The biggest problem facing the desert tortoise is extinction due to being hit by automobiles. Of course, they're a protected species and there are a few rules that have to be followed by us humans.

First of all, if you spot one on the road you're supposed to stop and carefully pick it up and move it to a safe location. Not only do you have to take it out of harms way but you are required to report its location and which direction it was headed to wildlife officials. If you want to "adopt" one for your backyard that's alright, as long as you have an enclosure from which they cannot climb out of. After all, they might be hit by a car cruising down your street. You'll also see many low fenced off areas in places that aren't built up. These are to make sure that the tortoises that supposedly live within the fences' confines won't get out and become traffic statistics.

Now, we're all for protecting wildlife but don't you think that this is another case of a government on the loose that's reaching the lunatic fringe? In Nevada, at least, you're probably in less trouble if you kill a person than a desert tortoise.

LAUGHLIN

Many Vegas tour operators offer you a chance to do the exact same thing you'd do in Vegas – gamble – in the small town of Laughlin, some 90 miles to the south. But Laughlin isn't a smaller version of Las Vegas in one respect. It's got the Colorado River flowing through town, separating Nevada's southernmost city from Bullhead City, Arizona on the eastern bank of the river, and that means a wide variety of water fun right in front of you.

Most Vegas hotels have literature on Laughlin excursions in their lobby. You can check out the list of tour operators in the *Getting Around* chapter for phone numbers.

Las Vegas is not the only southern Nevada community with a nearby dam: Laughlin has **Davis Dam** at the edge of town holding back Lake Mojave to the north from the Colorado River to the south. Self guiding tours of the dam are available. From desert oasis just a decade back – there were only 90 residents in 1983, to today's sprawling town, Laughlin has come a long way. Although the building boom of the 80's has ended there are more than 10,000 hotel rooms and ten major hotel/casinos. Many of them are Vegas offshoots such as the Golden Nugget, Flamingo Hilton and Harrah's.

Just about all of the casinos in Laughlin are lined up alongside the Colorado River. There's a riverfront promenade that's a nice place for either a long or short stroll as long as the weather isn't too hot. You can get around in Laughlin nicely by foot (the hotels that are furthest away from the center, like Harrah's, have shuttle bus service. However, the coolest way to travel is by river taxi. These small boats ply the river and can stop at most of the bigger hotels. You can also get across the river to Bullhead City, Arizona, if the fancy strikes you. The **Ramada Express Hotel** has an old-time railroad circling the property that has good views and will keep the kids amused for a little while. It's free of charge. Consult the operating schedule outside the hotel. Laughlin also has some shopping.

Gambling is the main activity in Laughlin (that's why they'll bus you in from Vegas for free and throw in a free lunch) but tourists and many southern Nevadans also like the idea of outdoor fun being within easy reach (not that Vegas outdoor excursions are difficult to get to). Fishing, swimming, boating and various water sports are all just a few minutes away on the Colorado.

So, is it worth the trip? Keep in mind that the round trip takes almost four hours and that the sights in Laughlin aren't anything near what you can see in Vegas. Given all that we have some serious doubts as to whether it warrants the effort to get there but the choice is yours. It's probably a better idea if you're staying in Vegas for a week or more and need something different to do, or if you're on your second or third trip to Las Vegas. If you plan to go and would like more information contact the **Laughlin Visitor Center**, *1555 S. Casino Drive; Tel. 702/298-3321.*

Directions: Take US 93/95 south to where they split (just before Boulder City) and then follow US 95 south about 90 minutes to Route 163 east into Laughlin. The last part of the trip descends steeply and is quite scenic.

LAUGHLIN CASINOS AT A GLANCE

Bayshore Inn, Tel. 702/299-9010; 800/733-6644
Colorado Belle, Tel. 702/298-4000; 800/458-9500
Edgewater, Tel. 702/298-2453; 800/67-RIVER
Flamingo Hilton, Tel. 702/298-5111; 800/FLAMINGO
Gold River, Tel. 702/298-2242; 800/835-7903
Golden Nugget, Tel. 702/298-7111; 800/237-1739
Harrah's, Tel. 702/298-4600; 800/447-8700
Pioneer Gambling Hall, Tel. 702/298-2442; 800/634-3469
Ramada, Tel. 702/298-4200; 800/272-6232
Riverside Resort, Tel. 702/298-2535; 800/227-3849

PRIMM

If you want to get out into the desert for a while and do some gambling too, but without going as far as Laughlin is, then try Primm. It's much closer (actually on the way in or out of Las Vegas if you're coming from Southern California) and just as much fun. Actually, Primm isn't so much a town as it is a group of three casino hotels, a golf course and a factory outlet mall sitting astride both directions of the Interstate highway. It used to be known as Stateline, but was changed in 1996 at the behest of the Primm family who founded the place, and to avoid confusion with a Stateline located at Lake Tahoe in northern Nevada.

The route from Las Vegas is through pleasant mountain and desert scenery. Once you leave Vegas, civilization ends fast, although there are a couple of casinos about midway to Primm at Jean. The three Primm casinos are **Whiskey Pete's**, **Primm Valley Resort** and **Buffalo Bill's**. They're connected by shuttle bus, monorail or miniature train ride but you can even walk if the weather isn't too hot. Whiskey Pete's has the "death car" of Bonnie and Clyde as well as a John Dillinger owned vehicle on display. Buffalo Bill's has an interesting old west interior (including animated characters around a hanging tree) and some wild rides – a log flume and one of the world's highest and fastest roller coasters, The Desperado. The casinos have the usual amenities found in Las Vegas. Name entertainment appears in the Arena at Buffalo Bill's. *Fee charged for amusement rides.*

The new shopping mall is called the **Fashion Outlet of Las Vegas** and contains many of the most recognizable names in fashion. The exterior is absolutely ugly – it looks like a bunch of billboards at best. The interior, however, is architecturally interesting and contains many oversized figures gazing down on shoppers. Unless you are an outlet mall specialist, we wouldn't make the trip to Primm just for this place. However, if you're coming here for a few hours or the day to see the casinos or are passing by, then it's a good stop.

Directions: Take I-15 south to the Primm exit (#1). It's a distance of about 40 miles from The Strip and should take less than 45 minutes.

GHOST TOWNS & INDIAN RESERVATIONS

Most of southern Nevada's ghost towns were once thriving silver, lead or zinc mining centers built to support the mining industry. The prosperity, however, was short lived. Many of these towns did not last very long at all, places like **Poatosi**, **Sandy** and **Searchlight**. The main ghost town we'd recommend (most of the other ghost towns have little or nothng to show for themselves) is **Goodsprings**, 35 miles southwest of Las Vegas.

The combination of a natural spring and the wanderings of one Joseph Good combined to fix the town's name. Good mined the area in 1861. Prospectors from Utah arrived about 25 years later and there were more than 40 mines established. It had several thousand residents by the early 1900's but a flu epidemic in 1918 took many lives. This was soon followed by the collapse of metal and mineral prices. About 100 people still call Goodsprings their home. The big tourist attraction is the old **Pioneer Saloon**.

Directions: Take I-15 south to Jean, turn west on Route 161 for seven miles to Goodsprings.

We'll also mention up front that, if you are taking the trip to Death Valley, then the ghost town of **Rhyolite** (near the present town of Beatty just outside the National Monument) is one of Nevada's best. A word of caution is in order for those who like to explore these types of places. There are many abandoned mines in southern Nevada but all must be considered as dangerous. Several people usually lose their lives each year in accidents involving these places, so **keep out!**

Although there are three Indian nations that have lived in Nevada for hundreds of years or longer, there are few significant reservations among the 25 or so that still exist. They generally are not set up for visitors the way many in Arizona or New Mexico are. This is, depending upon your outlook, either good (Native Americans are not reduced to tourist attractions) or bad (opportunity for interaction and understanding between cultures is reduced).

The largest reservation in proximity to Las Vegas is the **Moapa Reservation**, about an hour north of town via I-15 to the exit for the Valley of Fire State Park. Other than the fireworks stand by the side of the road there isn't much to see or do here. However, some tribes occasionally hold pow-wows and perform ceremonial dances in Las Vegas and Boulder City.

GRAND CANYON

You're close to one of the most majestic pieces of real estate in the United States, but it's not exactly around the corner – roughly 300 miles away. To call the Grand Canyon a Vegas area attraction is analogous to New York calling Boston a New York area attraction. Still, who can blame the city elders for wanting to claim the **Grand Canyon National Park** as their very own backyard? You can choose to visit either the North Rim or the South Rim, maybe both if you've got the time.

The Canyon runs 277 miles in length, is a mile deep and almost 20 miles across at its widest point. It's a breathtaking, beautiful place. We're assuming here that you're mainly interested in a brief visit, so we'll limit our remarks to the very basics since huge volumes exist on the history, attractions, lodging, etc. The South Rim is the more heavily visited portion of the park although the "experts" will tell you that the relatively lightly traveled North Rim may even be more spectacular. Most visitors from Vegas don't drive to the Grand Canyon because that generally requires an overnight trip and they don't have the time to do so. There are ground tours that do it in a single day but we think that's a real knockout and doesn't even give you the time to properly appreciate what there is to see. So, how do you visit the canyon on a day-tripper? Read on.

Grand Canyon Air Tours From Las Vegas

"Flight-seeing" tours of the Grand Canyon depart from a number of places in the Las Vegas area, including McCarran Airport, the North Las Vegas Airport (most tours have relocated there in the past couple of years to relieve congestion at McCarran), and the Henderson Executive Airport (formerly Sky Harbor). In addition to flying over either one or both Grand Canyon rims, these flights usually include a pass over Lake Mead and Hoover Dam. Flights are no longer allowed to go into the canyon for safety and environmental reasons. Therefore, you should enhance the overall experience of your flight-seeing adventure by taking a trip that includes some time on the ground at the Grand Canyon. (There is an airport located there.) These trips aren't cheap. Prices start at about $80 for air only and at around $120 for trips that spend some time at the canyon. Helicopter tours are even more expensive.

Airplane tour operators include:
- **Lake Mead Air**, *Tel. 702/293-1848*
- **Las Vegas Airlines**, *Tel. 702/647-3056 or 800/634-6851*
- **Scenic Airlines**, *Tel. 702/638-3300 or 800/634-6801*

Helicopter tour operators include:
- **Discount Helicopter Tours Adventure**, *Tel. 702/471-7155*
- **Grand Canyon Tours**, *Tel. 702/655-60608 or 800/512-0075*. This company also offers plane and bus tours.
- **Papillon Grand Canyon Helicopters**, *Tel. 702/736-7243 or 888/635-7272*

In addition to the above operators, the general tour operators listed earlier in this book can book you on Grand Canyon flights.

Directions: If you're the stubborn type and plan to make the round-trip on your own (or are smarter and will do it with a stayover at the Canyon or elsewhere), the route there and back is quite simple. For the South Rim take US 93 south to I-40 at Kingman and then take the Interstate eastbound to Arizona Route 64 north into the park. For the North Rim take I-15 north to Utah 9 east (north of St. George) to US 89 at Mount Carmel. Go south to the Arizona 67 turnoff and follow it to the end. Combining the north and south rims by car really requires a three day trip and is beyond the scope of this book to describe.

DEATH VALLEY

Let's begin by telling you that a trip to the highlights of Death Valley can be done in a single day but you'll have to leave early and return late to make it worth the drive. You're better off making it an overnighter. Accommodations are available within Death Valley and in the town of Beatty. We strongly urge you not to go to Death Valley between late May and mid-September. Temperatures can be in the 120's and the unprepared visitor can be in for a rude surprise – even a dangerous one. Those temperatures are also hard on cars. The common wisdom is that the only people you see in Death Valley during the summer are German tourists. On the other hand, wintertime in Death Valley is delightful and spring and fall are definitely managable.

Death Valley National Park is a natural wonderland with tons of beautiful scenery. The diversity of the landscape comes as a surprise to most people who figure it's just a barren wasteland. Perhaps so, but the valley is surrounded by towering mountains that soar more than 12,000 feet above the valley, and within the valley there is a surprising variety of interesting and colorful rock formations. Besides stopping at **Badwater**, the lowest point in the United States, visitors should take a ride on **Artist's Drive**, an easy one way loop road; and drive up to the incredible **Dante's View** where the panorama of mountains and valley is spread out before you. **Zabriskie Point** has gold colored rocks and makes you feel like you're not on this planet anymore. **Scotty's Castle** is a mansion built in the early part of the century by an eccentric millionaire. However, it is in the northern part of the Monument and is too far to include on a day trip. Services within Death Valley are available at Furnace Creek.

Directions: The quickest way to get there is to take I-15 south to Blue Diamond Road and then head west on State Highway 160. Just north of the town of Pahrump turn left on Highway 210 which crosses into California. At Death Valley Junction pick up California Highway 190 which takes you into the heart of the Monument. Return the opposite way. If you're taking a two-day jaunt and want to see more of Death Valley then proceed as above as far as Pahrump and then follow Nevada 372 and California 178 through Shoshone and into the southern entrance of the Monument. Exit via Nevada 267 (from Scotty's Castle) or Nevada 374 (via Rhyolite and Beatty) to US 95. Then take US 95 south all the way back to Las Vegas.

SOUTHWESTERN UTAH

Some of the most amazing and beautiful scenery in the entire world will be found in the southwestern corner of the state of Utah, part of which goes by the name "Color Country." Unfortunately for Vegas visitors, it definitely requires at least two days to do properly although it is feasible to do at least Zion National Park in a single day. It's well beyond the scope of this book to even begin to thoroughly describe the scenic attractions of this area, so we'll give you a capsule listing of the most important attractions that are reachable in a mini-trip:

Brcye Canyon National Park: Simply put, one of the most beautiful places in all the world. A fairytale-like setting of multi-colored rock pinnacles in a natural amphitheater.

Cedar Breaks National Monument: A smaller and less spectacular version of Bryce.

Snow Canyon State Park: Colorful rock formations and outdoor recreation. Not as spectacular as the other places in southwestern Utah but it is the closest to Las Vegas.

Zion National Park: A dramatic narrow canyon flanked by massive walls and towering rock formations of different colors. Another section of the park outside the valley has splendid views into the valley as well as its own share of unusual geologic formations.

Some of the above, especially Zion, can be combined with a trip to the North Rim of the Grand Canyon.

Directions: I-15 north into Utah. Snow Canyon can be reached by taking Utah 18 north from the town of St. George. Take Utah 9 (north of St. George) east to Zion National Park. If you're continuing to Bryce then follow Utah 9 from Zion to US 89 and then go north to Utah 14 and then east to Bryce. Return via Utah 14 to Cedar Breaks and then rejoin I-15 at Cedar City for the return trip south to Las Vegas.

17. LAS VEGAS FOR KIDS

Las Vegas seems to have a Jekyll and Hyde attitude when it comes to children. At first it was an adults only sort of place. Then came the big push to attract families. Then some of the casino moguls decided that wasn't such a good idea after all. The result is that there are plenty of things for families with small children to do but you have to avoid certain places where children aren't so welcome or will be uncomfortable. That's what this chapter will try to help you out with.

In general, Las Vegas isn't appropriate for children under the age of six. Between that age and around 15 there are lots of enjoyable activities for them. Older teens present a special problem because they're old enough to want to try and sample things that they're legally not old enough to try. On the other hand, there are also many activities for children in that age group. We would be leading you astray if we told you that Las Vegas is as good a place to bring children on vacation as Disneyland. It isn't. But if you have children and you're planning on coming to Vegas, there isn't any reason that you shouldn't bring them along.

CHILD CARE FACILITIES

Several major hotels have on-premise facilities and supervised activities for children. If you want one on or near The Strip your best bets are the **MGM Grand**, **Las Vegas Hilton**, **Gold Coast** or **Orleans**. In addition, all four **Station Casinos** (Boulder, Palace, Sunset and Texas) have an extensive "Kids' Quest" facility.

If you're staying at a hotel other than the above and need a place to drop the kids for a few hours or a whole day, it's best to inquire with the hotel concierge or front desk personnel. Every hotel will be able to recommend a reliable child care giver that you can rely on.

ARCADES

There are countless arcades in the hotels along The Strip and in other locations throughout the Valley. In fact, you would be hard pressed to find a major hotel that doesn't have one of these electronic child sitters. Even some of the hotels that try not to gear themselves towards children usually give in on this one. Children, of course, from ages six and up will have no trouble occupying themselves in almost any arcade for hours on end. That's the good part. However, we caution parents that there is often little or no supervision of the arcades. You may leave your children there but do you know that they will remain there if you go off to gamble or do something else? Our point is that, used appropriately, the arcades can be an enjoyable part of your child's visit to Las Vegas. However, they are not a substitute for parental supervision and shouldn't be treated as such.

Clark County regulations bar children under the age of 18 from being in an arcade after 10 pm (midnight on weekends) unless they are accompanied by an adult.

With all of that in mind, it's time to let the kids have some fun. The Strip's **Gameworks** in the Showcase Center is the biggest arcade and town and has even more options than any of the hotel arcades.

AMUSEMENT & THEME PARKS

Hours and prices for amusement parks tend to vary quite a bit depending upon the season so it is always best to call in advance, especially during the winter.

Adventuredome/Circus Circus, *see Chapter 12 for details.*

Las Vegas Mini Grand Prix & Family Fun Center, *1401 N. Rainbow Blvd., Tel. 702/259-7000.* A different kind of amusement park that can be loads of fun for all ages. It has kiddie karts for drivers under the age of four, go karts for the bigger kids, Gran Prix cars and super stock cars for those 16 and over. Except for the kiddie karts, you drive over an actual "race" course. By the way, the Las Vegas Mini Grand Prix hosts competition races that are open to everyone. Prizes are awarded. A game arcade and snack bar are on the premises. *Open year round.*

MGM Grand Adventures, *see Chapter 12 for details.*

Mountasia Family Fun Center, *2050 Olympic Avenue, Henderson (one block north of Sunset Road and Mountain Vista), Tel. 702/898-7777.* The usual assortment of mini-rides, slides and so forth. Best for smaller children.

Speedworld, *in the Sahara Hotel. Tel. 702/737-2471.* Not exactly an amusement park, but rather a high-tech facility with virtual reality and 3/4-scale Indy style simulated auto racing. Prices vary according to type of attraction, with the Indy cars costing $8. *Daily from 10 am to 10 pm (11 pm on Friday and Saturday).*

Scandia Family Fun Center, *2900 Sirius Avenue, Tel. 702/364-0070.* Features miniature golf, bumper cars and boats, bating cage and a video arcade. *Children under five are allowed in for free.*

Wet 'N Wild, *2601 Las Vegas Blvd. S., Tel. 702/734-0088.* Located adjacent to the Sahara Hotel, this place has swimming, floating and sliding on 26 acres of pools, lagoons and waterslides. More than 1.5 million gallons of water beckon you to get wet and act wild. Try the Blue Niagara, a waterslide inside a 300-foot long blue loop, a wave-maker, the Black Hole water ride and Bomb Bay. It's a nice place to cool off from the blazing summer sun. *Open April through September.*

ATTRACTIONS FOR KIDS

We won't bother going into a lot of detail repeating what has already been said in the Seeing the Sights chapter. However, to make things easier for you to plan, we'll give you a brief rundown on those previously described attractions that will be enjoyed by children.

The Strip itself, either by day or night, is a magical experience for any age. Just keep a tight rein on the little ones. (There is a curfew on The Strip that is in effect at all times. Those under the age of 18 are not allowed to be on The Strip without being accompanied by an adult after 9 pm, and it is enforced.) At Caesars, the **Sinking of Atlantis** as well as all the simulator rides are the focus for kids. Just about everything except the casino at **Circus-Circus** and the **Excalibur** is excellent, as are the simulator and theater at the **Luxor**. The **Secret Garden of Siegfried & Roy** and the **Tiger Habitat** at The Mirage are among the best kiddie destination's as is, of course, the **Battle of Buccaneer Bay** at Treasure Island. The **New York, New York** roller coaster and the thrill rides atop the **Stratosphere Tower** can take up some time as will the **Star Trek Experience** at the Las Vegas Hilton. Two other Strip attractions where children will be at home are all of the segments of the **Showcase** complex and the **Magic & Movie Hall of Fame** at O'Sheas. Masquerade Village's **Show in the Sky** is a good choice along with the dazzling lights of the **Fremont Street Experience**.

The museums near downtown, **Lied Discovery Museum** and **Museum of Natural History**, are both entertaining as well as educational. The Henderson **Factory Four** is another group of attractions that are likely to find favor with your little ones.

When it comes to excursions, the best one for children is **Hoover Dam**. This is something that will amaze people of all ages. The natural attractions around the Las Vegas area can be enjoyed by children if they aren't too small. Nature doesn't seem to impress those under the age of around eight.

Note that the Bellagio and Mirage hotels do not allow anyone under 18 years of age to be in the hotel unless they are registered guests. That also means you can't take a stroller inside unless you're staying there. We think they've gone a bit too far with the adult atmosphere.

SOME HOTEL SUGGESTIONS

Where to stay in Las Vegas when you have children with you is a different question than if only grown-ups are visiting. There are some hotels that have a deserved reputation for being kid-friendly and some that seem to go out of their way to make children unwanted, although the majority lie somewhere in between these two extremes.

The most suitable hotels for children include **Circus Circus**, the **Excalibur**, the **MGM Grand** and **Treasure Island**. The hotels that we would suggest avoiding if you have small children are Bellagio and the Desert Inn. We haven't had enough exposure to the newest places (Mandalay Bay, Venetian and Paris) to come to any conclusions but we think that they'll be somewhere in the middle along with all the other hotels we didn't mention in this section. Surprisingly, the upscale **Four Seasons** provides a package of children's amenities upon check-in for guests toting little ones with them.

18. WEDDING CHAPELS

Imagine exchanging vows on a 175-foot high bungee jumping platform adjacent to Circus Circus and then, literally, taking the plunge to get the marriage off to a good start. Or getting married in a helicopter, or by a singing Elvis, or in a hot tub at the back end of a stretch limo. These and almost countless other possibilities can all be reality in the wacky world of Las Vegas. Las Vegas is a place of extremes and if you want to do it, you can. If you have a suggestion for an unusual wedding try mentioning it to the staff of one of the more unusual wedding chapels, and they might (for an extra fee) do exactly what you want. Believe it or not, about five percent of all weddings in the United States take place in Las Vegas! Most, however, are rather ordinary.

About 100,000 couples exchange vows in Las Vegas each year. Valentine's Day is always a big wedding day in Las Vegas, with more than 2,500 weddings taking place annually on February 14th. No other city can boast as many wedding chapels – about a hundred in all.

Actually, most chapels do not have Elvis performers or other such gimmicks. Many are of the standard, old-fashioned quickie marriage variety. Whether you're planning to tie the knot here, or are just curious, take some time to visit one or more of these chapels. It's a fun break from all the faster-paced action in Vegas. You'll frequently see bride and groom, all dressed up for the occasion, walking through the hotels or down The Strip. Often they're at the tables or slot machines spending all of their wedding money. Wedding parties are frequently to be seen in front of some of the major hotel's best picture taking spots doing just that – snapping the official wedding photobook.

GOING TO THE CHAPEL

State law does not require a blood test. There is no waiting period. If you're 18 years old, you're in (if you're under 18 you need a parent's or guardian's notarized consent). Just get a license from the **Clark County Marriage License Bureau**, *200 S. 3rd Street; Tel. 702/455-3156*. Remember that both you and your intended have to apply in person. The license fee is $35. The license bureau is open from 8 am to midnight, Monday through Thursday and from 8 am Friday to midnight Sunday (i.e., all weekend). If you want a Justice of the Peace and nothing fancy, walk about a block to the **Commissioner of Civil Marriages**, *309 S. 3rd Street; Tel. 702/ 455-3474.* They'll get you wedded in a jiffy before you know it for a mere additional $35.

Many of the better known chapels are grouped together at the northern end of Las Vegas Boulevard South, the bulk of them starting a short distance after the Stratosphere Tower and continuing for about a mile to between Charleston Boulevard and Downtown. This isn't the pretty side of town and mixed in among the chapels are seedy motels, pawn shops, adult video stores and less than gourmet dining. The atmosphere, however, doesn't seem to bother anyone and the chapels do a booming business. The chapels run the gamut from simple to beautiful. If you want something on the fancier side then you might want to consider using a wedding chapel in one of the big hotels. Many of the hotels have them and they're often tied to the theme of the hotel itself.

Besides Valentine's Day, New Year's Eve and the entire month of June are the busiest times for Las Vegas weddings. Depending on what you're looking for you can spend as little as $100 for the entire package, including the license, chapel fee, minister's or judge's fee and tip. (The latter runs about $25-50.). Not a bad deal, considering the cost of weddings these days. On the other hand, you could easily spend well into four digits. The choice is yours.

Some of the best known of Las Vegas' wedding chapels are briefly reviewed here. First we'll do the independent chapels, followed by a few of the better hotel-based establishments.

INDEPENDENT CHAPELS

A LITTLE WHITE CHAPEL, *1301 Las Vegas Blvd. South. Tel. 702/ 382-5943.*

Perhaps no other wedding chapel in Las Vegas has so many crazy ways to get married on their "menu" as this place does. Their minister will come to your place, no matter where in the area that may be. At the chapel itself you can drive (or even roller skate) through the Tunnel of Love for a drive-in ceremony. You can get married right in the front seat (and, no doubt for some, have the honeymoon in the back seat). The Little White Chapel in the Sky is a colorful hot air balloon for those who want an airborne wedding experience. (This chapel also claims the record for the most marriages performed in a helicopter.) They even have a branch at the Las Vegas Motor Speedway. Among the celebrities who've tied the knot here were Demi Moore/Bruce Willis, Joan Collins (we forget which husband) and basketball great Michael Jordan.

CANDLELIGHT WEDDING CHAPEL, *2855 Las Vegas Blvd. South. Tel. 702/735-4179.*

Because of its Strip location (right across the street from the Riviera Hotel), this is one of the most frequented wedding spots in Las Vegas. The chapel provides a nice touch by offering free limousine service from your hotel. Join the ranks of Bette Midler, Whoopi Goldberg and Michael Caine, who all were married at Candlelight.

CHAPEL OF THE BELLS, *2233 Las Vegas Blvd. South. Tel. 702/735-6803.*

This pretty little chapel has been featured in many movies and lots of famous people have been married here. A good place for a more straight forward ceremony than say the Little White Chapel.

CHAPEL L'AMOUR, *1901 Las Vegas Blvd. South. Tel. 702/369-5683.*

Both a chapel and a wedding store. If you're into red velvet then this is the place for you. They also own a long trailer called Weddings on Wheels where, among other things, you can watch the volcano blow its top at the Mirage while you exchange vows for richer or poorer (and in Vegas the latter is a definite possibility if you're not real careful).

CHAPEL OF LOVE, *1431 Las Vegas Blvd. South. Tel. 702/387-0155.*

Very nice facility with four separate chapels so you rarely have to wait for your next. The name says it all for those romantically inclined. Each chapel has a different color scheme.

CUPID'S WEDDING CHAPEL, *827 Las Vegas Blvd. South. Tel. 702/598-4444.*

Often photographed, Cupid's is also one of the better known establishments. They'll make reservations for you if you're coming in from out of town.

GRACELAND WEDDING CHAPEL, *619 Las Vegas Blvd. South. Tel. 702/474-6655.*

What more could a bride and groom want? Elvis belts out a tune and serves as your witness. Bon Jovi got married here and growing numbers of rockers are following his lead, making this one of the more hip wedding chapels in town. But you don't have to be a famous rock-and-roll star to get in the door here – they'll take anyone!

LITTLE CHURCH OF THE WEST, *4617 Las Vegas Blvd. South. Tel. 702/739-7971.*

The most historic of Las Vegas chapels (dating back to 1942) and now on the National Register of Historic Places. The Little Church of the West started out next to the old Last Frontier Hotel and then moved (literally – the whole building headed down The Strip) to a site on the grounds of the Hacienda. When they imploded that hotel the chapel moved a few blocks south to its present location. Simple, no gimmick weddings. Free champagne is given to the happy couple.

SHALIMAR WEDDING CHAPEL, *1401 Las Vegas Blvd. South. Tel. 702/382-7372.*

This is another of the nice chapels without gimmicks. They have a pretty gazebo if you want to get married outdoors.

SILVER BELL WEDDING CHAPEL, *607 Las Vegas Blvd. South. Tel. 702/382-3726.*

The price here includes the cost of your marriage license so it's one of the better buys. They've been in business for nearly 40 years, making it one of the oldest chapels after the Little Church of the West. It has been nicely refurbished.

BEST HOTEL WEDDING CHAPELS

BALLYS (BALLY'S CELEBRATION CHAPEL), *Tel. 702/892-2222.*

The Bally's monorail has "a touch of class" written on its side and the same can be said of their chapel. No glitz, just a very pretty and formal setting for what is, after all, a serious affair.

BELLAGIO (BELLAGIO WEDDING CHAPEL), *Tel. 702/693-8787.*

The new Bellagio's chapel has the kind of elegance found throughout the hotel. There are two chapels, one seating 35 and the other 135 persons. Prices are high (more than $1,000 to start), but this is a first class operation. They even video the entire proceedings from behind mirrors and you receive the edited tape immediately upon leaving the chapel.

IMPERIAL PALACE (WE'VE ONLY JUST BEGUN CHAPEL), *Tel. 702/733-0011.*

This was one of the first major hotels to have a chapel on the premises. The name is kind of corny but they do a real nice job.

EXCALIBUR (CANTERBURY CHAPELS), *Tel. 702/597-7278.*

Two attractive chapels, one large and one small where you can have a traditional ceremony or you can get all dressed up as the lord and lady of the castle for a Medieval style ceremony.

FLAMINGO HILTON (GARDEN CHAPEL), *Tel. 702/733-3232.*

Located in its own little building, the pretty chapel overlooks the hotel's spacious and beautiful grounds. A trellis lined walkway faces the chapel entrance.

MGM GRAND (FOREVER GRAND CHAPEL), *Tel. 702/891-7950.*

No theme here, but the chapel is beautiful and the arrangments are excellent.

MONTE CARLO (MONTE CARLO WEDDING CHAPEL), *Tel. 702/730-7575.*

Getting married here is like the prelude to a French Riviera honeymoon.

RIO HOTEL (RIO WEDDING CHAPEL), *Tel. 702/247-7986.*
Like most things at the Rio, part sophistication, part fun.
TREASURE ISLAND (TREASURE ISLAND CHAPELS), *Tel. 800/527-6393.*

The chapels are real nice but for something really special (at a substantial extra fee), how about exchanging vows in a ceremony on board the deck of the *HMS Britania*? Don't worry, they don't fight the pirate ship when weddings are taking place.

TROPICANA (ISLAND WEDDING CHAPEL), *Tel. 702/798-6151.*
On the same idea as the Garden Chapel at the Flamingo Hilton and almost as nice. The wood-beamed interior is supposed to be like a Polynesian meeting hall.

DIVORCE, LAS VEGAS STYLE

We're not trying to break up the marriage so soon after the wedding, but the flip side of the easy marriage laws in Nevada are the quickie divorce laws. With only a six week residency period required for divorce (and then six weeks more to get your final papers), a lot of people check into a hotel or extended-stay motel in order to make the qualification. In fact, after the 1931 Nevada law that liberalized wedding and divorce regulations, there was a time when more people came to Nevada to take advantage of the divorce regulations than marriages. It's how the state earned its title of the "Divorce capital of the world." While the laws haven't changed and plenty of people still come to Vegas to break up, family supporters will be glad to learn that in recent years the number of divorces performed in Las Vegas is only about one-tenth of the volume of marriages. Ain't love grand?

19. ANNUAL EVENTS

The calendar of annual events keeps getting more and more filled. From the rodeo to poker tournaments to crafts shows, Las Vegas has plenty of things to do all year round. The only problem you'll have is finding the time to fit them in with everything else there is to do!

Here's the month-by-month breakdown on many of the more significant events that are held on an annual basis. Since the schedule for events is often subject to change (and the exact days usually vary), check with the folks holding the event or the **Las Vegas Convention and Visitor's Authority**, *Tel. 702/892-0711*, for exact days and times. Venues for annual events also change in many cases (which is why you won't always see the location in the list below), so, once again it's wise to contact the LVCVA. They publish a list of events that covers two months at a time which can be found in many hotels. The visitor authority has an office at the Convention Center where you can stop by and find out what's happening. Also be sure to scan local publications and newspapers for other annual as well as special events that may be taking place while you're in town.

Although some of the events in this list are unique to Las Vegas because of their gaming nature or tie-in, one of the nicest things about some of them is that they are, by and large, for locals. However, visitors are welcome and this is one way to learn that people in Las Vegas live just like those in other parts of the country. You can get a true taste of the southern Nevada life-style and find that it, too, is a whole lot more than gambling.

JANUARY
Consumer Electronics Show, *Las Vegas Convention Center*, is a showcase for new and often unusual products that will soon be available on the open market.

Super Bowl Sunday generates as much excitement in Las Vegas as in the city hosting the big game. It's one of the busiest weekends of the year and thousands of people jam their favorite race and sports book to watch the game on big screen TV. Dozens of hotel/casinos large and small host Super Bowl parties.

FEBRUARY

Autorama Antique Car Show, *Cashman Field.*

Bridal Spectacular Show, *Cashman Field.* See the latest in bridal wear and wedding catering, then go out and tie (or re-tie) the knot at a local wedding chapel!

Great American Train Show, *Cashman Field.* A must for little train lovers.

Ladies Professional Golf Association Tournament, *Desert Inn Hotel.* Sometimes held in March.

CONVENTION CITY

Las Vegas is one of the most popular spots in the world for convention planners large and small. The attractions of Las Vegas that appeal to most visitors are only part of the reason that so many conventions are held here. Another important reason is that there are few places that can match the facilities that Las Vegas possesses for holding large conventions. In additon to the behemoth sized Las Vegas Convention Center, there's the Sands Convention Center and the Cashman Field Center. And if that's not enough, throw in the majority of The Strip hotels, which have their own extensive convention facilities.

Most conventions don't have much impact on non-convention visitors but one of the important exceptions is the annual computer show called **Comdex** *that is held around the middle of November. The number of visitors to Comdex now exceeds 200,000. It obviously takes a lot of hotel space and convention space to pull off such an affair and Las Vegas may be the only city that could do it so well. But that many visitors means that you, as an individual, would have trouble finding a hotel room during Comdex.*

Even if you could get a room you might not want one. Because Comdex dominates the tourism industry during its five day run, it has a negative effect on many traditional aspects of Las Vegas. Perhaps the most obvious example is that most shows are dark during Comdex because the typical Comdex attendee doesn't go for that sort of entertainment. It's been said that Comdex conventioneers arrive in town with one clean shirt on their back and $20 in their pocket and don't change either! – you get the idea.

MARCH

Native American Arts Festival, *Clark County Heritage Museum, Henderson*, is the largest Native American event of the year in southern Nevada.

Crafts Festival, *Cashman Field*.

St. Patrick's Day Parade and Block Party. There's a parade downtown for the major event but dozens of little celebrations dot the town as well.

Hoover Dam Square Dance, *Boulder City*.

Las Vegas 400-NASCAR Winston Cup Series, *Las Vegas Motor Speedway*, was first held in 1998 and promises to become one of the biggest annual sporting events to be held in "Glitzville".

Las Vegas Big League Weekends, *Cashman Field*, helps close out the Exhibition season of Major League Baseball. Usual dates are the end of March as well as the first few days in April.

APRIL

Art-A-Fair and Festival of Arts, *Canyon Gate Country Club*.

Henderson Heritage Days, *Henderson*, includes a parade down Water Street and food and craft fairs, antique auto show and more at several different venues in and around town.

World Poker Championship Series, *Binion's Horseshoe Hotel* (finishes in May) attracts some of the world's best players who compete for huge prizes. Lots of people like to watch.

Boulder City Spring Jamboree and Craft Show, *Boulder City* (sometimes held in May).

MAY

Helldorado Days and Rodeo, *various venues*, celebrates the old west with rodeo, parades, cooking contests, dances and general partying.

Clark County Fair and Rib Burn-off, *Sunset Park*.

Clark County Artists Show, *Boulder City Bicentennial Park*.

JDF Monopoly Tournament benefits the Juvenile Diabetes Foundation.

Snow Mountain Pow Wow is held by the Las Vegas Paitue Tribe on their reservation north of Las Vegas at the Kyle Canyon Turnoff of US 95.

Senior Classic Golf Tournament, *Desert Inn Hotel*.

JUNE

Sand Bash Open Golf Tournament, *Canyon Gate Country Club*.

Green Valley "Concert Under the Stars" is a jazz show held in various parks around Henderson throughout the summer.

Las Vegas International Film Festival. It isn't Cannes, but the industry is increasingly recognizing this as an important cinema event.

JULY

 Fourth of July Family Pops Concert featuring the Las Vegas Symphony Orchestra, *Cashman Field.*

 Fourth of July Damboree, *Boulder City.*

 Green Valley "Concert Under the Stars" features classical music this month.

AUGUST

 Hoedown Concert Series, *Las Vegas Jaycee Park,* features bluegrass and country & western music.

SEPTEMBER

 Shakespeare in the Park, *Foxridge Park.* Who says Vegas lacks culture? For Bard lovers and those who like old-fashioned entertainment events.

 Oktoberfest, *Las Vegas Art Museum.*

 KNR Craftswork Market, *Henderson Convention Center.*

 Las Vegas Cup Unlimited Hydroplane Races, *Lake Mead.* See these jet-like boats whiz by on the lake.

OCTOBER

 Jaycess State Fair, *either Cashman Field or Convention Center.* Sometimes held in late September.

 Art in the Park, *Boulder City.*

 Fairshow, *North Las Vegas.* Music, food, crafts and a carnival.

 Las Vegas International Golf Tournament, *Summerlin, Tournament Players Course and other courses.*

 Harvest Festival, *Cashman Field.* (Sometimes held in early November).

NOVEMBER

 Antique and Classic Car Sale, *Imperial Palace Hotel.*

 Magical Forest, *Opportunity Village* (mid-November through late December), benefits the mentally retarded. Begun in 1992 this extraordinary display of Christmas is a wonderland for all ages – three million lights, crafts, gingerbread houses, a train ride and even artificial snow.

 Wendy's Three Tour Challenge, *Reflection Bay at Lake Las Vegas, Henderson,* is one of the nation's big golf tournaments and attracts a big crowd.

DECEMBER

Christmas Parade, *Boulder City.*

National Finals Rodeo, *Thomas & Mack Center and other venues.* This is one of the largest and most prestigious rodeo events in the country. The whole town seems to take on a western theme (even the Imperial Palace's "Legends in Concerts" show goes all-country during the NFR). Lot's of fun with all those cowboys in town.

Nevada State Championship Chili Cookoff.. A really hot time!

New Year's Eve Celebrations are a big thing in Las Vegas which is, after all, party city. There's a big to-do Downtown under the canopy of the Fremont Street Experience but the real party is on The Strip. Hundreds of thousands of visitors and residents promenade up and down Las Vegas Boulevard in a celebration that rivals the one in Times Square in New York. The Strip is closed to vehicular traffic in what has become the world's biggest block party.

HOTEL IMPLOSIONS – THE NEW VEGAS EXTRAVAGANZA!

When Las Vegas gets ready to rid itself of an old hotel, they don't call in the wrecking ball – that wouldn't be dramatic enough for this city. They IMPLODE and it's become a big attraction in itself. It began quite a few years ago with The Dunes Hotel. This was a daytime implosion and it attracted so many people that it scared the city fathers so much that when it came time for the next two implosions, they were done in the middle of the night. That still didn't keep at least some people from witnessing the demise of The Landmark and the venerable Sands. (Footage from the Landmark implosion was used in the zany sci-fi spoof movie Mars Attacks!)

Then Circus Circus Enterprises decided that attracting people was a good idea after all. So they imploded the Hacienda to coincide with the nationally televised New Years' Eve celebration on December 31, 1996. This was "the mother of all implosions" and was deliberately slowed down and enchanced with flames and other pyrotechnic displays to thrill the quarter-of-a-million estimated onlookers. Most recently, in April of 1998, the old Aladdin came down at sunset to the cheers of happy spectators.

While it only takes seconds to reduce a big building to a pile of dust through implosion, the process isn't as fast or simple as it looks. It takes several weeks of meticulous work to strategically place the explosives. While we don't know of any impending implosions, it's only a matter of time before some hotel developer decides that something has to give to make way for another mega-resort. And if you can be here for it, all the better.

INDEX

Adventure Dome 174-175
Airfares 33-35
Airlines 35-36
Airport, *see McCarran International Airport*
Airport transportation 47
Aladdin Hotelo & Casino 193
Alcoholic beverage laws 37
Alexis Park Resort 78-79
Amtrak 50
Annual Events 264-268
Antiques 226
Appian Way 172, 224
Arcades 256
Arizona Charlie's 92
Art works 227-228
Auto Racing 235

Babysitting services 255
Baccarat, how to play 157-160
Bally's Las Vegas 65, 168
Banking 37-38
Barbary Coast Hotel & Casino 70
Baseball 235
Bellagio Hotel 60-61, 168-171
Belz Factory Outlet World 226-227
Best of Las Vegas 20, 131
Bicycling 230
Binion family 26
Binion's Horseshoe 87, 198
Blackjack, how to play 137-141
Boating 231
Bonnie Springs Ranch 245
Boulder City 242
Boulder Station Hotel & Casino 89-90
Boulevard Mall 226
Bowling 231

Boxing 235
Bryce Canyon National Park 254
Buffets 123-131
Bungee jumping 231
Bus service: inter-city 48; Las Vegas area 53-54; Strip 54

Caesars Palace 66, 171-174
California Hotel & Casino 86
Camping & RV Parks 94-95
Car rentals 48
Carroll Shelby Factory & Museum Tour 201
Casino basics 132-133
Casino only establishments 206
Chamber of Commerce 32
Children 255-258
Chinatown 201
Circus Circus Hotel & Casino 76, 174-175
Citizens Area Transit (CAT) 53-54
Clark County Heritage Museum 205
Climate 29-30
Commercial Center 122
Comps 45
Convention & Visitors Authority 32, 264
Conventions 29, 265
Craps, how to play 142-148
Crowne Plaza Hotel 79

Dalitz, Moe 26
Dancing 218-220
Death Valley National Park 253-254
Desert Demonstration Gardens 201
Desert Inn Hotel & Casino 61, 175
Dining 96-131; see also individual hotel listings

Disabled, services for 44
Divorce laws 263
Don Pablo Cigar Company 195
Downtown 85-88, 118-119, 129-130, 198-200, 226
Driving to Las Vegas 49-50

El Rancho Vegas 25
Ellis Island Casino 206
Emergencies 38-39
Entertainment, *see Nightlife & Entertainment*; celebrity 217-218
Ethel M. Chocolates 204
Excalibur Hotel & Casino 7, 175-176
Excursions from Las Vegas 239-254

Fashion Show Mall 225
Favorite Brands Marshmallow Factory 204-205
Fiesta Hotel & Casino 92
Fitzgerald's Hotel & Casino 86
Flamingo Hilton 70, 176-177
Foreign visitors 39
Forum Shops at Caesars 173-174, 223-224
Four Queens Hotel & Casino 87
Four Seasons Hotel 61
Fremont Hotel & Casino 86
Fremont Street Experience 199
Fun Books & Discounts 40

Galleria at Sunset Mall 227
Gambling 132-166
Gambling paraphenalia 229
Gambler's Book Club 229
Gambler's General Store 229
Gaming laws 37
Getting Around Las Vegas 51-56
Ghost towns 251
Glitter Gulch: see *Downtown*
Gold Coast Hotel & Casino 83
Golden Gate Hotel & Casino 85
Golden Nugget Hotel 199
Golf 231-233
Grand Canal Shoppes 192, 224
Grand Canyon 252-253
Guiness World of Records Museum 195

Hard Rock Hotel & Casino 80, 195-196
Harrah's Las Vegas 71, 177
Health 40
Henderson 93-94, 122-123, 130-131, 202-206, 227
Henderson Factory Four 203-205
Hiking 233
History of Las Vegas 24-28
Holiday Inn Boardwalk 71
Hoover Dam 240, 242
Horseback riding 233
Hospitals 38
Hotels & Casinos 57-95, see also individual hotel listings
Hughes, Howard 26

Ice hockey 235
Ice skating 235
Imperial Palace Auto Collection 177-178
Imperial Palace Hotel & Casino 71-72, 177-178
Indian reservations 251
Itineraries, suggested 21-23

Jackie Gaughan's Plaza Hotel 87-88
Jerry's Nugget 206
Jewelry stores 228

Keno, how to play 151-153
Kerkorian, Kirk 26
Klondike Hotel & Casino 77

LaQuinta Inn 84
Lady Luck Hotel & Casino 88
Lake Las Vegas 204
Lake Mead 243
Lake Mead National Recreation Area 242-244
Las Vegas: accommodations, see Hotels & Casinos; moving to 28
Las Vegas Art Museum 201
Las Vegas Club Hotel & Casino 88
Las Vegas Events 32
Las Vegas Hilton 79, 196
Las Vegas Natural History Museum 200

Las Vegas valley, geography 46
Laughlin 248-250
Lee Canyon 246
Liberace Museum 198
Lied Discovery Children's Museum 200
Limousines 55
Lounge acts 214-217
Luxor Hotel & Casino 72, 178-180
Luxor IMAX Theater 179

Main Street Station Hotel & Casino 86-87, 199
Magazines 41
Magic shows 211-212, 213, 215
Majorie Barrick Museum of Natural History 198
Mandalay Bay Hotel & Casino 67, 180-182
Marriott Suites 78
Maxim Hotel & Casino 84
McCarran International Airport 46-47
MGM Grand Adventures Theme Park 183
MGM Grand Hotel 67-68, 182-184
Mirage, The 68, 184-185
Money management 134-135
Monte Carlo Hotel & Casino 72-73, 185
Mormons 24
Mormon Temple 201-202
Mt. Charleston 246-247
Mt. Charleston Lodge 246
Music 222

Nellis Air Force Base 28
Neonopolis 199-200
Nevada Commission on Tourism 32
Nevada Control Board 26
Nevada Gaming Commission 26
Nevada Palace Hotel & Casino 92
Nevada State Museum & Historical Society 202
Nevada Test Site 28
New Frontier Hotel & Casino 73
New York, New York Hotel & Casino 68-69, 185-186

Newspapers 41
Nick the Greek 2
Nightclubs 218-221; men's clubs 221-222
Nightlife & Entertainment 207-222

Ocean Spray Cranberry World West 204
Old Mormon Fort 200
Omnixmax Theater 172-173
Orleans Hotel & Casino 80-81

Paiute Indians 24, 251
Palace Station Hotel & Casino 81
Paris Hotel & Casino 69, 186-187
Parking 53
Places of worship 41-42
Poker, how to play 153-157
Primm 250-251
Production shows 208-214
Prostitution 18

Rafting 234
Red Rock Canyon Natural Conservation Area 244-245
Reservations, hotel 58-59
Reserve Hotel & Casino, The 94, 202-203
Resort at Summerlin, The 88-89
Restaurants: see *Dining*
Rio Suite Hotel & Casino 81-82, 197-198, 217, 220
Riviera Hotel & Casino 73-74, 187-188, 208, 210, 213-214
Roulette, how to play 160-163

Sahara Hotel & Casino 77, 217
Sam Boyd Stadium 236
Sam's Town & Gambling Hall 90, 220
San Remo 82, 209
Santa Fe Hotel & Casino 91
Sassy Sally's 206
Scandia Family Fun Center 257
Senior citizens 44-45
Shopping 223-229
Showboat Hotel & Casino 92-93
Showcase 194-195
Siegel, Benjamin "Bugsy" 25

Siegfried and Roy 213
Silver City Casino 206
Silverton Hotel & Casino 93
Simulator rides 173-174, 176, 196
Skiing 235
Sky diving 235
Slots, how to play 148-151
Souvenir shops 229
Spectator sports 235-236
Sports and Recreation 230-238
Spring Mountain Ranch State Park 245
Southern Nevada Zoological Park 202
St. Tropez Suites 82
Stardust Hotel & Casino 74
Stratosphere Hotel & Casino 74, 188
Strip, The 60-78, 97-113, 125-128, 167-195, 233-236
Strip Trolley 54
Sunset Station Hotel & Casino 93-94, 202
Swimming 236

Taxes 43
Taxis 55
Telephones 43
Tennis 237
Texas Station Hotel & Casino 91
Theater 222
Theme parks 174-175, 183, 256-257
Thomas and Mack Center 236
Time shares 95
Time Zone 43
Tipping 43-44

Toiyabe National Forest 246
Tortoise, desert 248
Tourism information 32
Tours, guided 56
Train service, see Amtrak
Traffic 52-53
Transportation 53-55
Treasure Island Hotel & Casino 75, 189-190
Trolley service 54
Tropicana Resort & Casino 75, 190-191

Universitgy of Nevada Las Vegas (UNLV) 236

Vacation Village 84-85
Valley of Fire State Park 247
Vegas Pointe Plaza 227
Venetian Hotel & Casino, The 64-65, 191-194
Video poker, how to play 163-166

Weather: see Climate
Wedding chapels 259-263
Westward Ho Motel & Casino 77-78
Wet 'n Wild 257
What's On magazine 41
Wild Wild West Gambling Hall & Hotel 85
Wynn, Steve 26

Zion National Park 254
Zoo 202

THINGS CHANGE!

Phone numbers, prices, addresses, quality of food, etc, all change. If you come across any new information, we'd appreciate hearing from you. No item is too small! Drop us an e-mail note at: Jopenroad@aol.com, or write us at:

Las Vegas Guide
Open Road Publishing, P.O. Box 284
Cold Spring Harbor, NY 11724